Mandolin Picking Tunes

LYRICAL GOSPEL SOLOS

by Dix Bruce

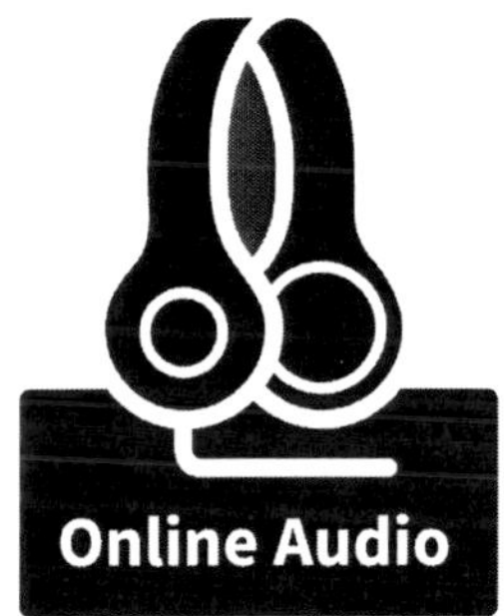

www.melbay.com/30870MEB

Special thanks to Kathi Bruce and Bruce Pettit for their helpful suggestions.

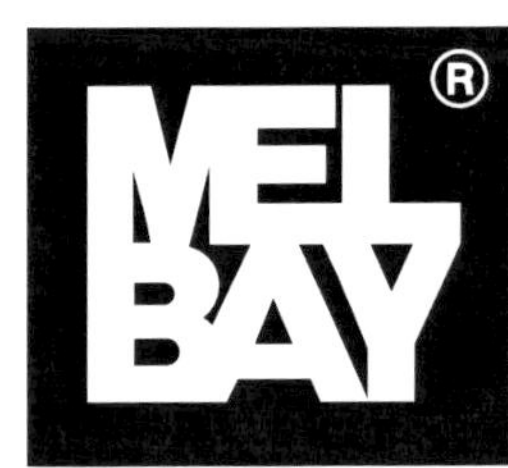

WWW.MELBAY.COM

Table of Contents

Introduction

As you work through these **Lyrical Gospel Solos** you'll explore a variety of techniques from simple single-note tunes through double stops, tremolo, up-and-down eighth-note picking, crosspicking, and chord melody. The comments that follow, beginning on page eight, include brief notes on the playing of each piece.

The tablature, or TAB line, is located under the standard notation. I added circles and ovals to the tablature to represent half or longer notes. Here are two excerpts:

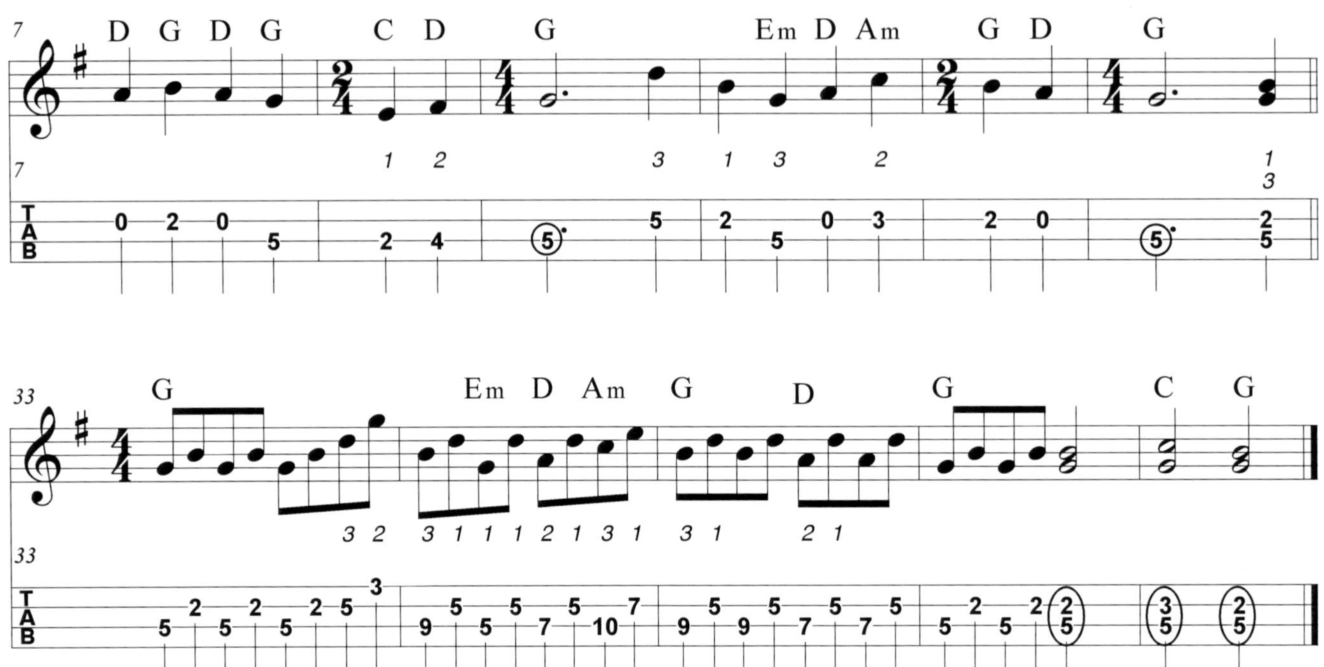

A single TAB number with a circle plus a stem indicates a half note. Ovals on more than one stacked TAB number indicate strums across more than one string. A circle without a stem indicates a whole note. Dots after circles or ovals work just like dots in standard notation and add half of a note's value to it. If a half note gets two beats, a dotted half gets three.

I included accompaniment chords in the music so that you can perform these songs in ensembles with chordal instruments. However, all of these arrangements work well as mandolin solos without any chordal accompaniment at all.

The rudimentary guitar parts on the recordings will give you a chordal background to play along with. These parts are quite simple and sometimes consist of just one or two chord strums per measure. Encourage your accompanist, on whatever instrument they play, to augment the parts as they see fit.

Measure numbers are shown above the treble clef sign on the left side of each song beginning with the second staff. I refer to these numbers in the text accompanying the songs. Numbering starts after any pickup measures.

Double and triple stops (when you fret and play two or three notes at the same time) are shown in the tablature as stacked numbers similar to the way they are shown as stacked notes in the standard music notation. If the double or triple stops have durations of half notes or longer, they'll have ovals in the TAB. Suggested fretting finger numbers for single notes, double, or triple stops are shown between the standard notation and the tablature staff. For double and triple stops the numbers will be stacked with the top number referring to the highest pitched note and lowest number to the lowest pitched note.

Generally speaking, when tremolo is used it's on notes longer than dotted quarters or halves. Tremolo gives a certain feel and sustain to a melody note. Tremolo can be a difficult technique, especially for beginners. It can be tough to start and stop the tremolo smoothly and, of course, that's something to work on. Practice may not make perfect, but it will make better!

All of the songs have been recorded and are downloadable. (See the URL on page one.) By adjusting the balance of your playback device, you can hear just mandolin (right channel), just guitar accompaniment (left channel), or both mandolin and guitar by listening in stereo. If you're listening on headphones, you can take one or the other side away from your ear to get a similar effect. Software called "Audacity" is available that allows you to import audio and control the pan of the playback through your computer of smart phone.

If these recordings are too fast for you to play along with, use "The Amazing SlowDowner" or similar software to slow them down. "Audacity" software can also be used to slow audio down.

When you begin working on a solo, practice it with a metronome at slower tempos. Online metronomes and downloadable apps are readily available. Learning to play along with a metronome is a valuable skill for any musician. Sight read through a piece a few times, then set the metronome to a speed slow enough to play it top to bottom without stopping and restarting. This slow speed should be set to a tempo where you can successfully play the most difficult parts of a song. As you become more familiar with a song or solo, gradually increase the metronome speed. The tempos of the recordings are only suggested tempos. If you feel the song faster or slower, play it as you wish!

Dix Bruce – Winter 2021

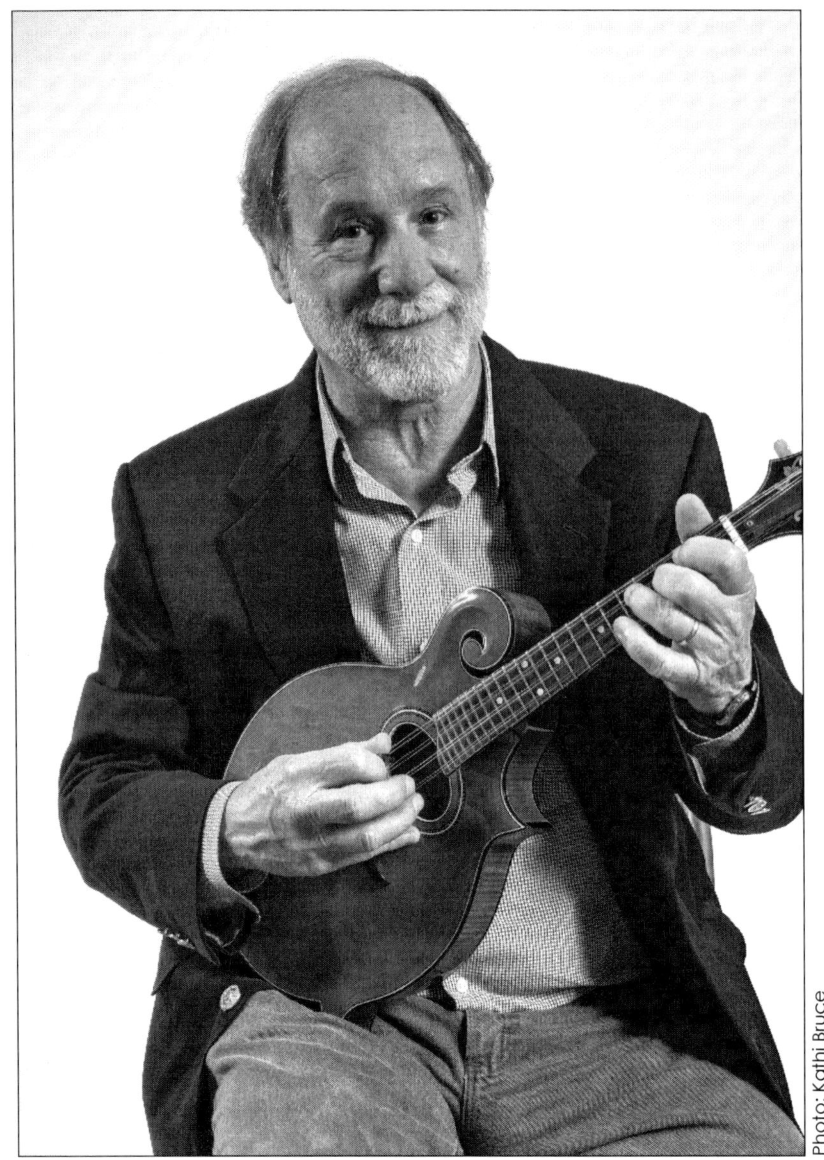

Photo: Kathi Bruce

Dix Bruce

About the Author

Dix Bruce is a musician and writer from the San Francisco Bay Area. He has authored over sixty books, recordings, and videos for Mel Bay Publications. All are available from his website: **musixnow.com**. Dix performs and does studio work on guitar, mandolin, bass, and banjo. He has recorded two albums with mandolin legend Frank Wakefield; eight big band CDs with the Royal Society Jazz Orchestra; his own collection of American folk songs entitled *My Folk Heart* on which he plays guitar, mandolin, autoharp, and sings; and a CD of string swing and jazz entitled *Tuxedo Blues*. He has released four CDs of traditional American songs and originals with guitarist Jim Nunally, including a collection of "brother duet" style recordings entitled *Brothers at Heart*. His CD with singer and mandolinist Julie Cline is entitled *Look at it Rain*. *Brothers at Heart* and *Look at it Rain* are available from iTunes, CDBaby, and from Dix's web site. Dix also arranged, composed, and played mandolin on the soundtracks to four different editions of the best-selling computer game *The Sims*.

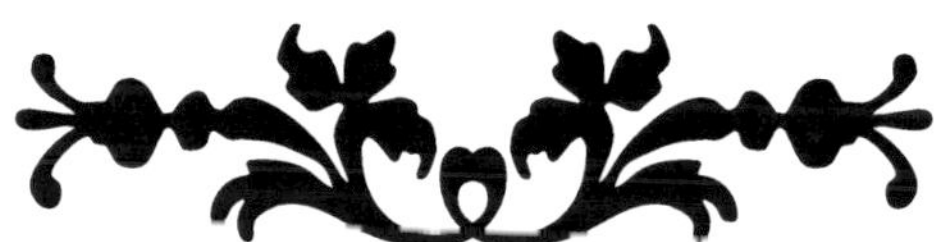

Notes on Lyrical Gospel Solos

Praise God from Whom All Blessings Flow, (p. 14) also known as "The Doxology" is played three times through with different techniques used on each pass. The first solo is a simple single-string statement of the melody. On the second solo I added in notes to make double stops. The third time through I split the notes of the double stops and turned them into eighth notes. Near the end at measure thirty-five we expand the form and give the G and D chords two beats each. This is followed by a "church" or "amen" cadence (IV-I chords) in the last measure. (See also "Have Thine Own Way, Lord" on pages 10 and 34.) "Praise God from Whom All Blessings Flow" is written in mixed meter with 2/4 and 4/4 measures. That gives the song a slightly unusual feel.

Amazing Grace (p. 16) is one of the most popular and best-loved hymns in the English language. I couldn't imagine leaving it out of this collection. I use tremolo on half notes or longer. Experiment with leaving out the tremolo altogether and see if you like the effect. This solo has no open-string notes – they're all fretted. Solos with no open-string notes can be moved relatively easily up and down the fingerboard to different positions and keys. The Em in parenthesis in measure thirteen is an optional chord.

Down in the Valley to Pray (p. 17) is an old, old song that found new life in the popular 2000 movie "Oh Brother, Where Art Thou?" where it was sung as "Down in the ***River*** to Pray." This solo is written in a bluegrass mandolin style with near continuous eighth notes. It's recorded at a moderate tempo, but you can play it at whatever tempo you prefer. "Down in the Valley to Pray" has both a verse and a chorus, and they're marked in the music.

Drifting Too Far from the Shore (p. 18) has both a verse and a chorus. The basic melody is augmented with short runs of notes throughout (see measures three, seven, eleven, etc.). Notice the hold or *fermata* in measure twenty-eight. The fermata looks like an eye and an eyebrow and is often called a bird's eye. A fermata indicates a pause or a stretching of time on the note it's placed over. How long the note is stretched is determined by the conductor or by the performer. Stretching a note to twice the written length is typical.

Softly and Tenderly (p. 20). Many of these traditional gospel songs have beautiful, simple melodies and I like to play them with very little added adornment. The arrangement of "Softly and Tenderly" is made up of a relatively simple statement of the melody with very few added phrases. It's played with no open-string notes, all fretted, rather high on the fingerboard. The mandolin has a beautiful, delicate timbre in this register. Try moving this solo down an octave for comparison.

As with "Drifting Too Far from the Shore" there's a *fermata* in measure twenty. In performance you can decide how long to hold or stretch the timing of this role.

This version of the melody is played on strings one and two. Since all the notes are played fretted and in a closed position, you can move this melody across the fingerboard and down in pitch to strings two and three and alternately to strings three and four. Simply play the same fret numbers but begin on string two or three instead of string one. Doing that will move "Softly and Tenderly" to the keys of C and F respectively.

Angel Band (p. 22) has a verse and chorus format. The verse is played with single notes, tremolo on notes with durations of dotted-quarters or longer. The chorus uses double stops. Fretting finger suggestions are shown between the standard and TAB staffs. The upper number represents the fretting finger for the higher note, the lower number for the lower note.

Bright Morning Stars are Rising (p. 24) is often performed vocally and unaccompanied in a slow, flowing, rubato (without strict adherence to tempo) style. The meter is mostly in 4/4 but measures seven and sixteen are in 3/4. That gives the song its unusual rhythm.

Part one, measures one through nine, is made up of single notes. Part two, measures ten through eighteen, includes double stops. If you have difficulty playing these double stops with tremolo, leave the tremolo out for now.

Bring Them In (p. 25) has two different recorded tracks – one with tremolo and one without. Together they demonstrate the different sounds you can get with and without tremolo.

Faith of Our Fathers (p. 26) has a verse and chorus, and each is played slightly differently. In the verse you'll play mostly single-string notes with a few double and triple stops here and there. Measures seven and fifteen have single-beat double stops. Tremolo is used on half notes or longer. The chorus has double and triple stops mostly without tremolo. It is more in the style of *chord melody* where chord notes are played in turn, from lowest to highest, with the highest note being the melody note. The lower notes of the chord should sustain and accompany the higher melody note.

This Little Light of Mine (p. 28) is one of my favorite Gospel songs. I love its joyful and positive message. This arrangement is in a continuous eighth note/bluegrass mandolin style. It's written in closed position without any open-string notes. That means that you can move it up and down the fingerboard as well as across the fingerboard to different keys with relative ease. Try moving the whole arrangement *down* by two frets to the key of F by starting this solo on string four, fret five. Keep your fretting fingers in the same relative positions. Next go back to the original key of G version and try moving the whole thing *up* in pitch by two frets to the key of A.

Try moving this solo *over* one string to start on the seventh fret of string three. This will move "This Little Light of Mine" to the key of D. Once at this new position you can also move the solo *up* and *down* the fingerboard to different keys. Using these two transposition methods, up and down or across the fingerboard, you can move the original arrangement to any key you wish.

Pass Me Not (p. 30) is played with double stops throughout. Once you can play it as written, try playing only the lower note of the double stop to make a single-note melody.

Give Me Oil (p. 32). The arrangement, with verse and chorus, is written in a bluegrass mandolin style. It's played with up and down picked eighth notes throughout and several blue notes added in measures two, six, seven, etc. Blue notes are generally the flatted third and seventh notes of the song's key, in this case the key of C. The flatted third note is an E♭. The flatted seventh note is a B♭. The blue notes can be identified in the standard notation with ♭ signs.

Have Thine Own Way, Lord (p. 34) is played twice through – the first time with single notes, the second with nearly all double stops. (See measure forty-three.) Tremolo is used throughout. Try playing it without tremolo and see which you prefer.

The ending in measures forty-eight and forty-nine has a "church," or "plagal" cadence where the chords of the melody follow a IV – I chord progression, which in this key means the G – D chords. Notice that the accompaniment doesn't include those chords. We could have included them but choose not to. This type of cadence is also called an "amen cadence."

What a Friend We Have in Jesus (p. 36) is presented here in a crosspicking arrangement. (See "Old Time Religion" on page 49 and "When I Lay My Burden Down" on page 76 for more crosspicking solos.) Mostly you'll use the pick direction pattern of "down – up – up" over sets of three strings: 3 – 1– 2 or 4 – 2– 3. The pick directions of the crosspicking pattern are shown in the first few measures. There will be non-pattern passages here and there of alternating "down – up" picking on neighboring strings. The suggested fretting finger numbers will steer you to the most efficient finger positions. Pay particular attention to the fretting finger position in measure twenty-one. It will probably be the most challenging section to maneuver.

Higher Ground (p. 38) has a verse and chorus and is played with single-string notes. I use tremolo on dotted quarters or longer. "Higher Ground" is in the key of A♭. If you're not used to playing in this key it can be a challenge. It will be worth the effort as it's important to be able to play in any key. Here's your chance to try out A♭. Notice that this arrangement has no open-string notes. They're all fretted, so this solo will lend itself to moving up the fingerboard to different keys.

I Shall Not Be Moved (p. 39). The solo to this wonderful old Gospel melody is built around a quarter note, two eighth notes rhythm pattern. There are also some phrases of consecutive eighth notes mixed in. They give the passages a bluegrass feel.

There Shall Be Showers of Blessing (p. 40). I heard this song in the Baptist church as a kid, and all these years I thought its title was "There Shall Be Showers of Blessing**s**." In doing research for this book I discovered that it was "blessing" singular, not plural. Always something new to learn!

This arrangement is in the key of B♭ and you'll play twice through the verse and chorus. The first time through is a basic statement of the melody with tremolo on half notes or longer but not on dotted quarters. With any of these songs the tremolo is up to you and what you think sounds best. You might leave tremolo out altogether, play it slowly or quickly, or add it in on shorter notes. The second time through you'll play almost continuous double stops. Try moving all the open-string notes to their fretted equivalents. Most of these new notes you'll play with your fourth fretting finger. This will be good exercise for this under used and underappreciated digit.

Holy, Holy, Holy (p. 42) has a more involved arrangement than most of the other songs in this book. We'll play through the melody three times with three different approaches. The first time we'll play single-string notes with tremolo on longer notes. The second time through is all double and triple stops, all strummed, with no tremolo. These double stops are constructed by adding a lower chord tone to the melody note. On the third time through we'll add in series of eighth notes placed around the melody notes. "Holy, Holy, Holy" is in the key of E♭, which may be a temporary challenge for some of you. If it is, keep working on it and it'll get better! This arrangement has no open-string notes. They're all fretted, so this solo will lend itself to moving up the fingerboard to different keys.

O Store Gud (p. 45) was written in the mid-1880s by a young Swedish pastor named Carl Boberg. Eventually English lyrics were added to his melody, and you may recognize the tune as "How Great Thou Art." You'll play it through twice. The first time through is a simple statement of the melody. The second time adds tremolo double stops. Double stops with tremolo can be a little tricky. The difficulty can be in getting a clean tremolo that covers two strings and also starts and stops smoothly. A great exercise is to simply start and stop tremolo over and over to work on getting up to speed and stopping instantly.

Jesus Loves Me (p. 48) features a slightly different technique that you can perform in more than one way. The solo is made up of all double stops and I play it with a flatpick, playing both strings of the double stop at the same time. I don't use tremolo. You could also play these double stops with your bare thumb and first or second finger in a pinching motion. The thumb would play the lower note of the double stop and the finger the upper. A third approach would be to hold a flatpick with your thumb and first finger, play the lower note with the pick and pinch with your second finger to play the upper note. Either way you do it, you'll get a very nice and quite unusual sound.

Old Time Religion (p. 49). This arrangement uses the crosspicking technique mentioned previously in the note to "What a Friend We Have in Jesus" on pages 10 and 36. The crosspicking technique on the mandolin was pioneered by Jesse McReynolds as a way to mimic the sound of a roll on the five-string banjo. You'll use a pick direction pattern of "down–up–up" through most of it, though there will be phrases of alternating "down–up" picking too. The pick directions of the crosspicking patten are shown in the first few measures, and you can extrapolate the others from there. Use the suggested fretting finger numbers, especially in measures six, seven, fourteen, and fifteen, to help you through some unusual finger positions. See also the crosspicking solo on "When I Lay My Burden Down" on page 76.

I Love to Tell the Story (p. 50) has a verse and chorus format and is recorded both with and without tremolo. When tremolo is used it's on half notes or longer. Be sure to try both and see which you like best.

I'm Working on a Building (p. 52) features the sound of blue notes. The blue notes in the key of D are C natural and F natural, the flatted third and flatted seventh notes of the D major scale. The solo, mostly in 4/4 time, has two measures of 2/4, at fifteen and twenty-four, mixed in with the 4/4 measures and that changes the song's rhythmic feel. The solo is made up of quarter and eighth notes. The eighth notes, especially those phrases with four or more eighth notes in succession, should be played with solid, even up and down pick strokes. This arrangement has no open-string notes. They're all fretted, so be sure to try moving it up and down the fingerboard to different keys.

Lord, I'm Coming Home (p. 54) has one of the most elaborate arrangements in the book and will give you the opportunity to explore and expand this beautiful melody. It's in the key of B♭ with a verse and chorus form that's played twice. The first time is a single-string melody with tremolo on half notes or longer. On the second time through, beginning in measure thirty-three, I added notes around the melody and tremolo on dotted-quarters or longer. On the second chorus, beginning in measure forty-nine, I added in double stops.

As I've previously mentioned, one of the main difficulties with tremolo, other than simply moving the pick up and down quickly, is to be able to start and stop the tremolo smoothly and accurately. You need to be able to instantly start your tremolo at whatever speed you choose and also be able to stop it cleanly and move on to the notes that follow. You can improve it with practice. Make up exercises of starting and stopping your tremolo on melodies or scales. Start with a slow tremolo and work your way to faster tremolos. You'll want to eventually be able to use a range of tremolo speeds, so practice them all. Listen to mandolinists that you admire and analyze how they play tremolo and especially how they use different speeds and feels to express different emotions. It can be helpful to have audio models in mind of just what you're trying to accomplish. David Grisman is my favorite. He's an incredible player and his tremolo is wonderfully expressive and dynamic.

In measures thirteen, twenty-nine, forty-five, and sixty-one, you'll see Gm chords in parenthesis. Try the progression with and without the Gm and see which you like better.

Just a Closer Walk With Thee (p. 58) is played through twice. The first time is a basic version of the melody with some added notes. The second time adds more additional notes and expands on the melody a bit more. Both solos have no open-string notes and can be moved to different positions and keys up and down the fingerboard. For example, you can move the whole piece down in pitch by a whole step from the key of A to G. As written, the first five notes are played on string two, frets four, five, six, and seven. To transpose down to the key of G, play these notes with the same fretting fingers two frets lower on the fingerboard at frets two, three, four, and five. Maintain your same fretting hand positions relative to the fingerboard. Do this same thing with all the subsequent notes, and you'll transpose the song from A to G.

Once you've done that, go back to the key of A position and try moving everything up in pitch the same way by one fret. This will transpose the song from the key of A to the key of B♭.

The Lily of the Valley, (p. 60) arranged here in the key of F, has a verse/chorus format. I suggest tremolo on half notes or longer. Notice that the melody is played on strings two, three, and four. Because mandolins are tuned in intervals of fifths, we can move this entire melody over one string and *up* in pitch to the key of C. Your first note will be on string two, fret three. All the following notes will be on the same frets as the key of F version, just one string over. Use the same fretting finger numbers that you used in the original key. Try moving other songs in this book to other keys in this same way.

Come, Ye Thankful People Come (p. 62) is a song we sang in elementary school, usually around the Thanksgiving holiday. Here it's arranged in a chord melody style where chords are played on almost every beat. See the "Faith of Our Fathers" note above on page 9.

Oh, How I Love Jesus (p. 64) is arranged in a modified chord melody style with mixed double and triple stops. In this style we drag the pick over two or more strings, lowest pitched to highest, let them ring out a bit, and end the strum on the melody note.

Sweet Hour of Prayer (p. 65). One of the special tools mandolinists have is tremolo. With tremolo we can stretch a note to any length. Tremolo is to a mandolinist what the bow is to a violinist. This arrangement is built around a straightforward stating of the melody. I recorded it with both continuous tremolo and no tremolo at all. Try both approaches.

The Old Rugged Cross, (p. 66). I took the basic melody and augmented it with additional notes and phrases as I would do in improvising a solo that stays close to the melody.

Just as I Am (p. 68) is played twice through. The first time is the very simple but very beautiful melody with no tremolo or double stops. For the second time through we'll add in double stops, all of them played with one motion of the pick to give a chime-like effect, again without tremolo.

Savior, Like a Shepherd Lead Us (p. 70) is played twice through. The first go-round is a simple single-string statement of the melody without tremolo. On the second time through we'll add in double stops, but again without tremolo. Try adding in tremolo on half-notes or longer.

The Wayfaring Stranger (p. 72) is another beautiful and haunting melody from the traditional Gospel repertoire. The melody, by itself, without much ornamentation, is stunning. So, the first time through you'll play a simple version of the melody with tremolo. The second time through is a vacation or improvisation on the first with some added phrases in place on the longer tied notes of the simple melody.

When I Lay My Burden Down (p. 76) is one more solo that uses the crosspicking technique. (See "Old Time Religion" on page 49 and "What a Friend We Have in Jesus" on page 36 for two other crosspicking solos.) I love this technique on the mandolin. It yields amazingly beautiful results at a variety of tempos. The pattern of roll is "down–up–up" and these pick directions are shown in the first couple measures. There are sections where you won't play this pattern exactly but for the most part, you'll use it throughout the solo. It's a short solo so play it through a few times when you perform it. Notice that the melody of "When I Lay My Burden Down" is virtually identical to "Will the Circle Be Unbroken?" You can use this solo on both songs.

Praise God from Whom All Blessings Flow

Doxology

Traditional
Arr. by Dix Bruce

Introductory note p. 8

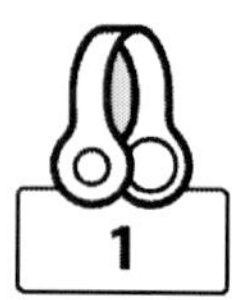

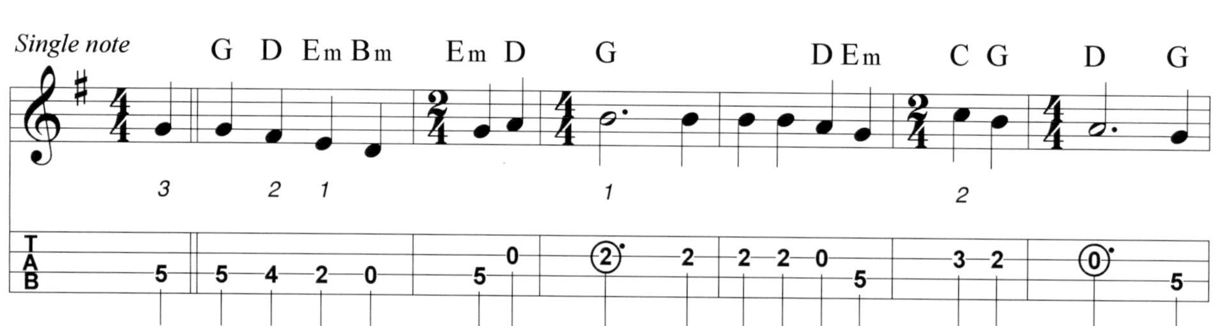

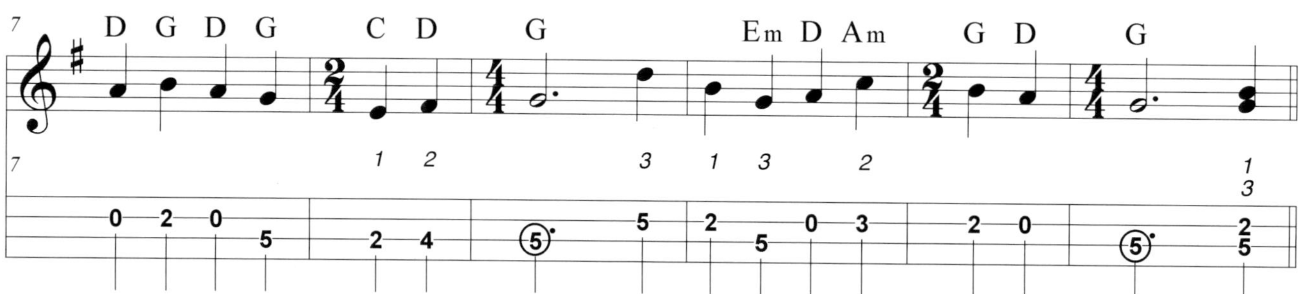

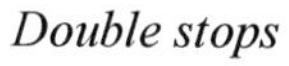

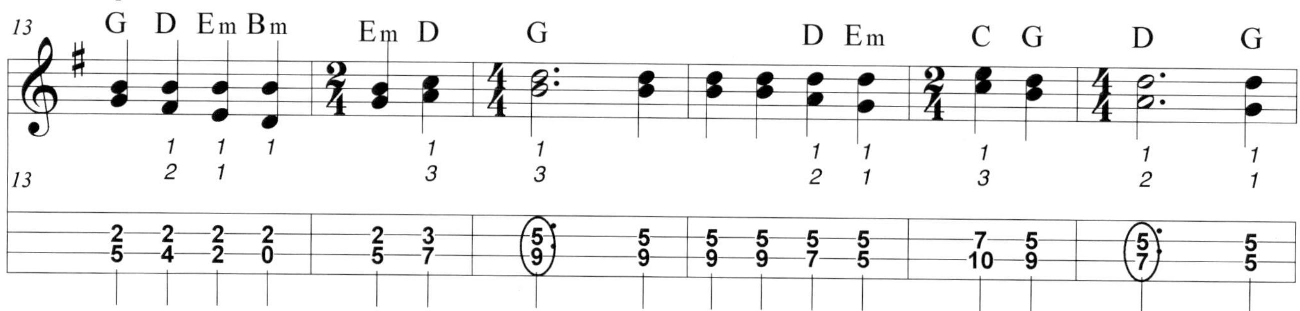

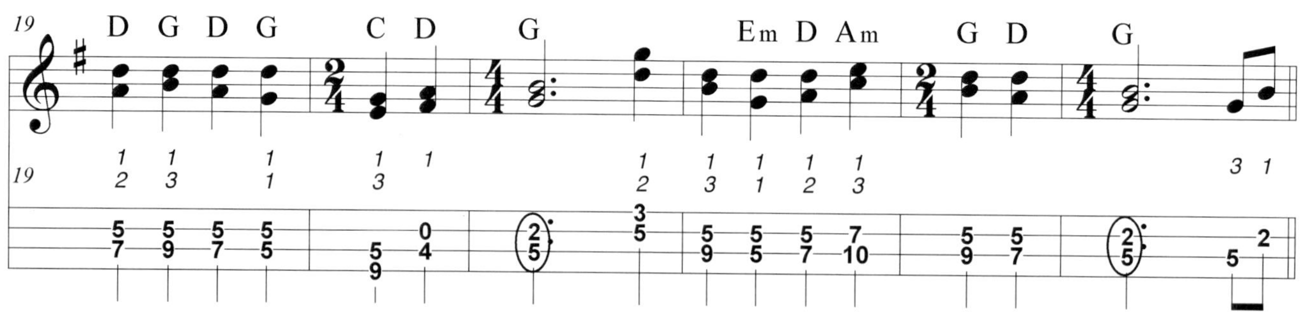

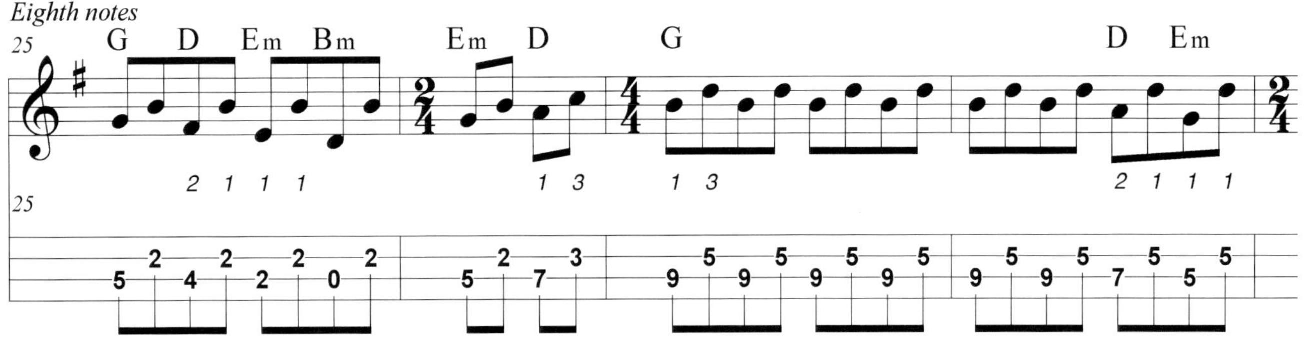
Eighth notes
25
G D Em Bm Em D G D Em

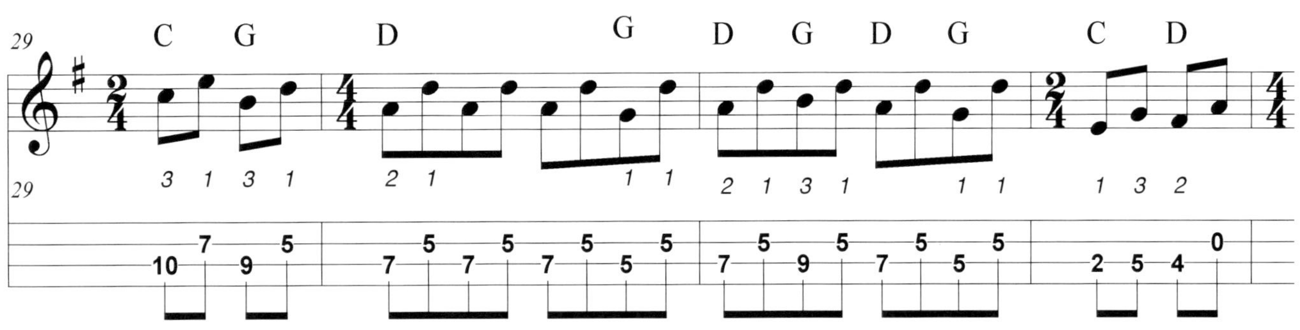
29
C G D G D G D G C D

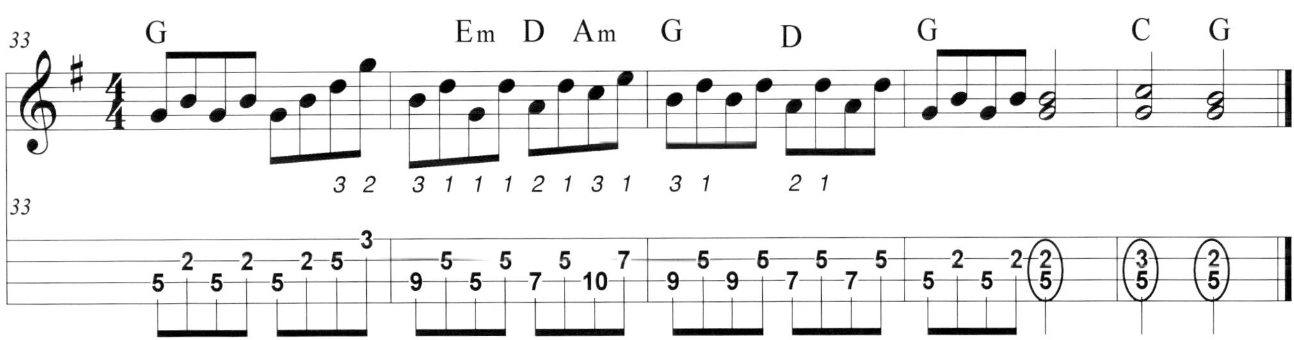
33
G Em D Am G D G C G

Amazing Grace

Introductory note p. 8

J. Newton - 1779
Arr. by Dix Bruce

2

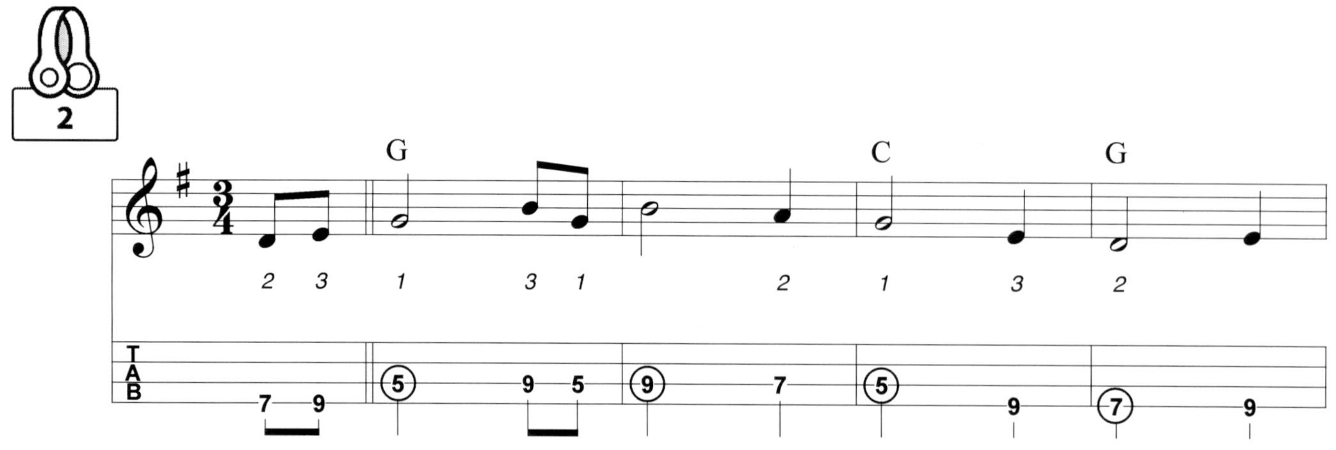

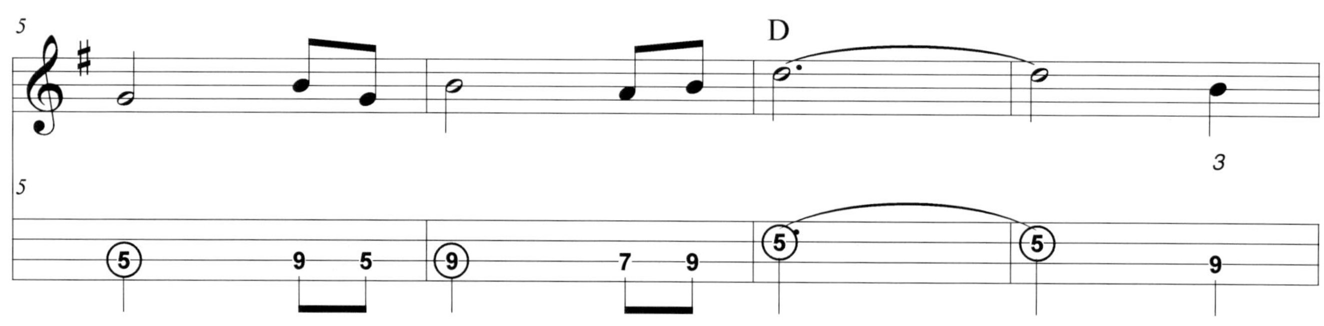

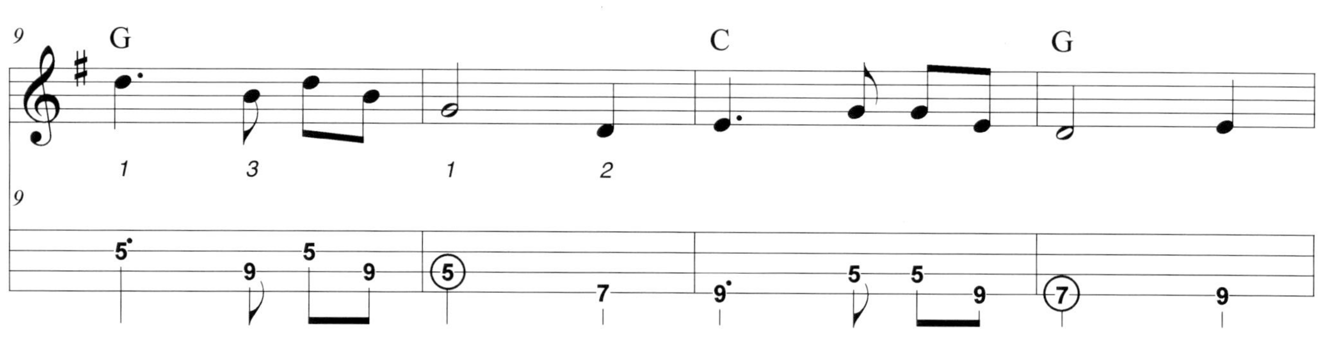

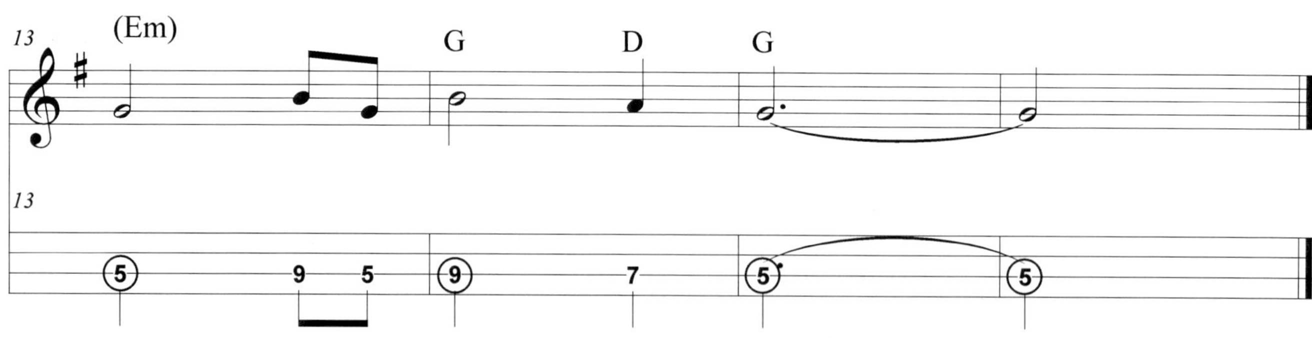

Down in the Valley to Pray

Introductory note p. 8

Traditional
Arr. by Dix Bruce

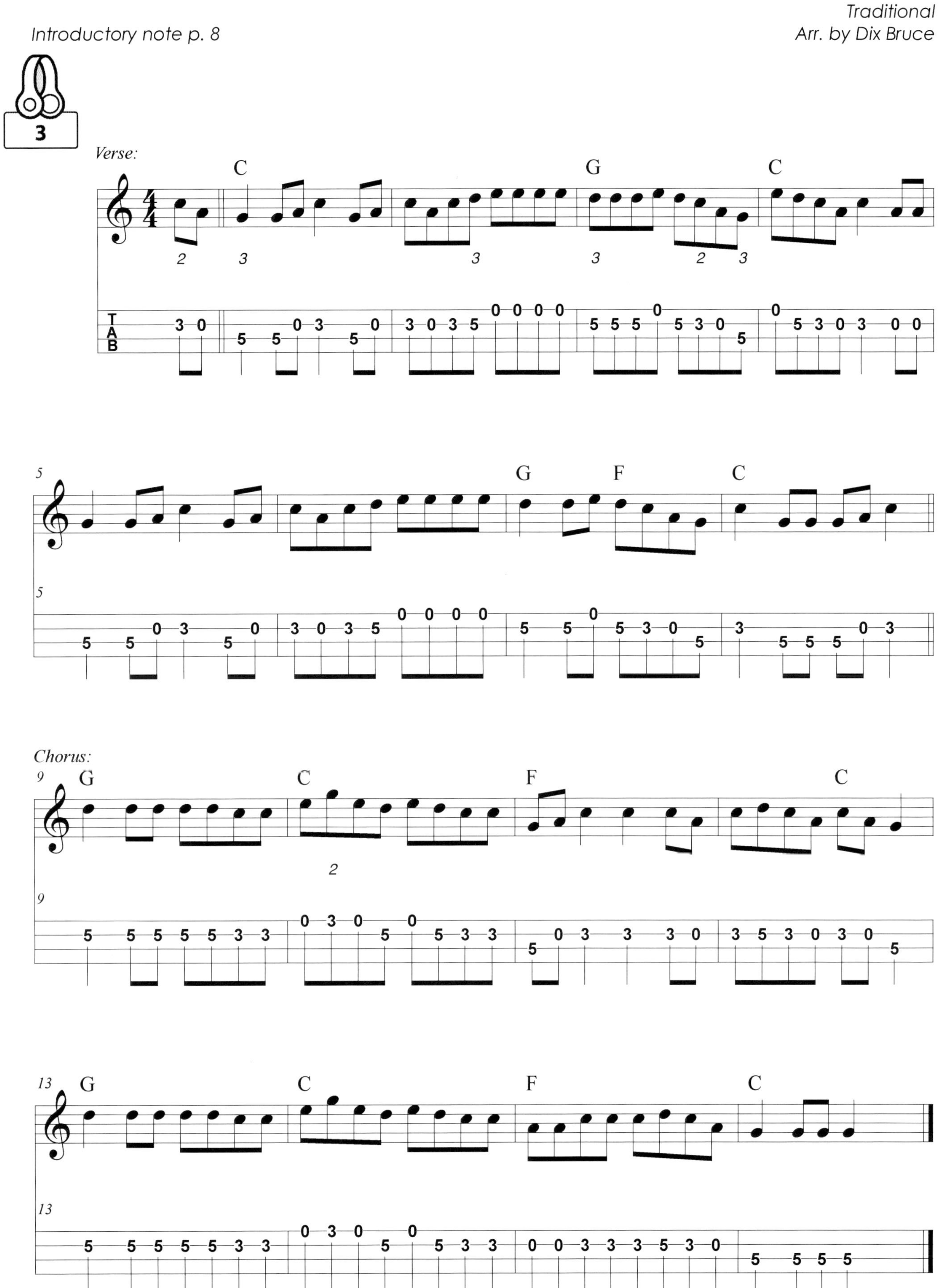

Drifting Too Far from the Shore

C.E. Moody - 1923
Arr. by Dix Bruce

Introductory note p. 8

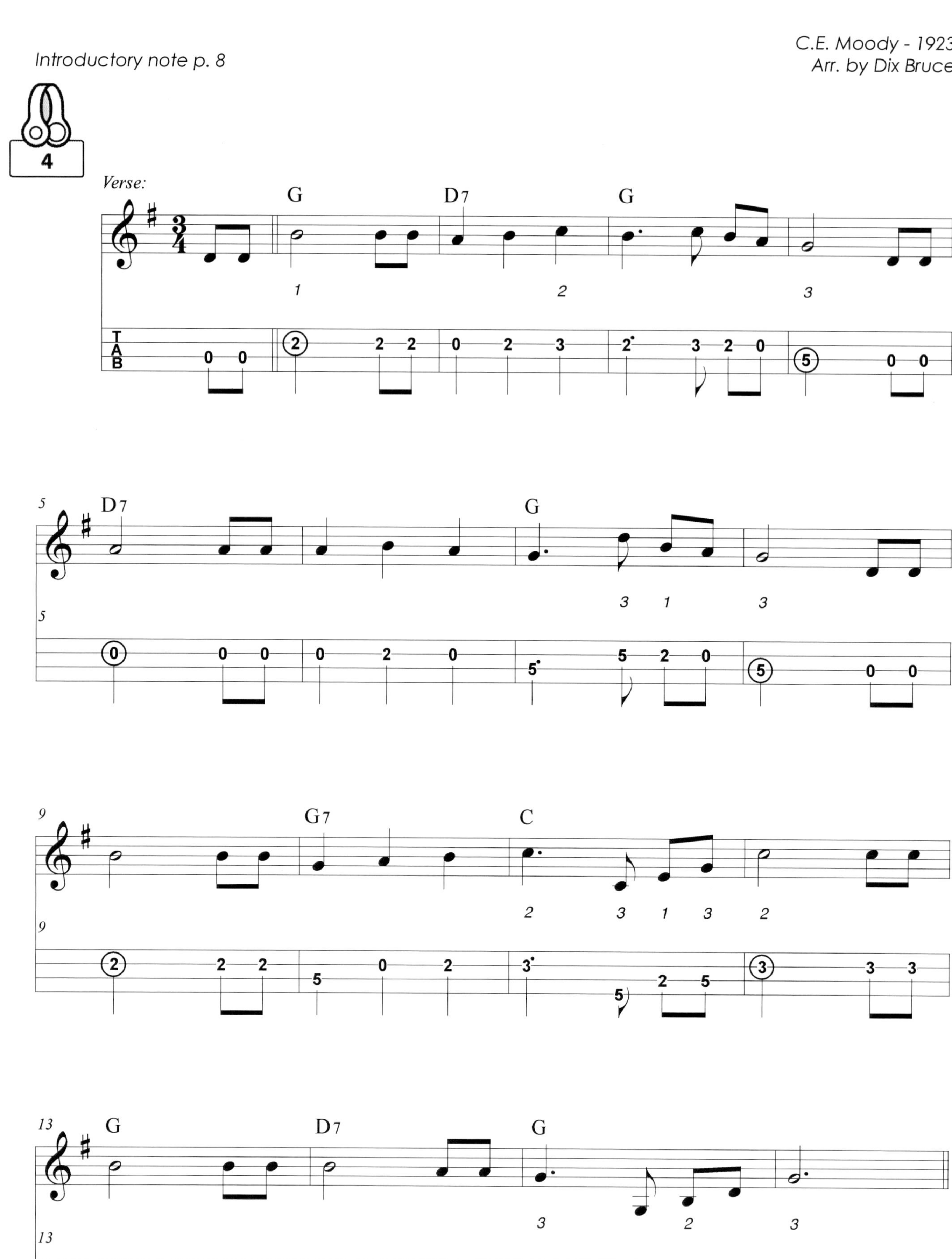

Chorus:

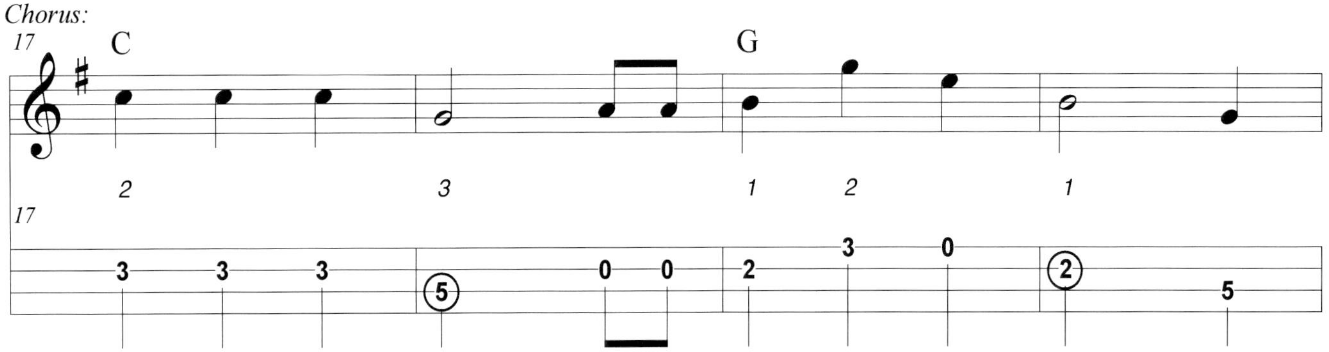

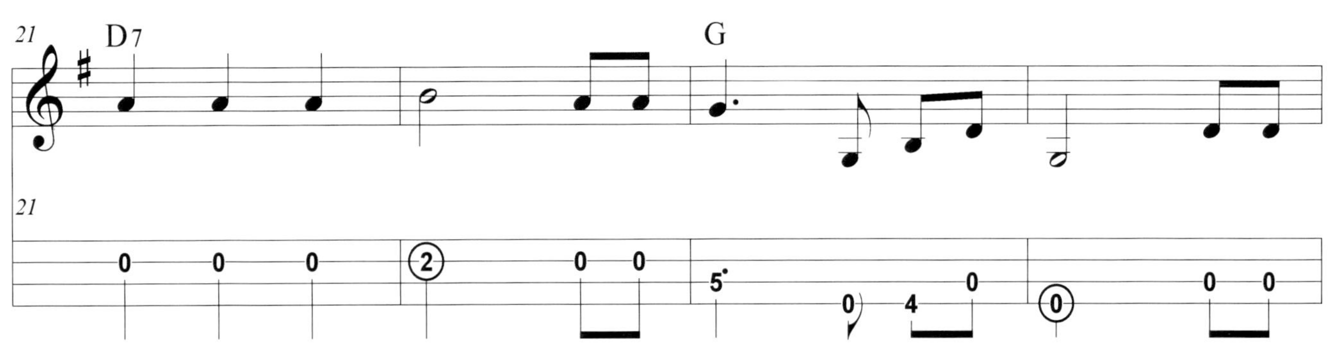

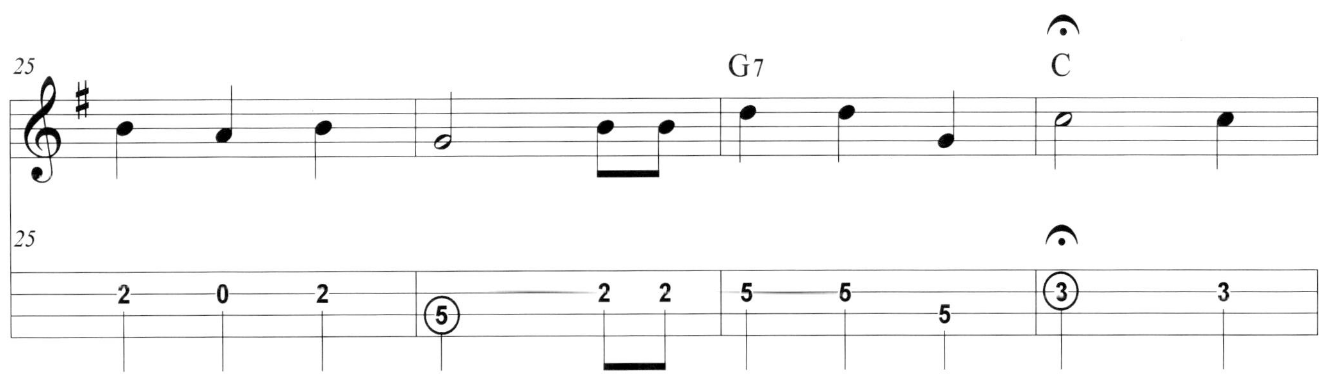

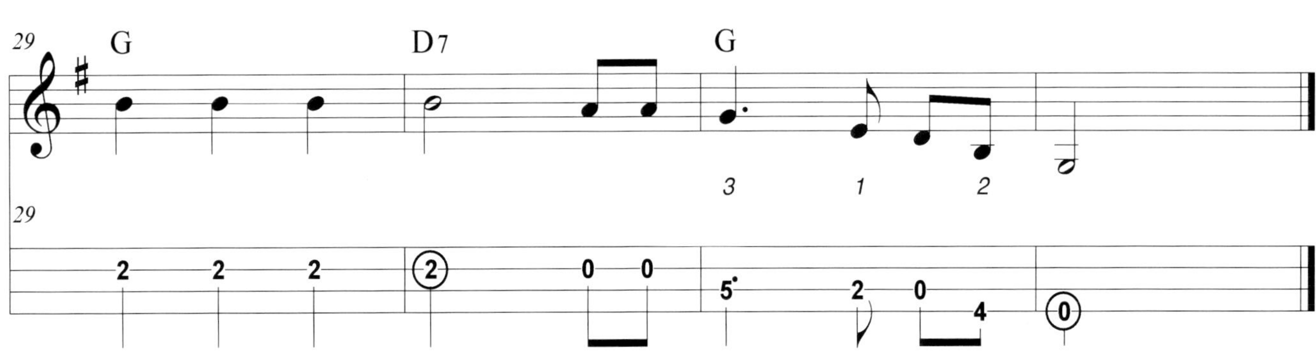

Softly and Tenderly

W. L. Thompson - 1880
Arr. by Dix Bruce

Introductory note p. 8

5

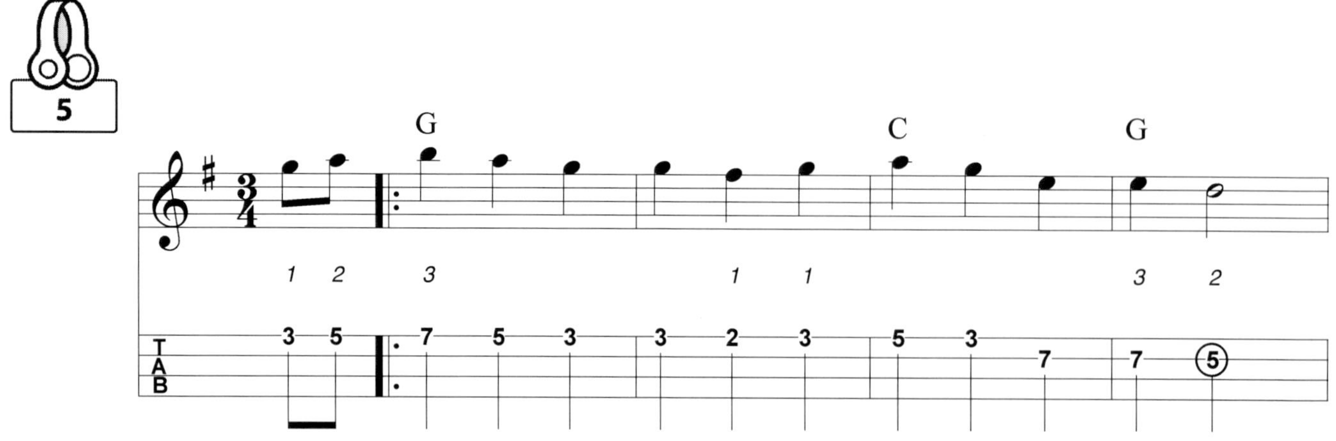

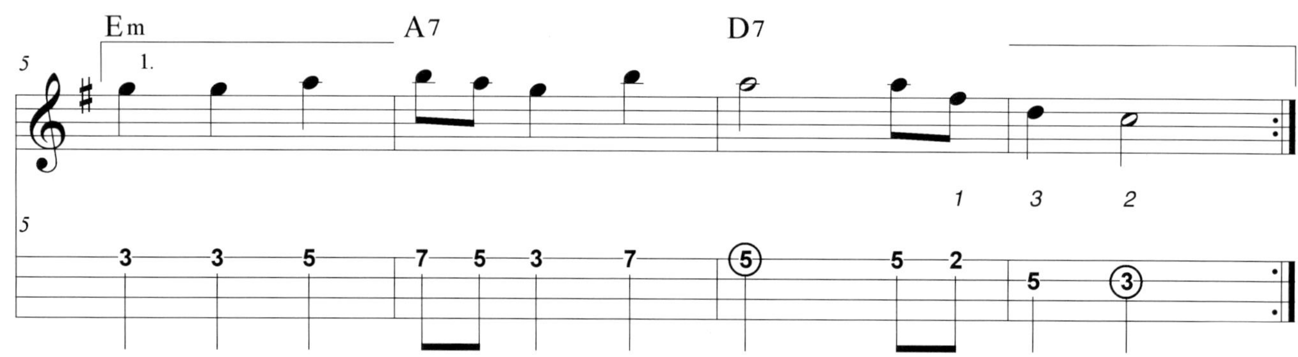

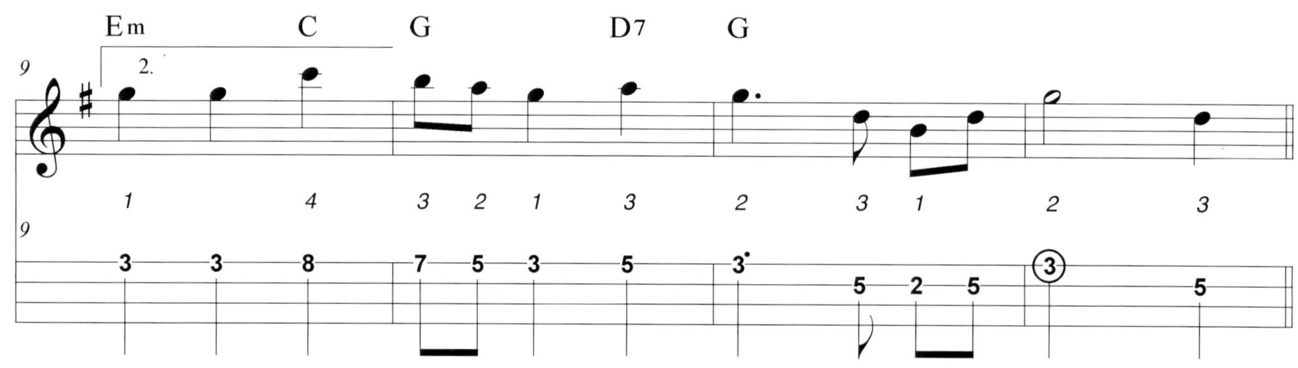

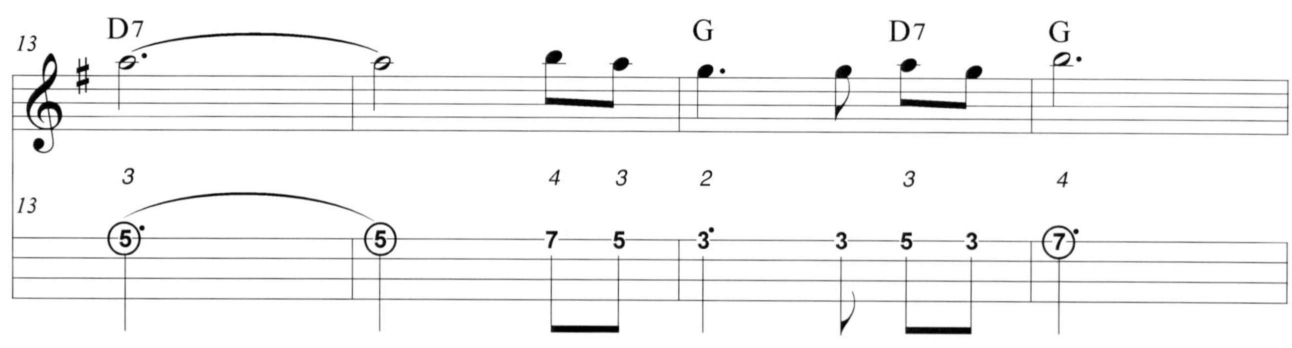

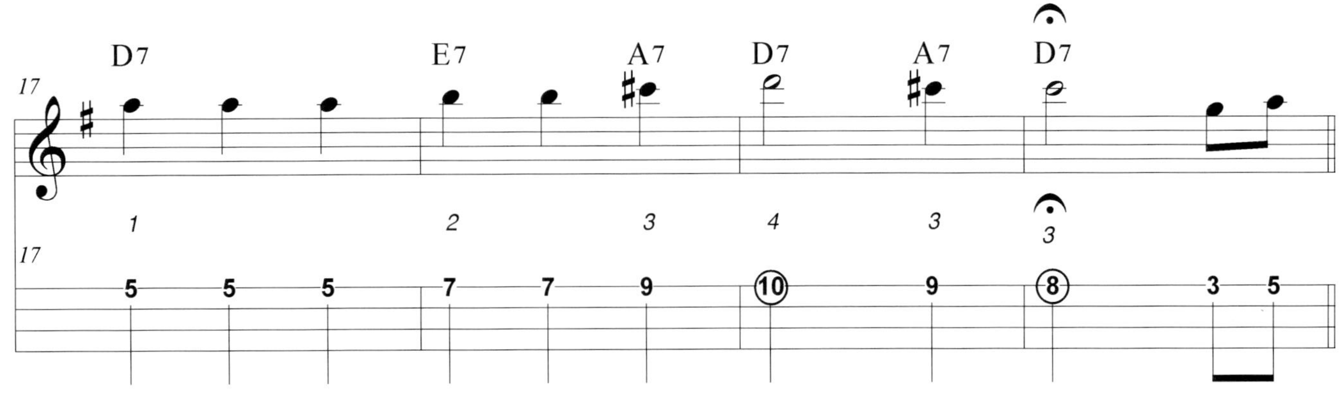
17
D7
E7
A7
D7
A7
D7
1 2 3 4 3 3
5 5 5 7 7 9 10 9 8 3 5

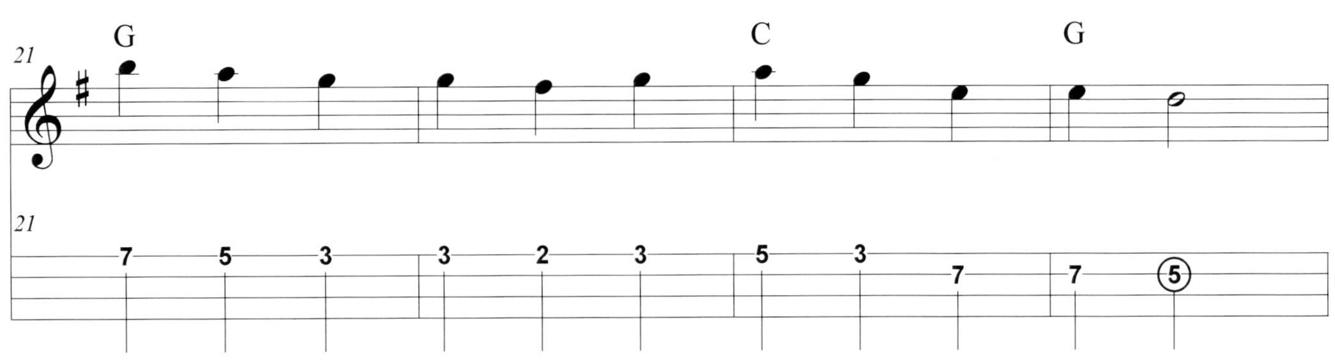
21
G
C
G
7 5 3 3 2 3 5 3 7 7 5

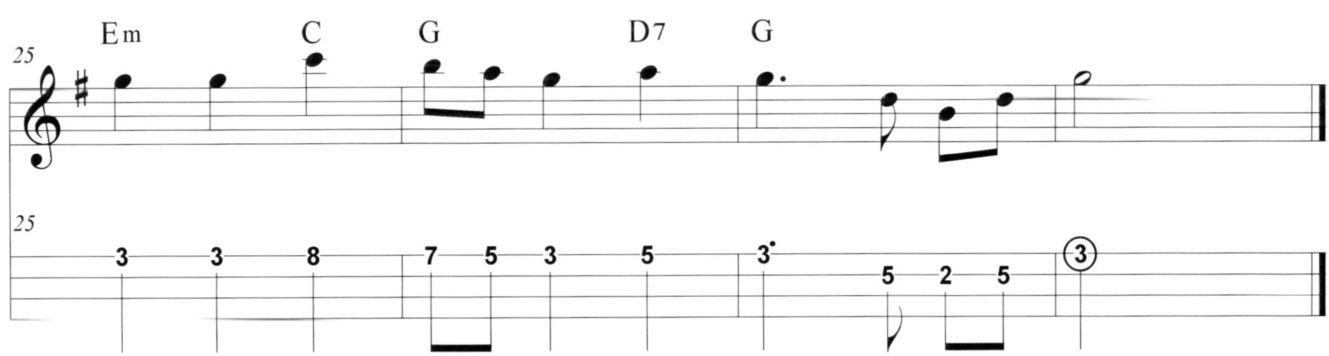
25
Em
C
G
D7
G
3 3 8 7 5 3 5 3 5 2 5 3

Angel Band

W. Bradbury, J.Hascall - 1862
Arr. by Dix Bruce

Introductory note p. 9

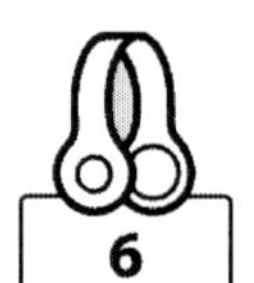

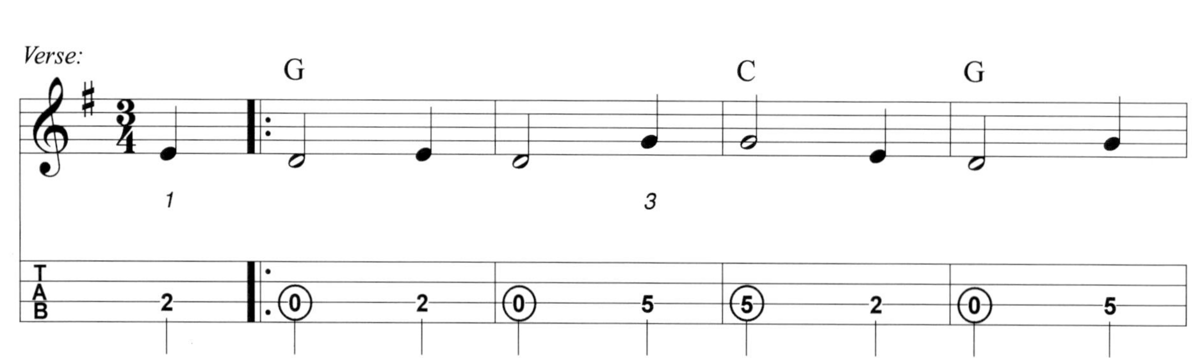

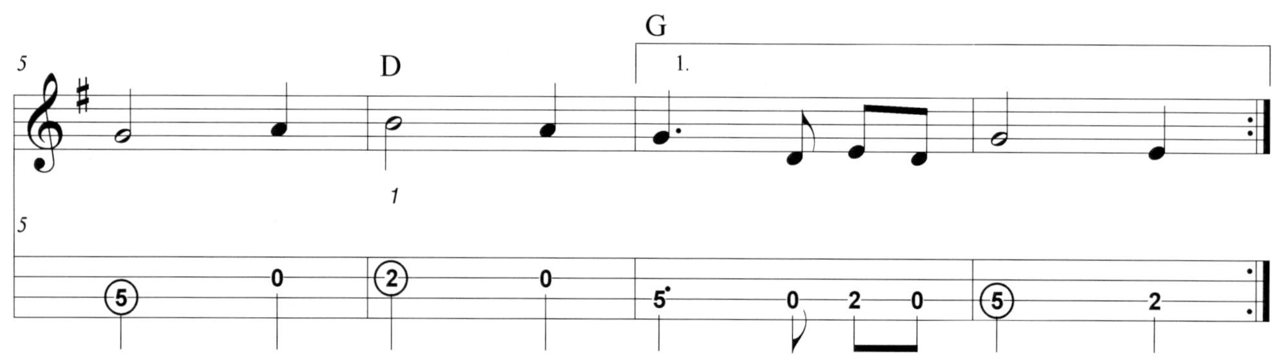

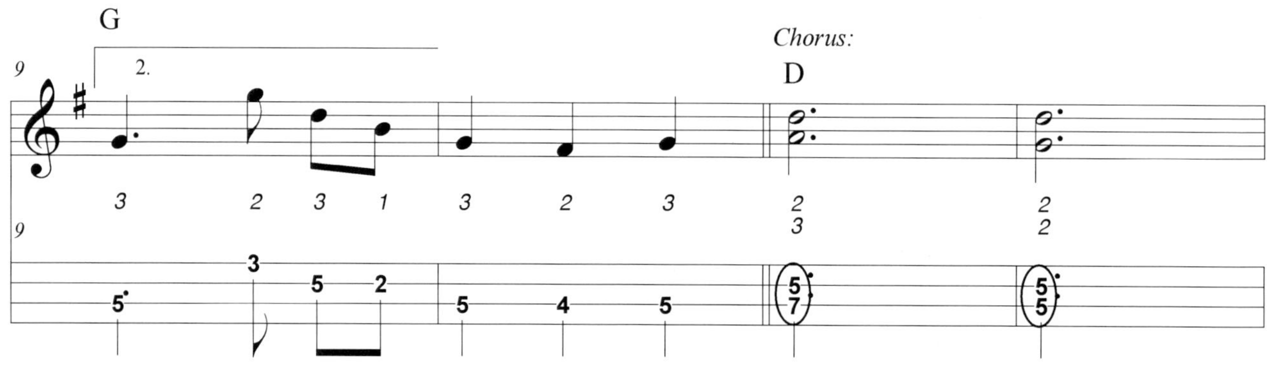

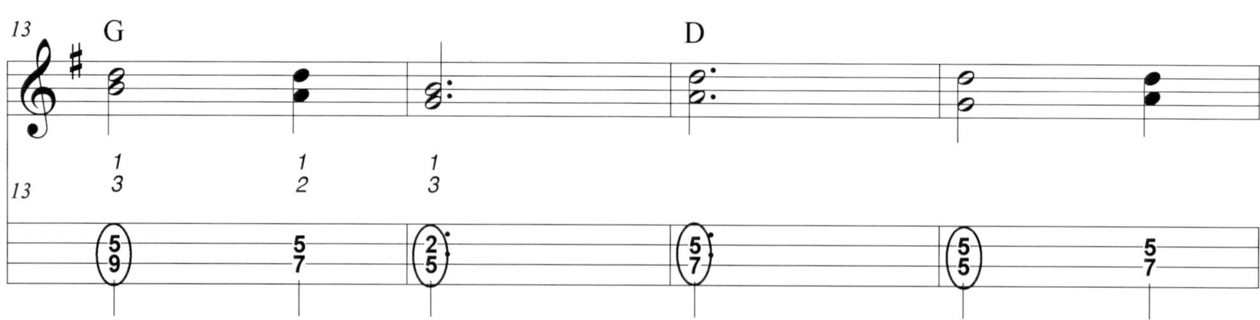

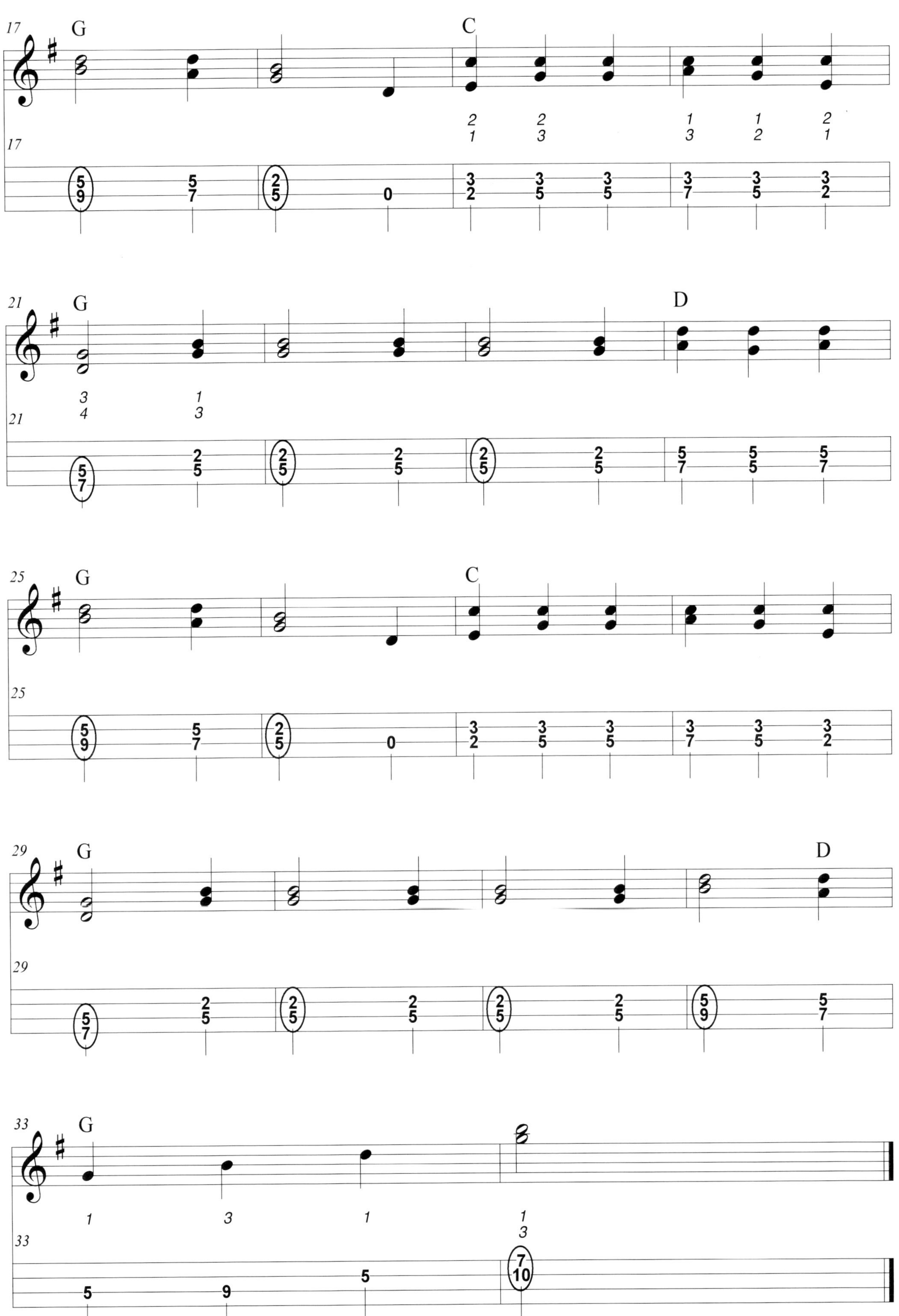
17
G
C
21
G
D
25
G
C
29
G
D
33
G

Bright Morning Stars are Rising

Traditional
Arr. by Dix Bruce

Introductory note p. 9

7

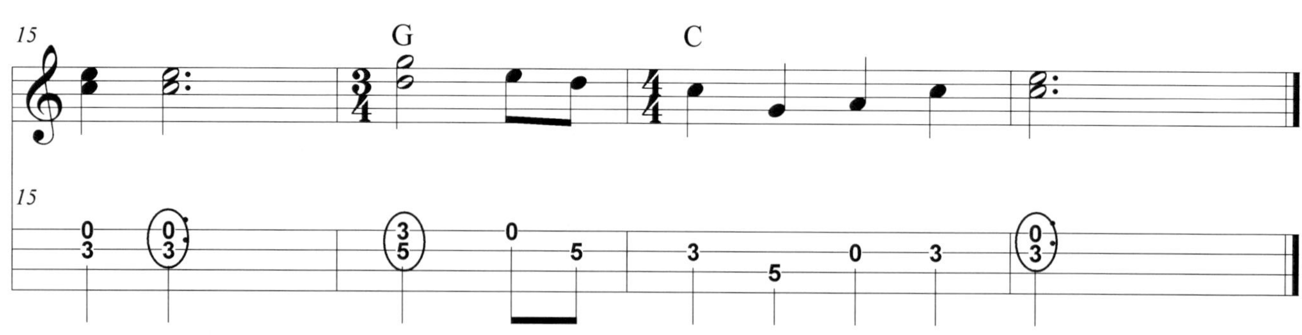

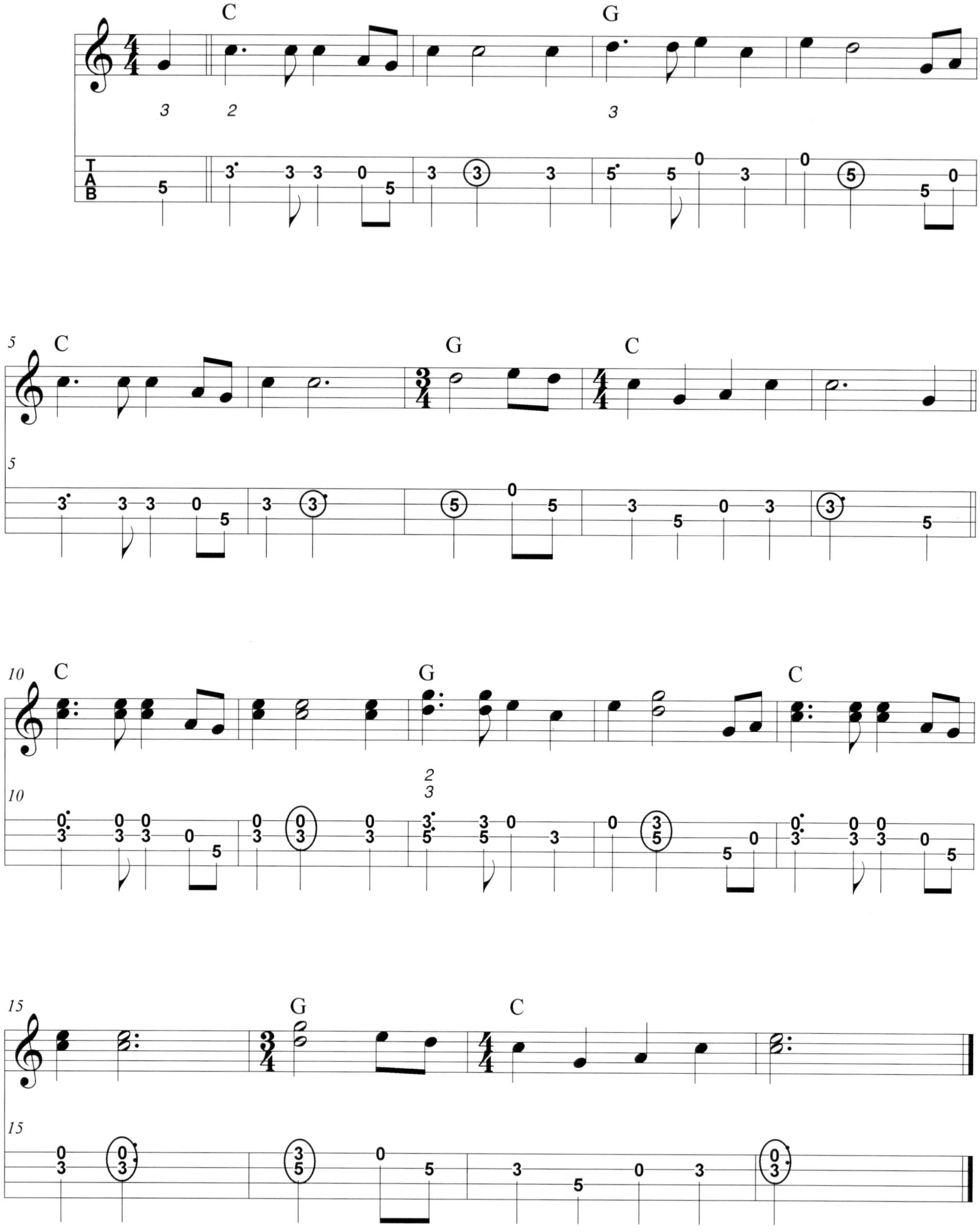

Bring Them In

Introductory note p. 9

A. Thomas, W.A. Ogden - 1885
Arr. by Dix Bruce

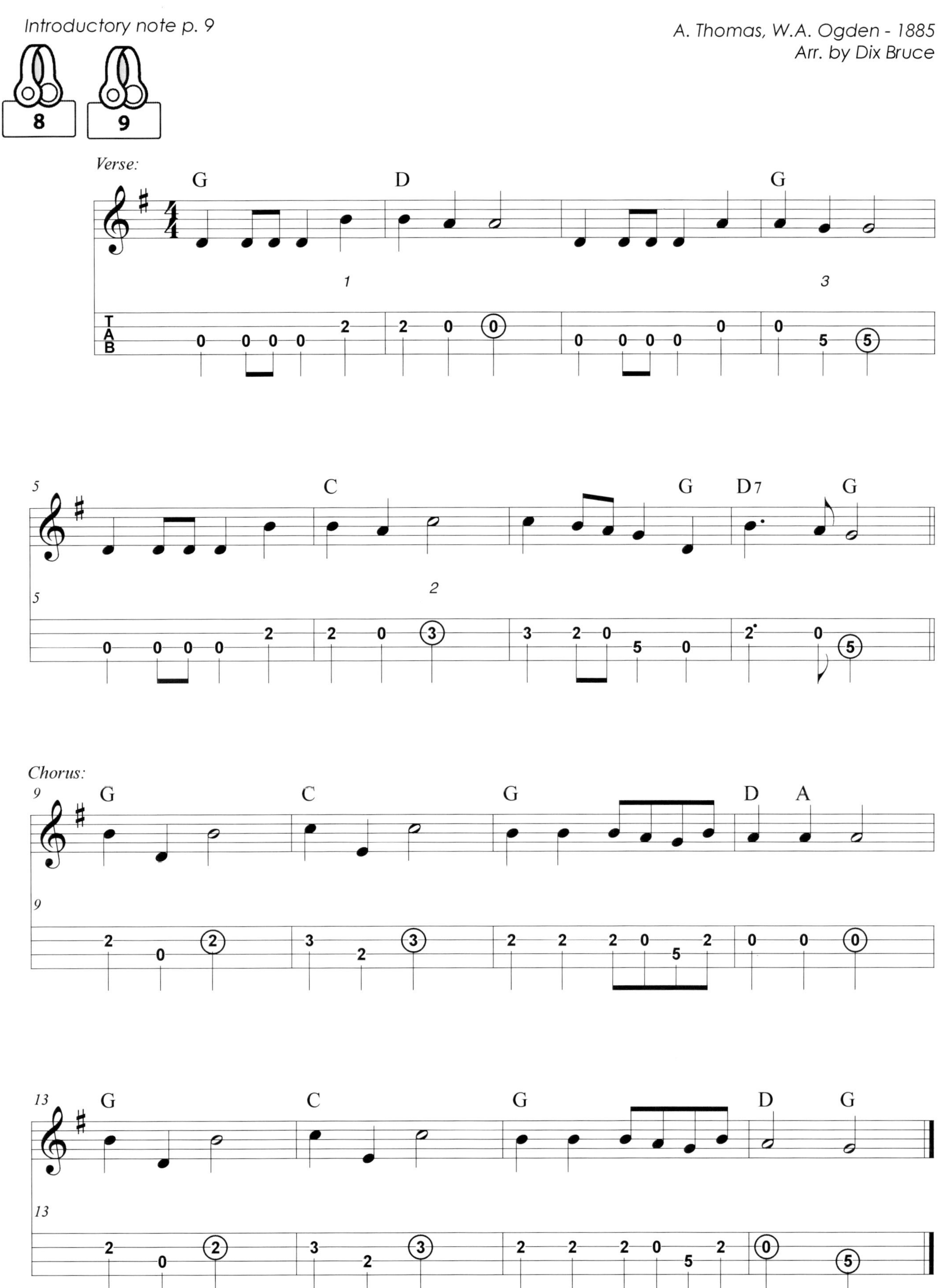

Faith of Our Fathers

F.W. Faber - 1849
Arr. by Dix Bruce

Introductory note p. 9

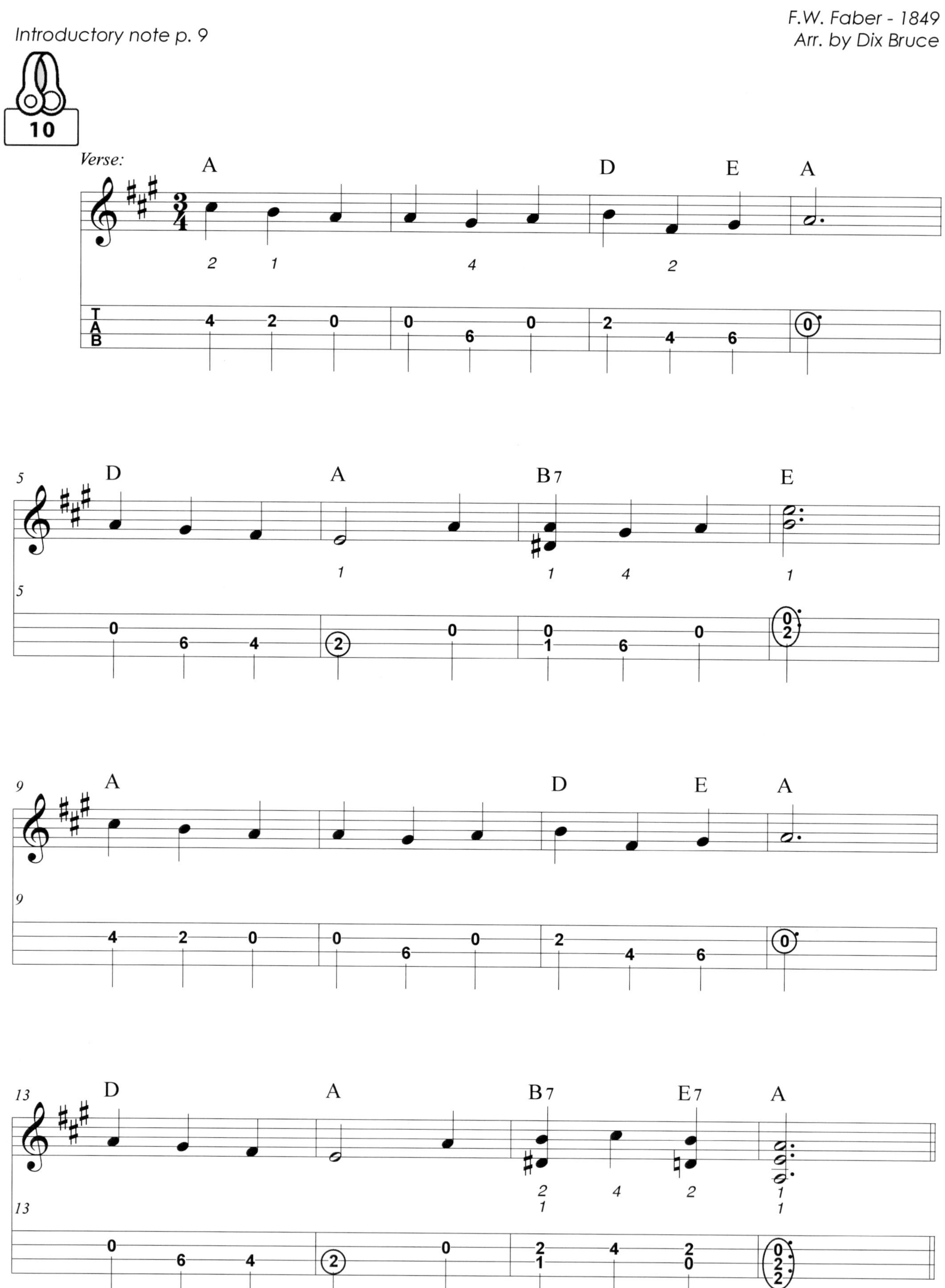

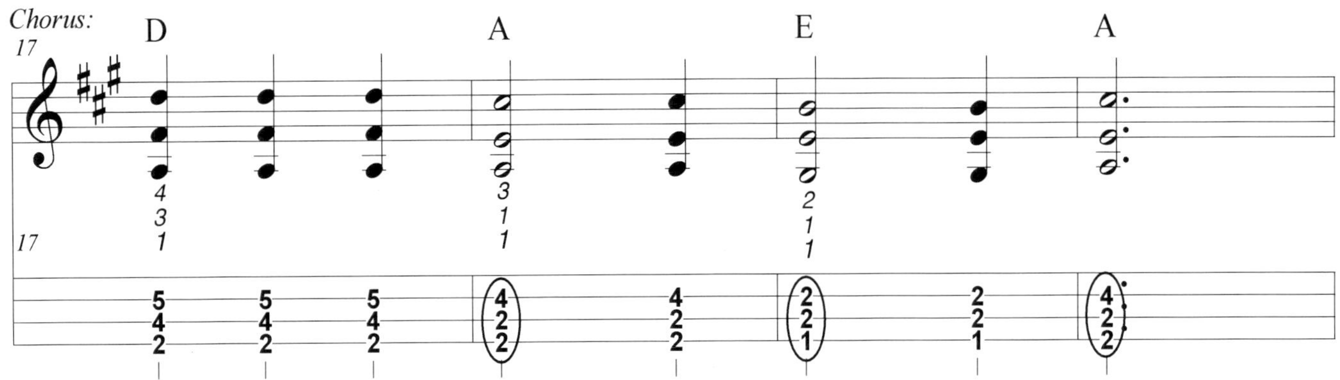

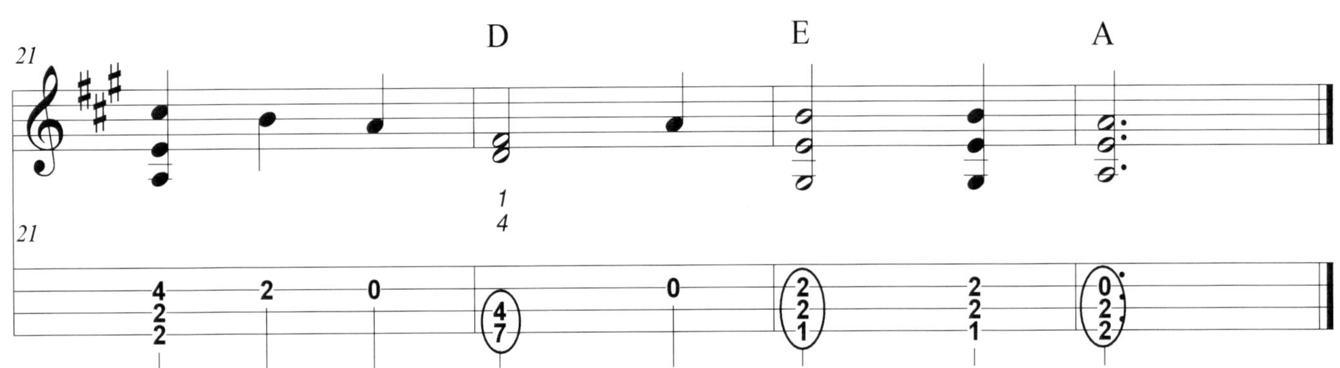

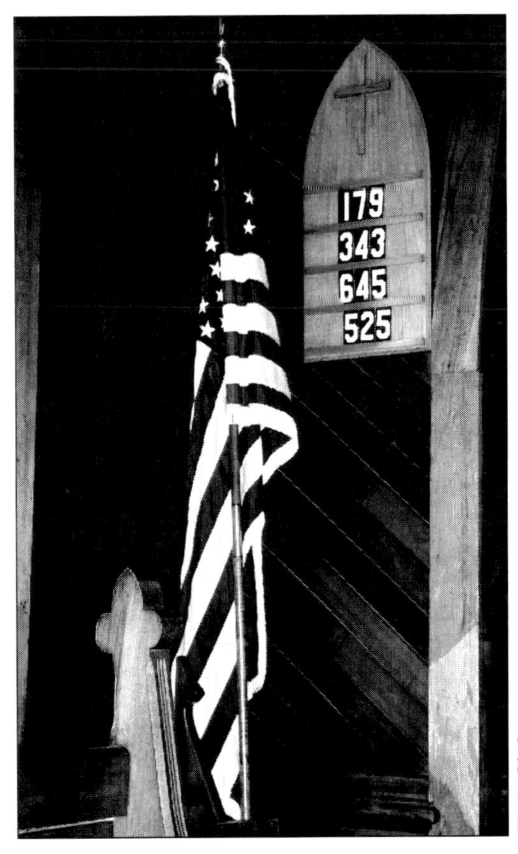

Photo: Dix Bruce

This Little Light of Mine

Introductory note p. 9

Traditional
Arr. by Dix Bruce

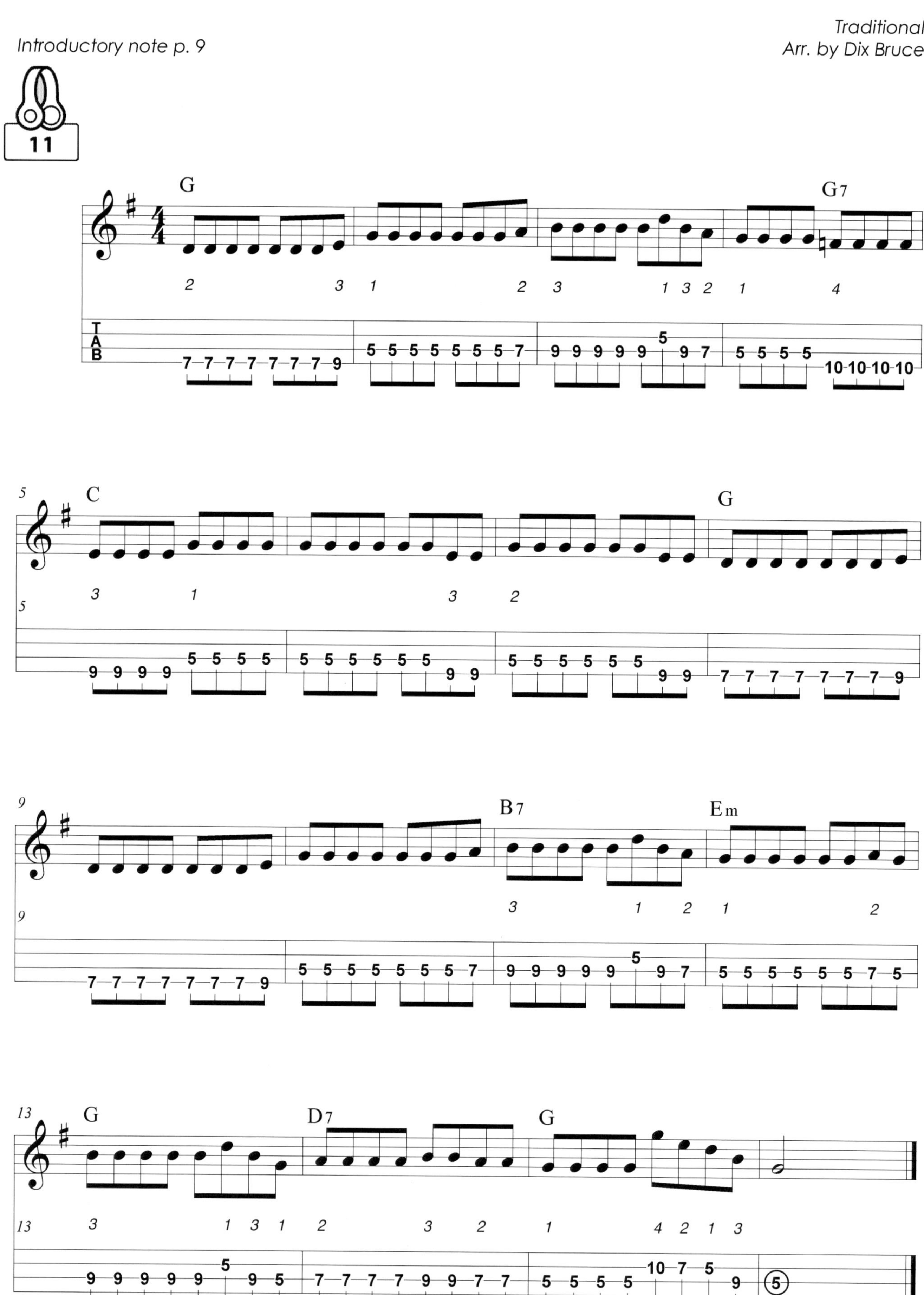

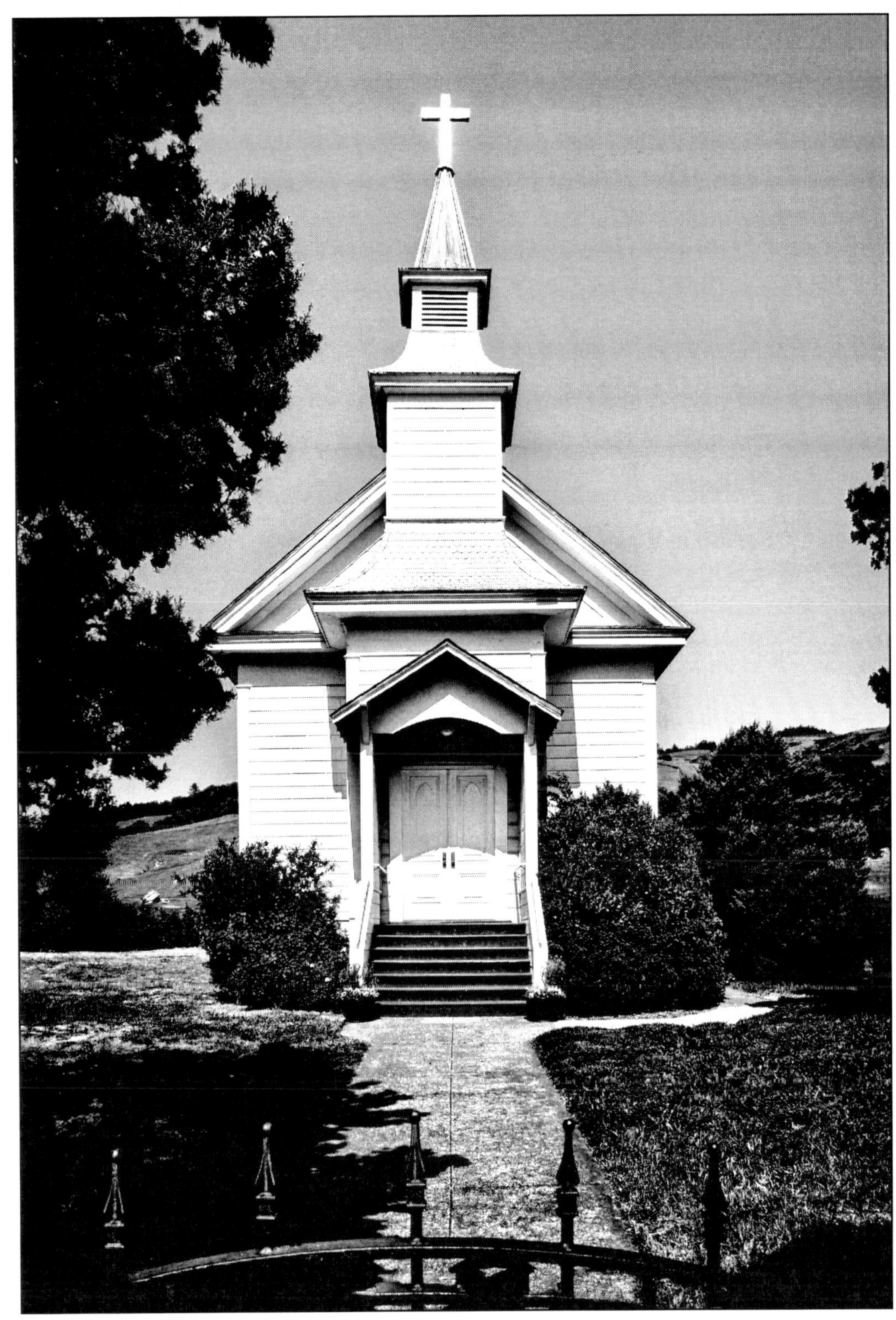

Photo: Dix Bruce

Pass Me Not

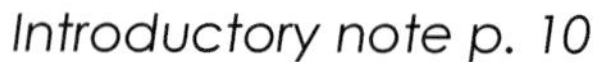
Introductory note p. 10

F. Crosby, W.H. Doane - 1868
Arr. by Dix Bruce

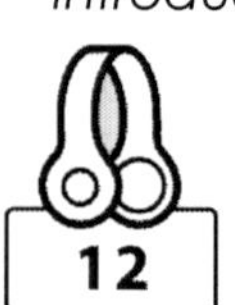

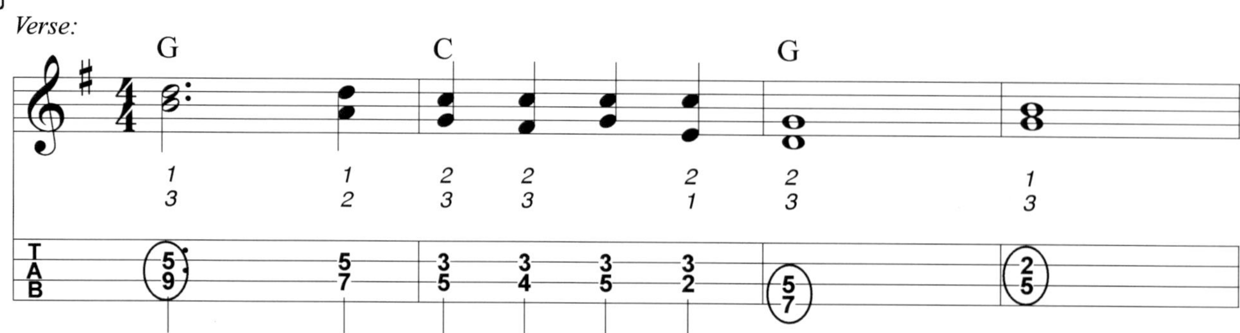

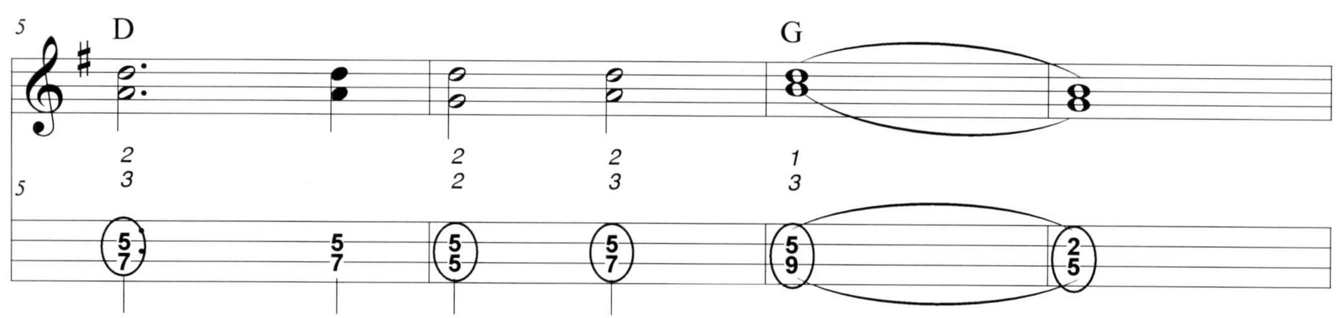

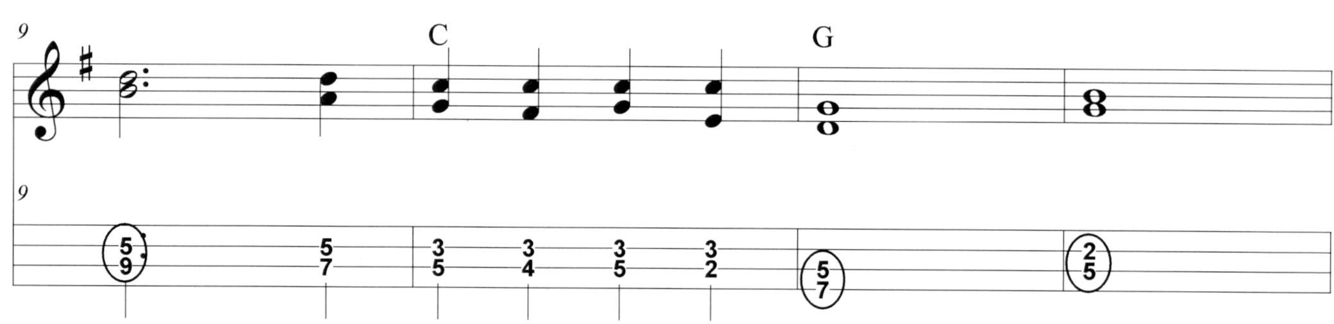

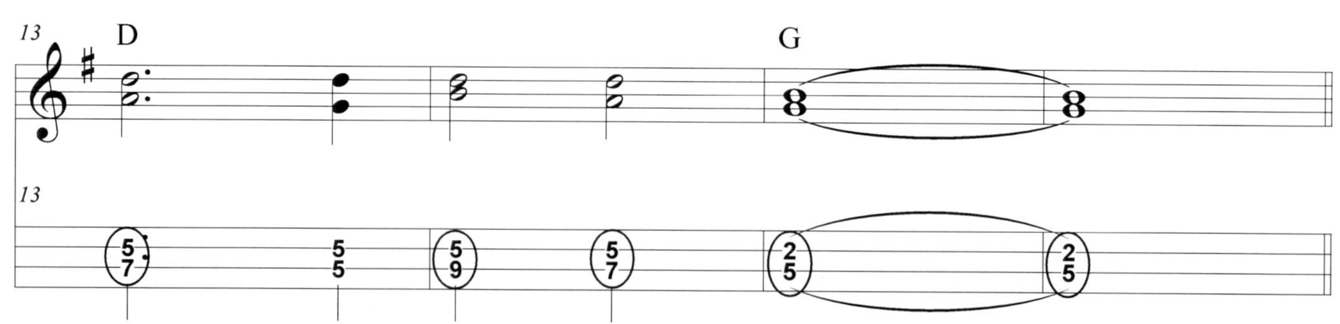

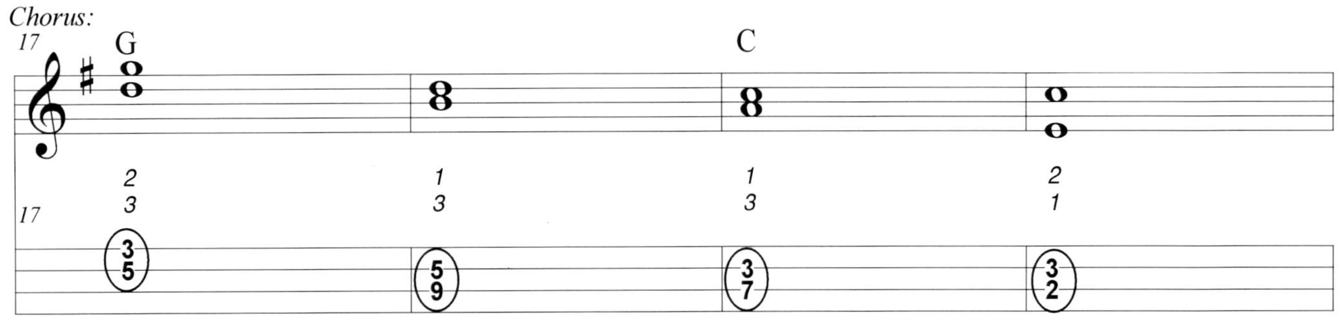
Chorus:
17
G
C
2 3
1 3
1 3
2 1
17
3 5
5 9
3 7
3 2

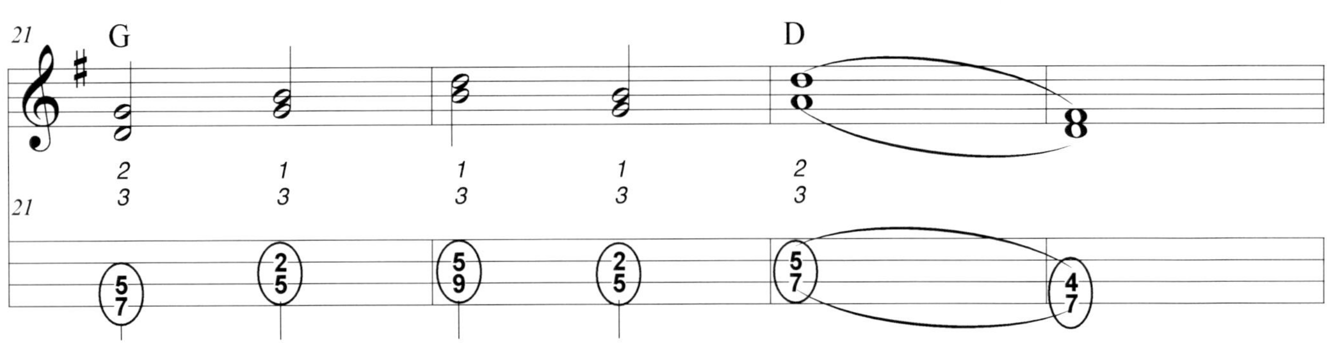
21
G
D
2 3
1 3
1 3
1 3
2 3
21
5 7
2 5
5 9
2 5
5 7
4 7

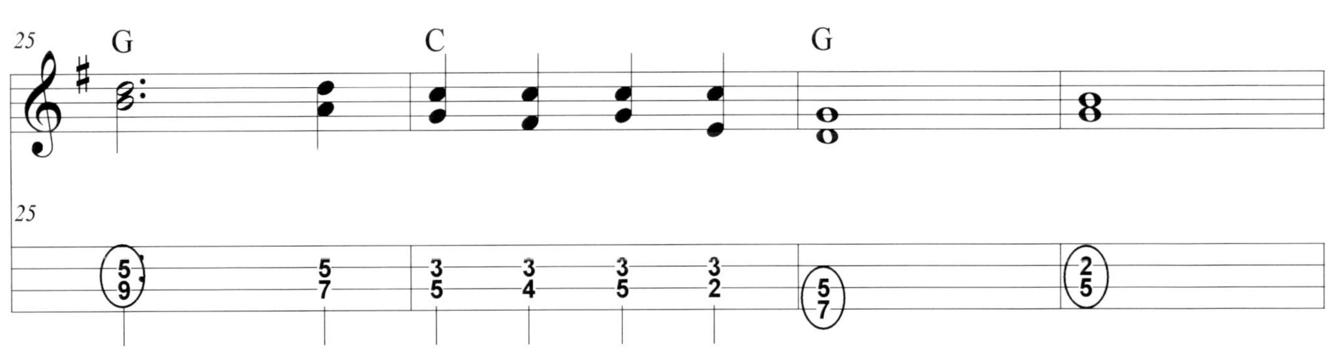
25
G
C
G
25
5 9
5 7
3 5
3 4
3 5
3 2
5 7
2 5

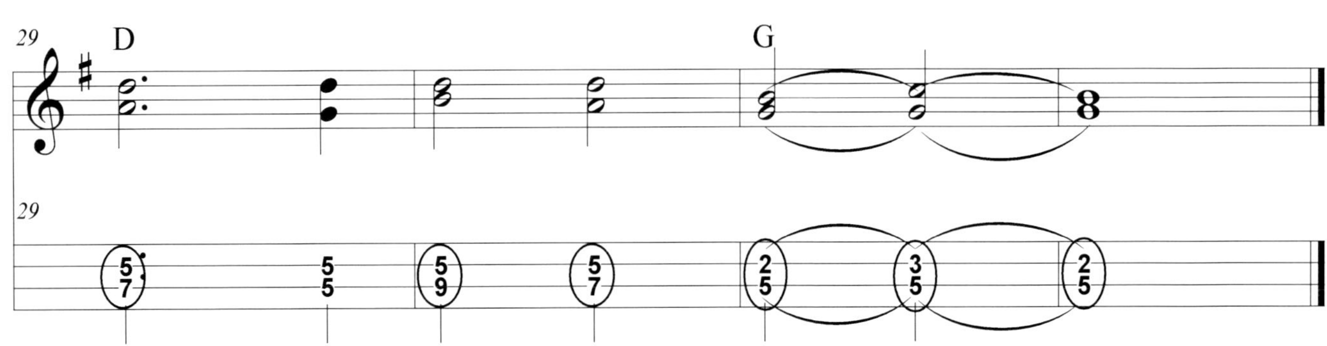
29
D
G
29
5 7
5 5
5 9
5 7
2 5
3 5
2 5

Give Me Oil

Traditional
Arr. by Dix Bruce

Introductory note p. 10

13

Verse:
F
B♭

5
F
C7

9
F
B♭

13
F
C7
F

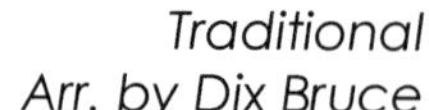

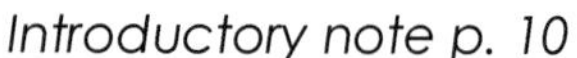

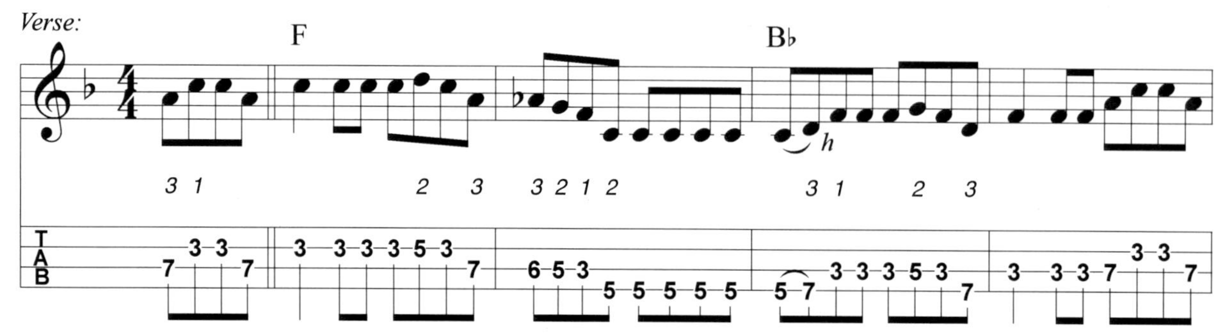

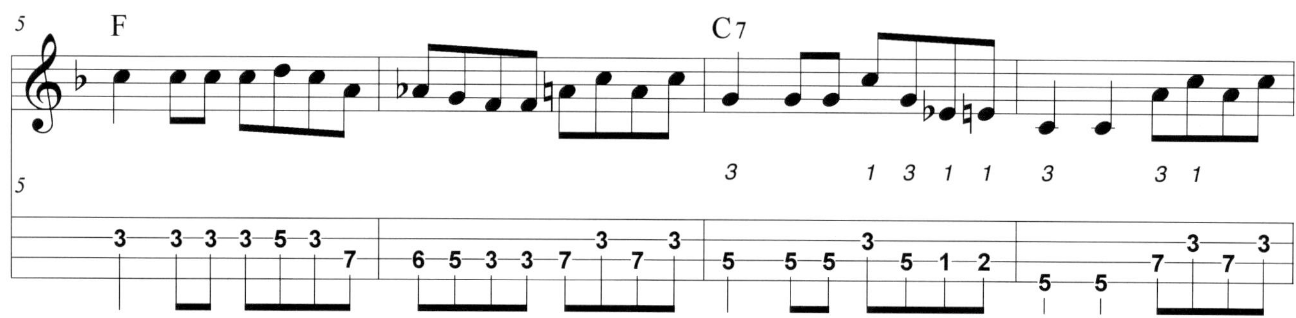

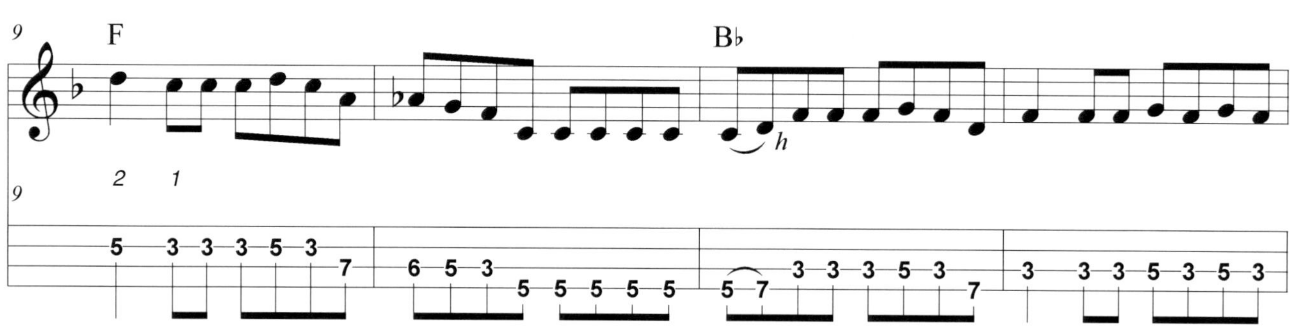

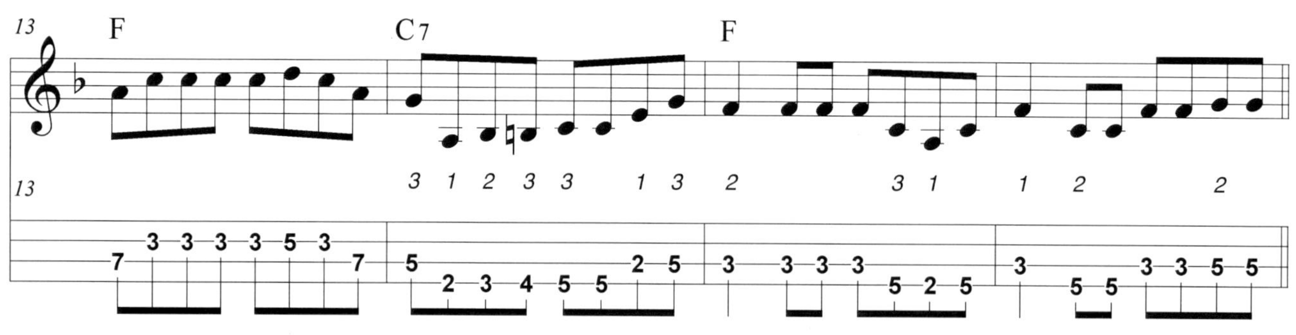

Chorus:

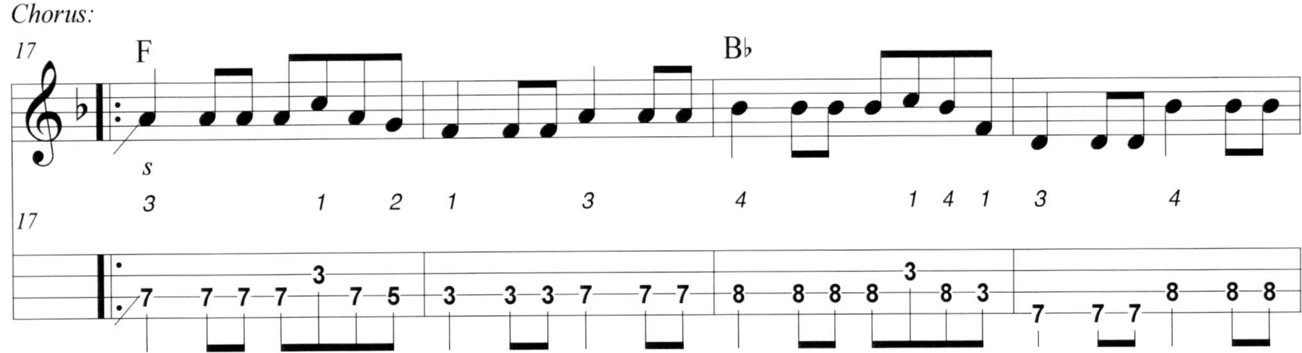

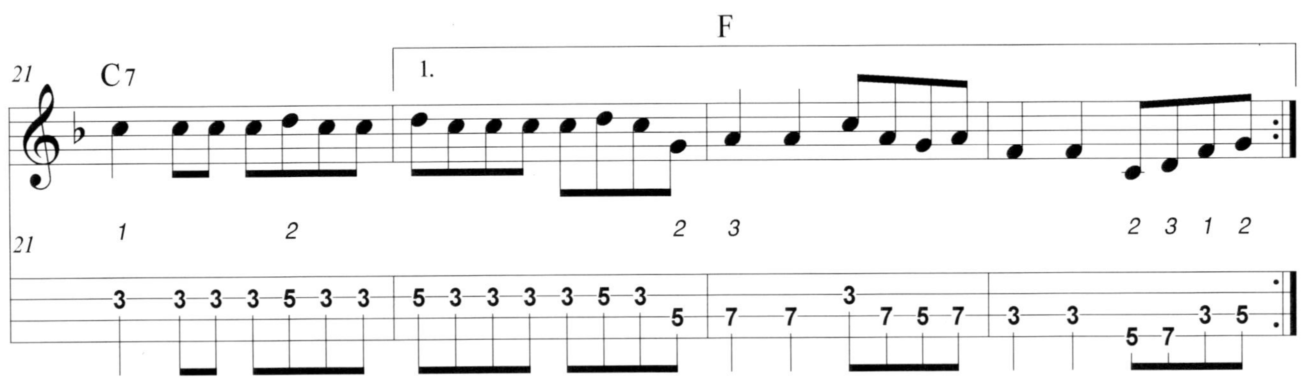

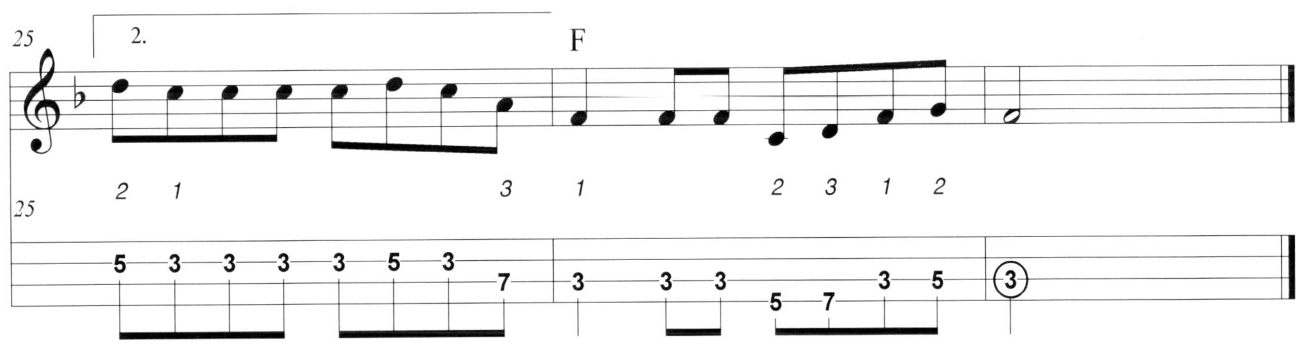

Have Thine Own Way, Lord

A.A. Pollard, G.C. Stebbins - 1907
Arr. by Dix Bruce

Introductory note p. 10

14

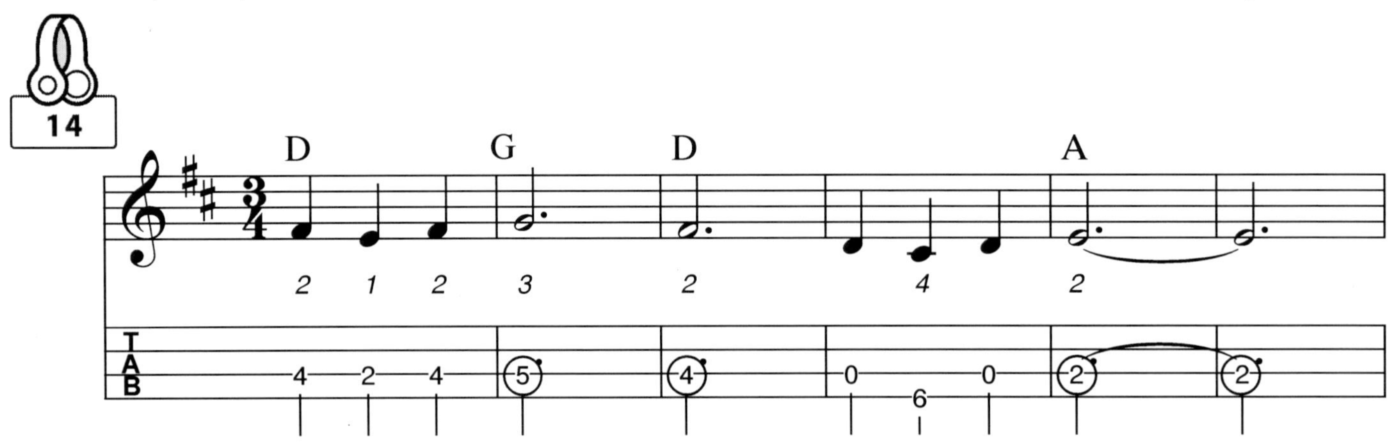

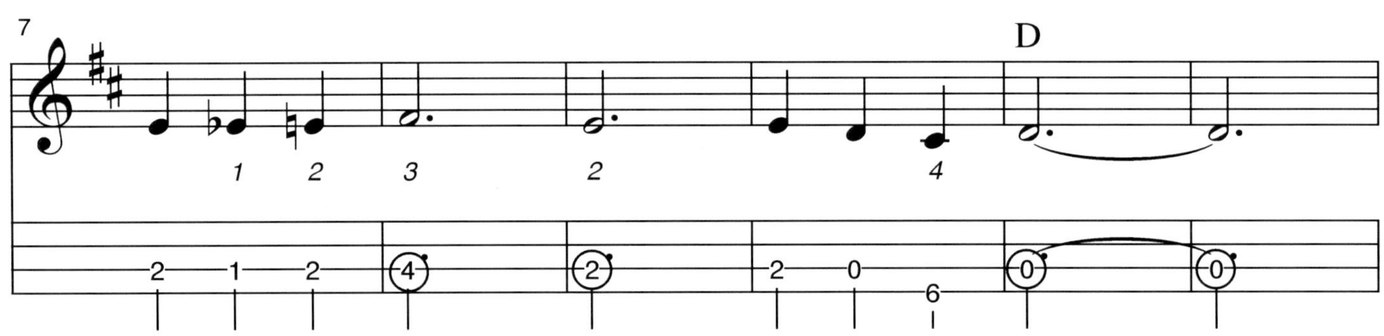

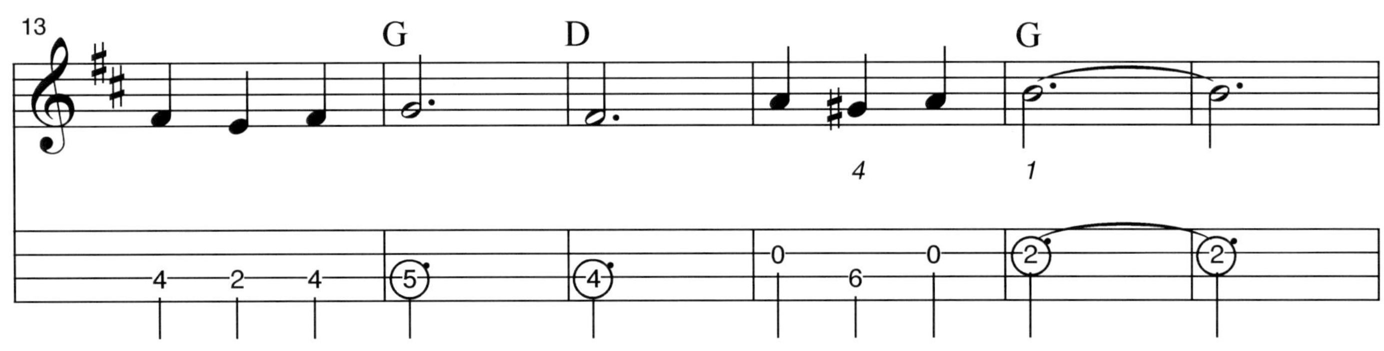

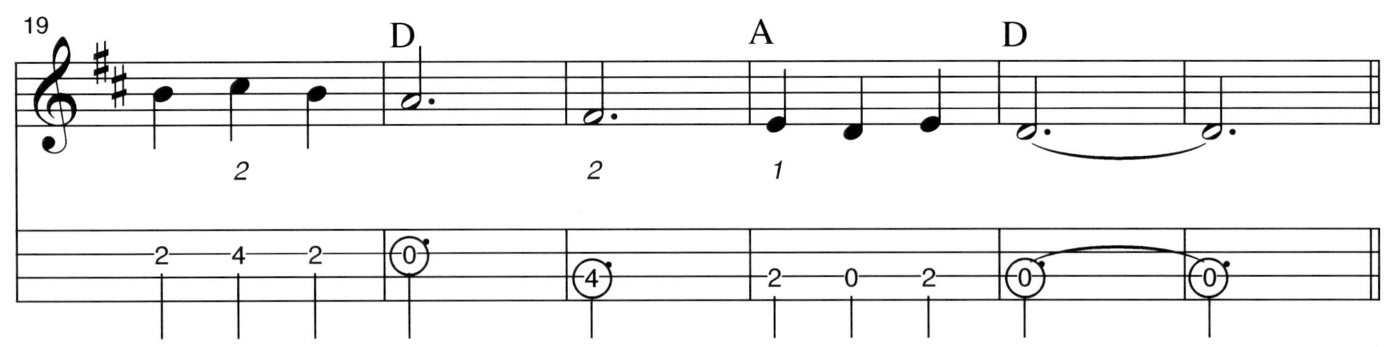

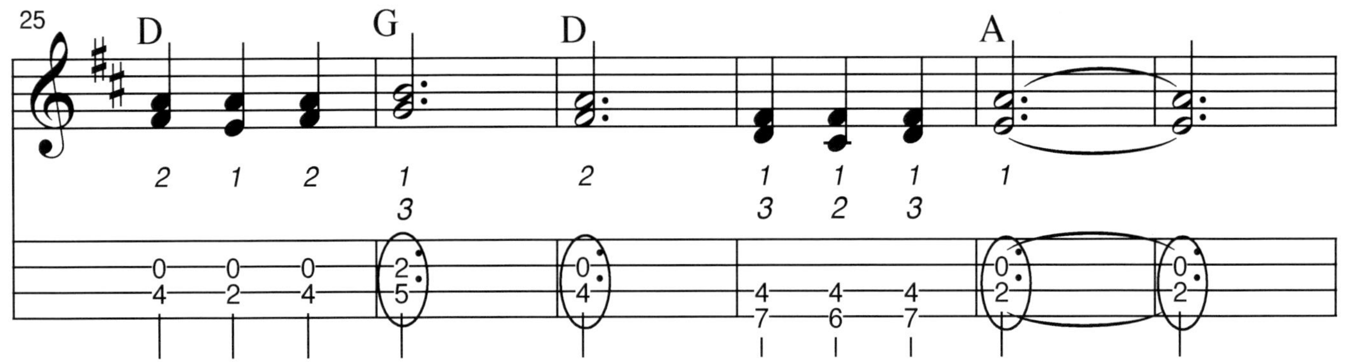
25
D
G
D
A

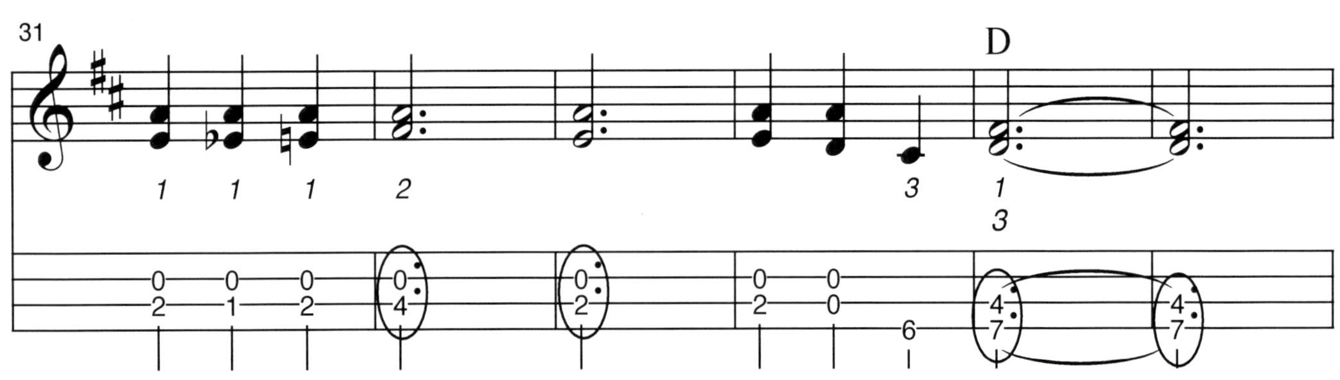
31
D

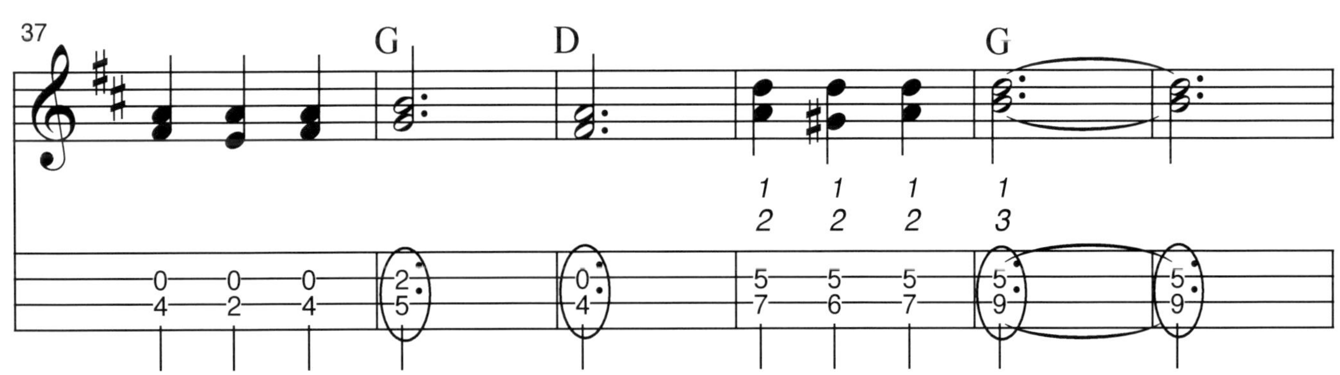
37
G
D
G

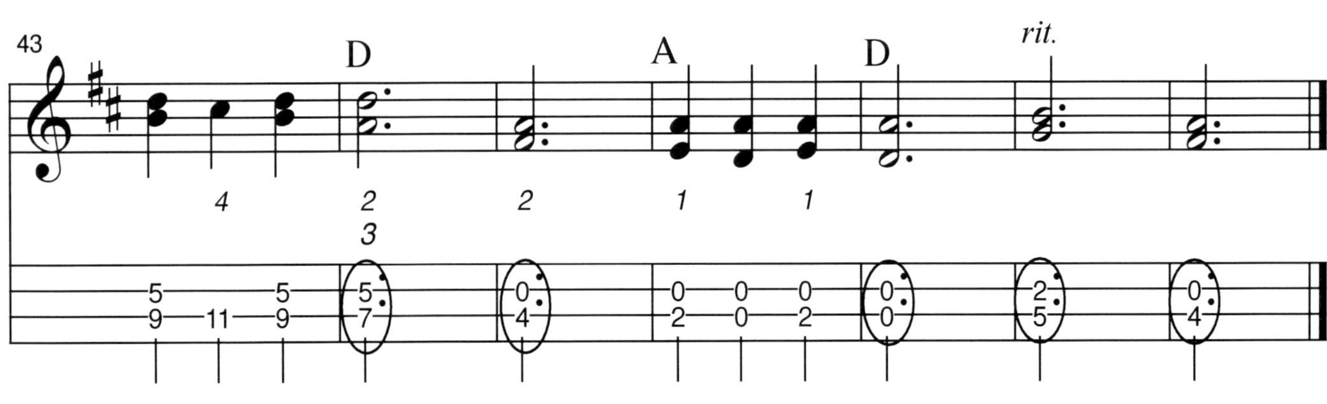
43
D
A
D
rit.

What a Friend We Have in Jesus

J.M. Scriven, C.C. Converse - 1870
Arr. by Dix Bruce

Introductory note p. 10

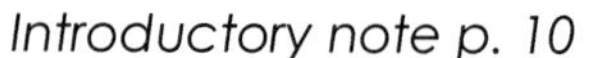

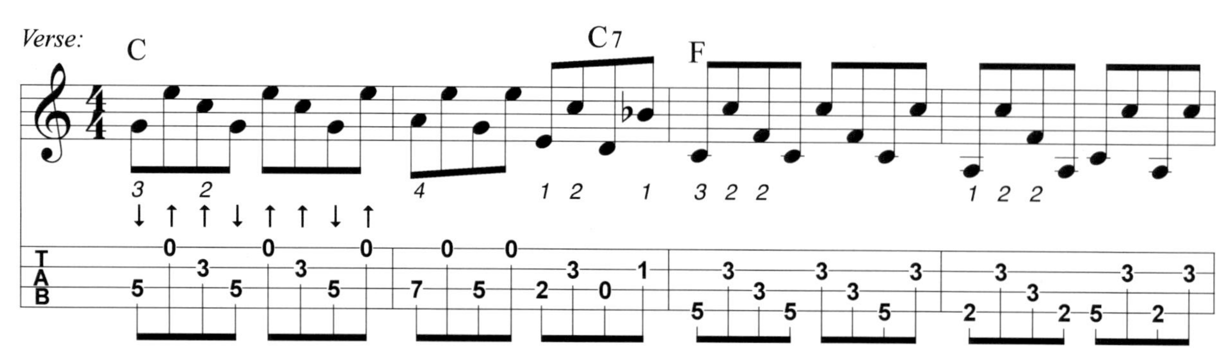

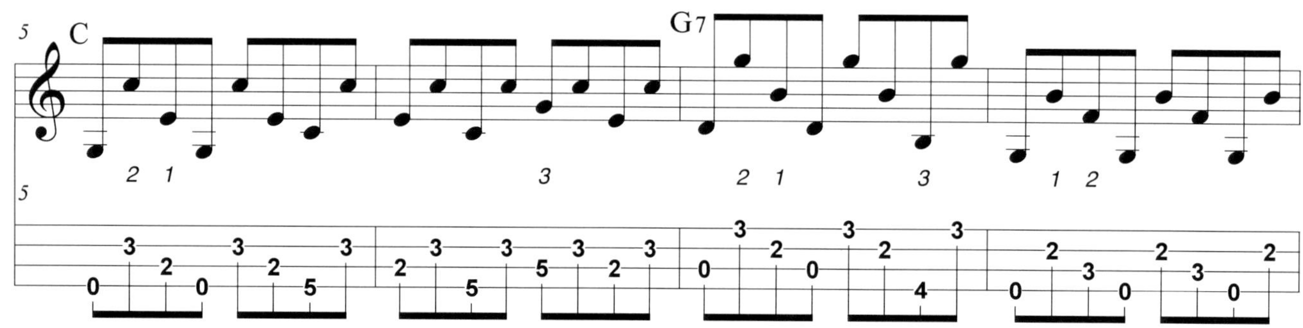

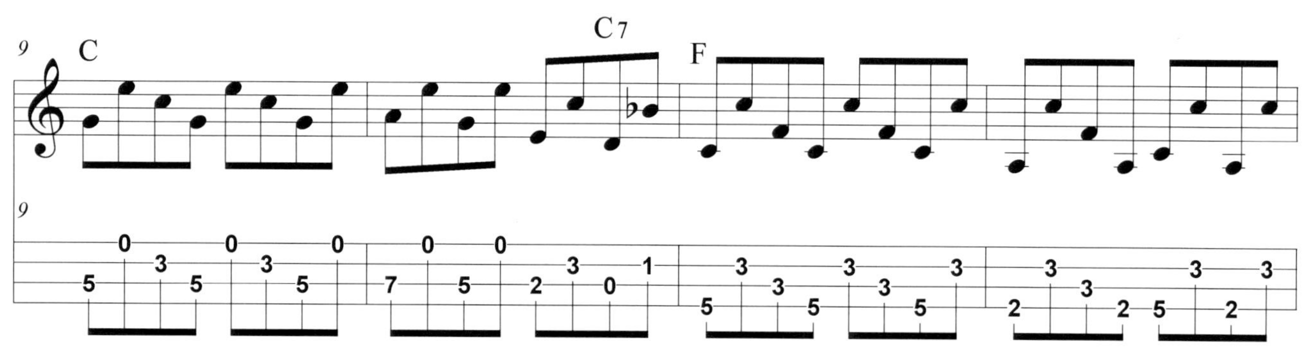

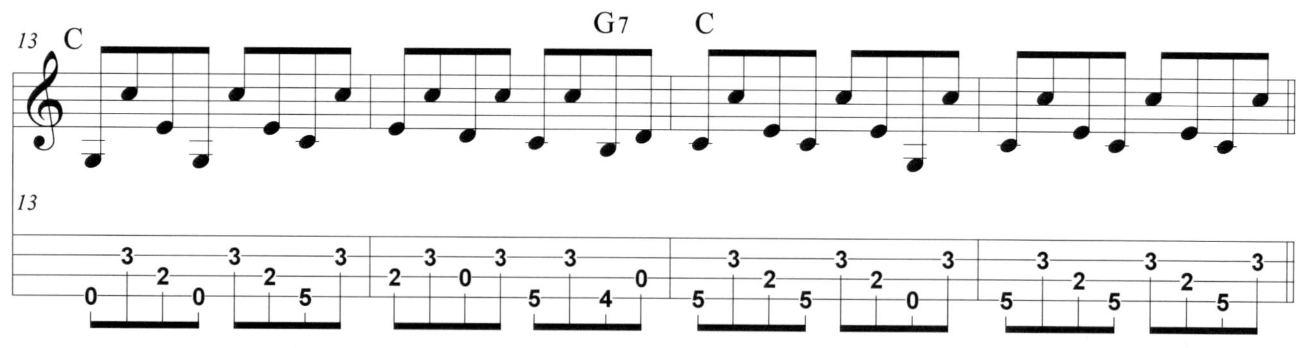

Chorus:

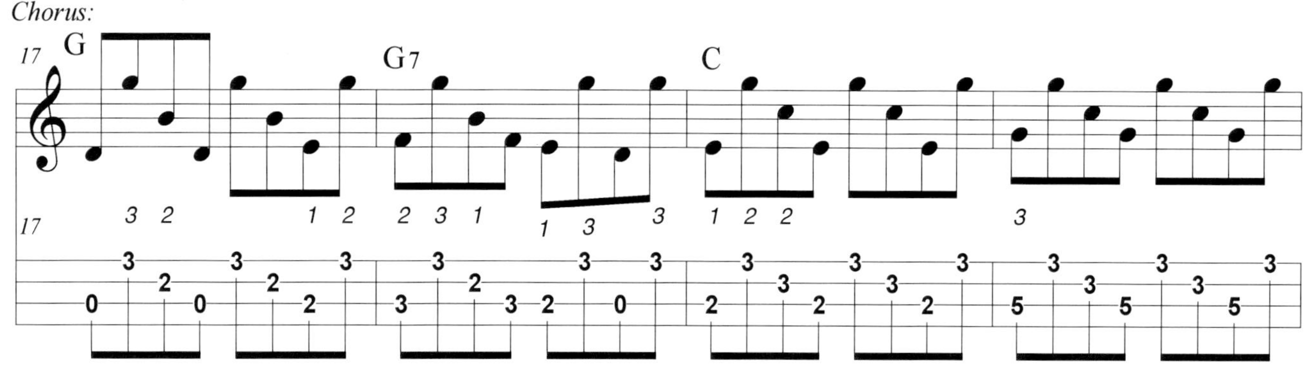

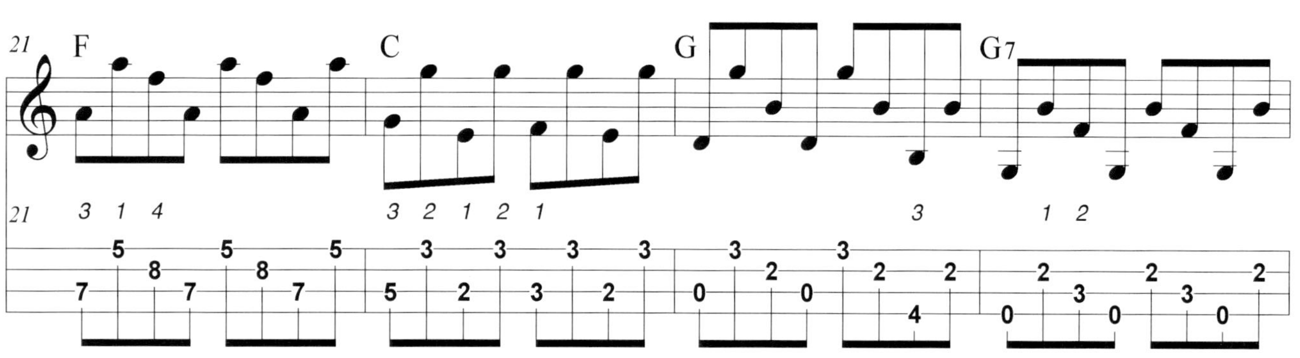

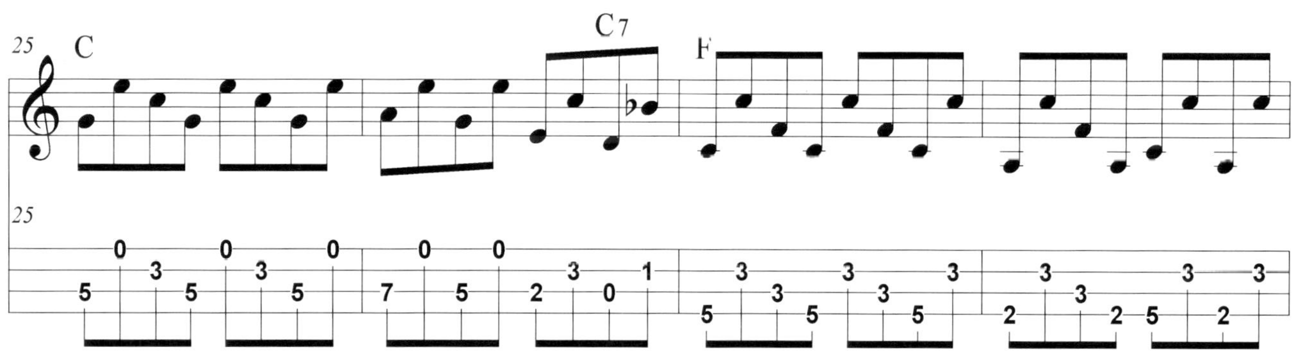

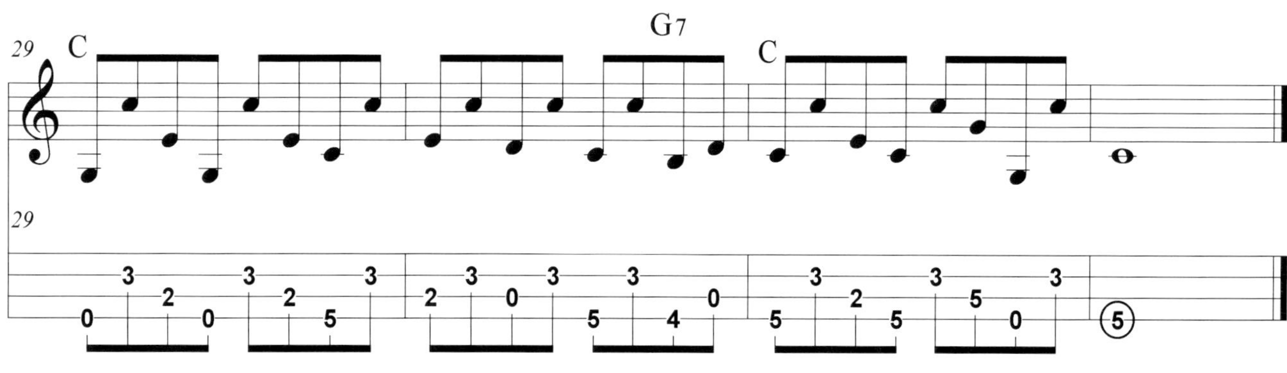

Higher Ground

J. Oatman, Jr. - 1898
Arr. by Dix Bruce

Introductory note p. 10

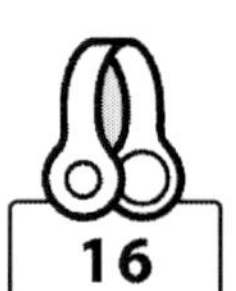

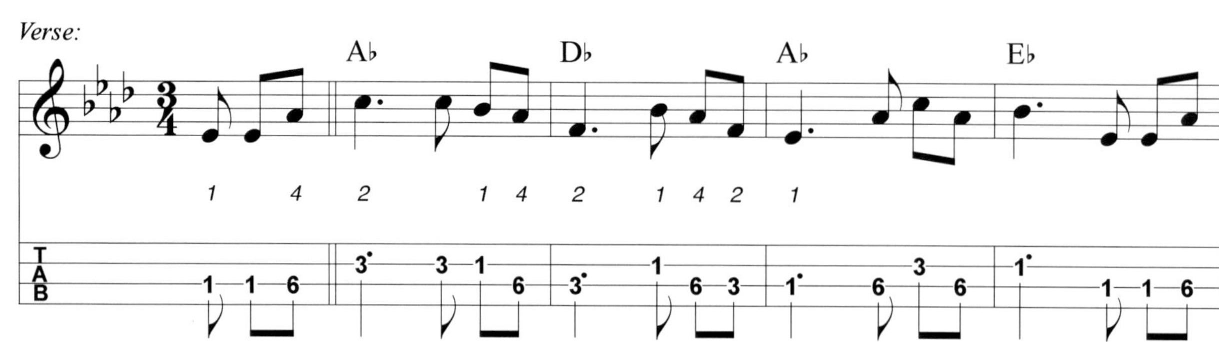

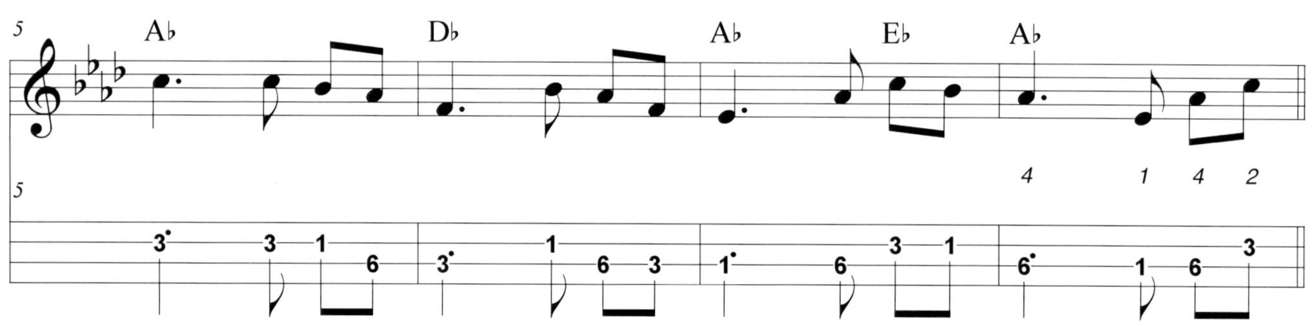

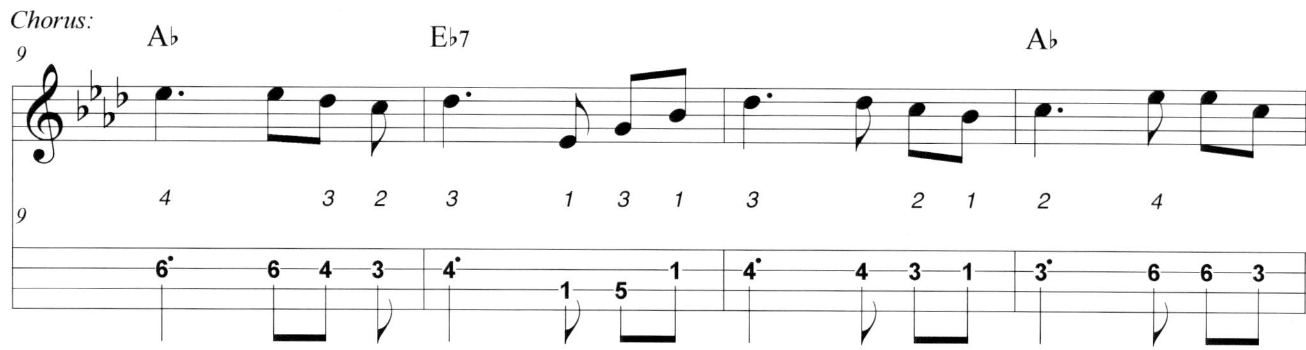

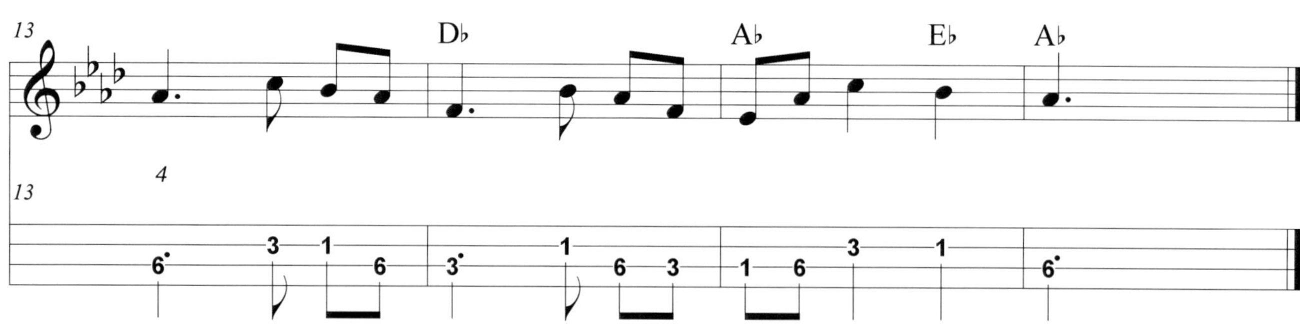

I Shall Not Be Moved

Introductory note p. 10

Traditional
Arr. by Dix Bruce

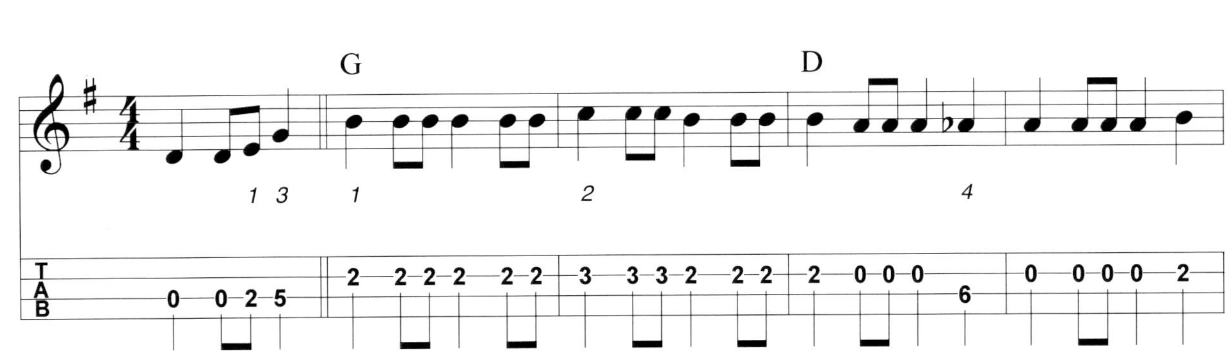

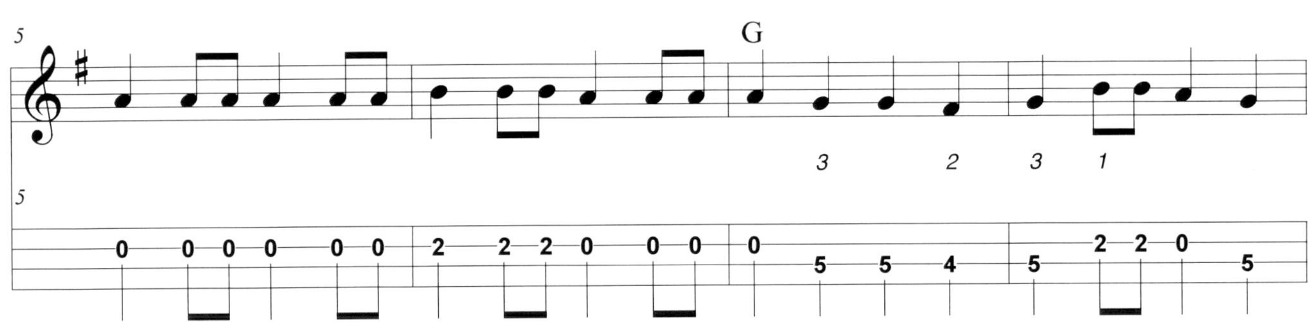

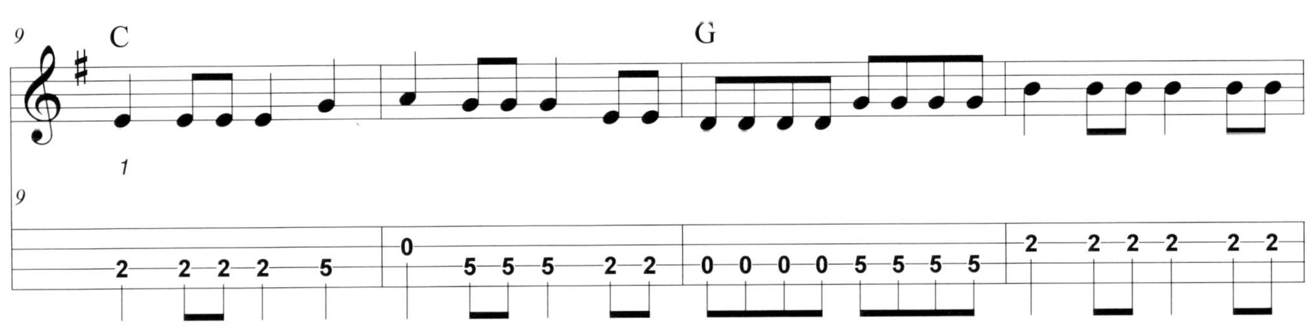

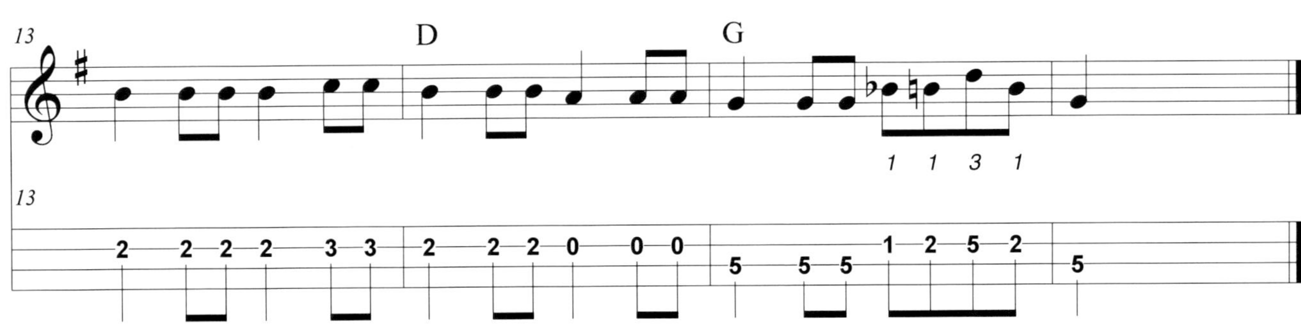

There Shall Be Showers of Blessing

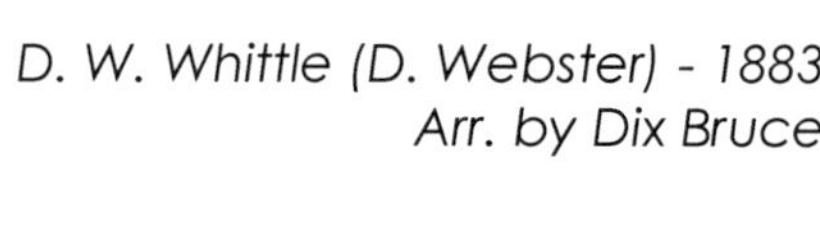

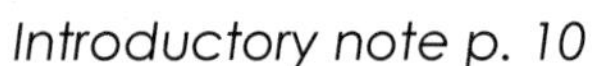

18

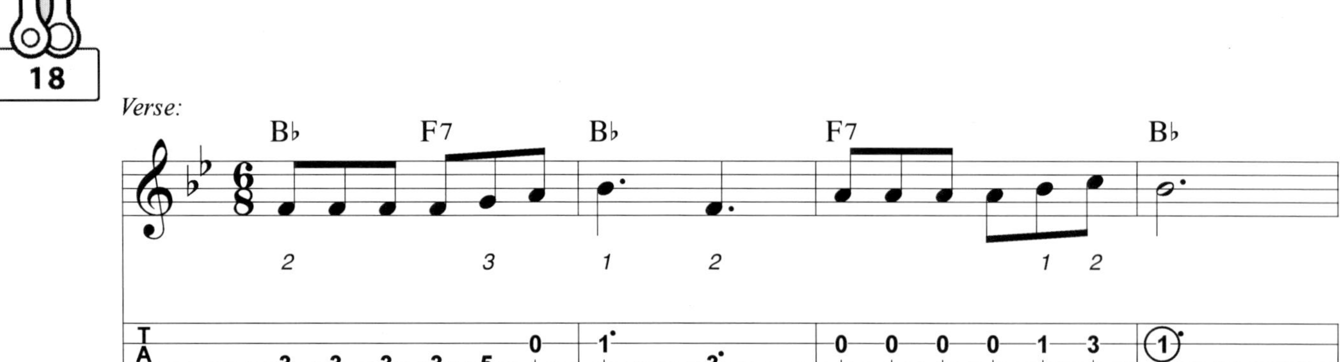

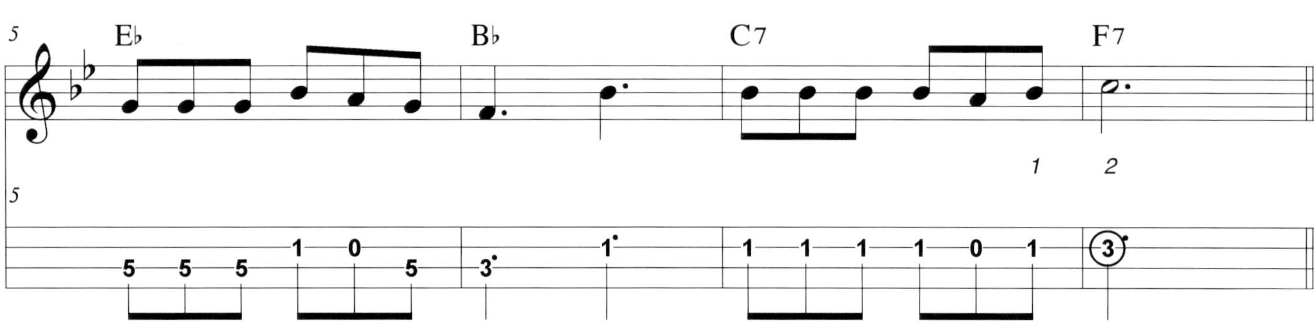

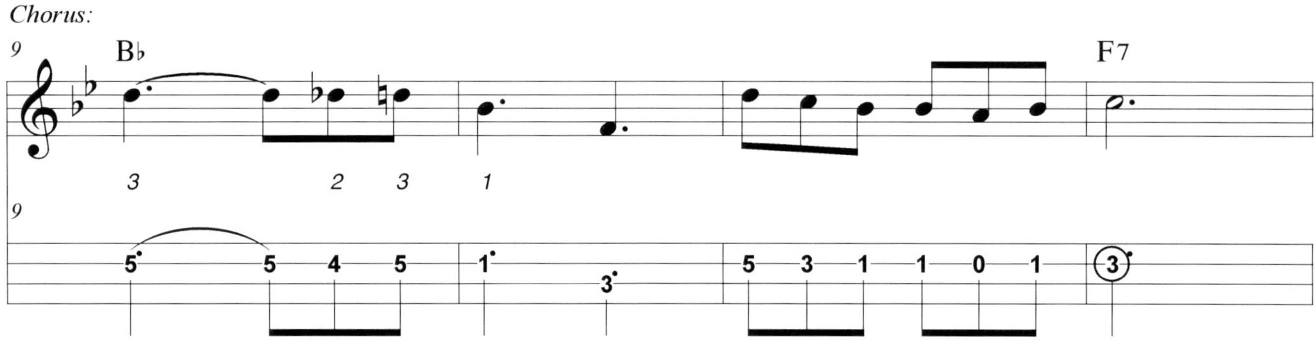

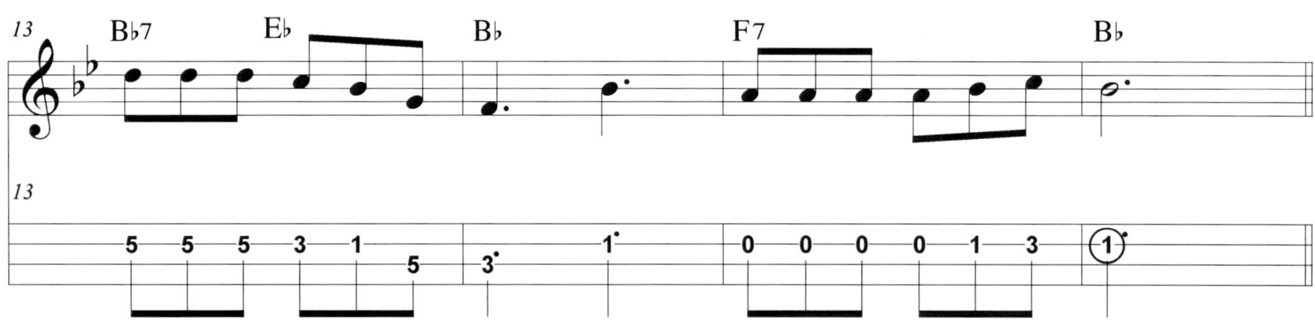

Verse:

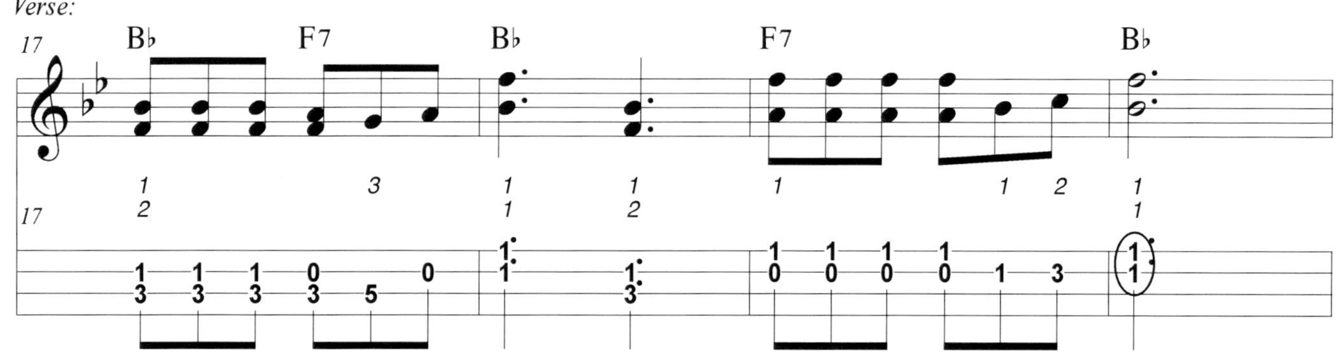

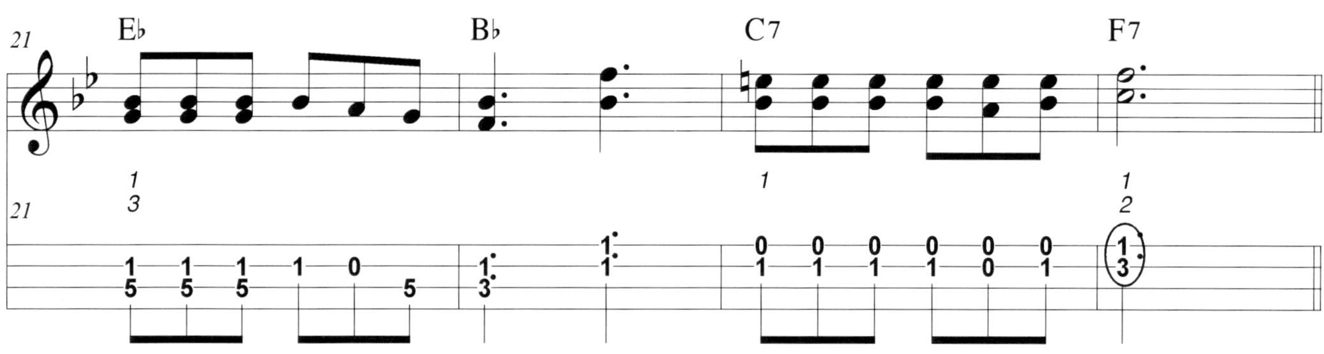

Chorus:

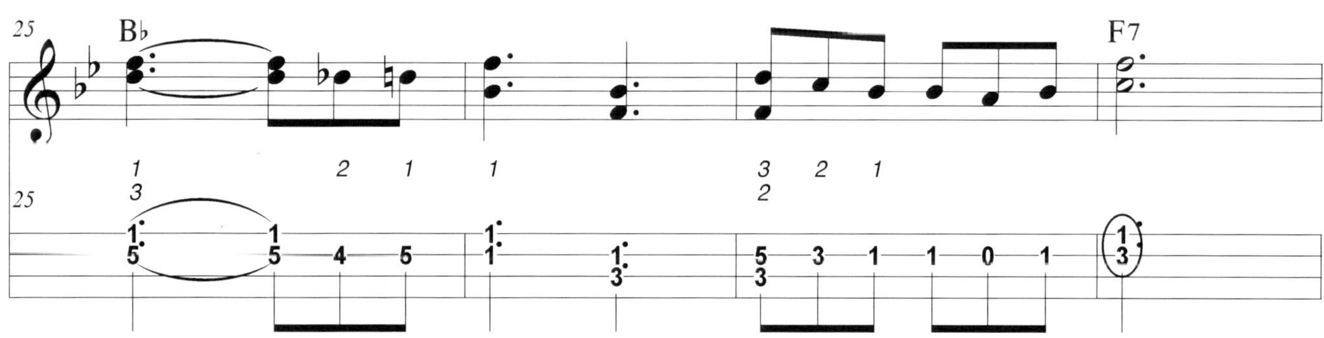

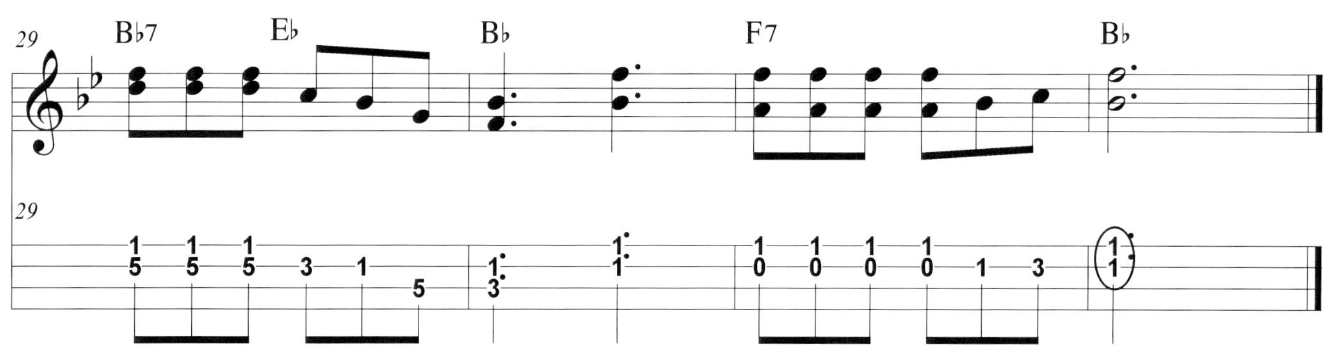

Holy, Holy, Holy

R. Heber, J. Dykes - 1861
Arr. by Dix Bruce

Introductory note p. 11

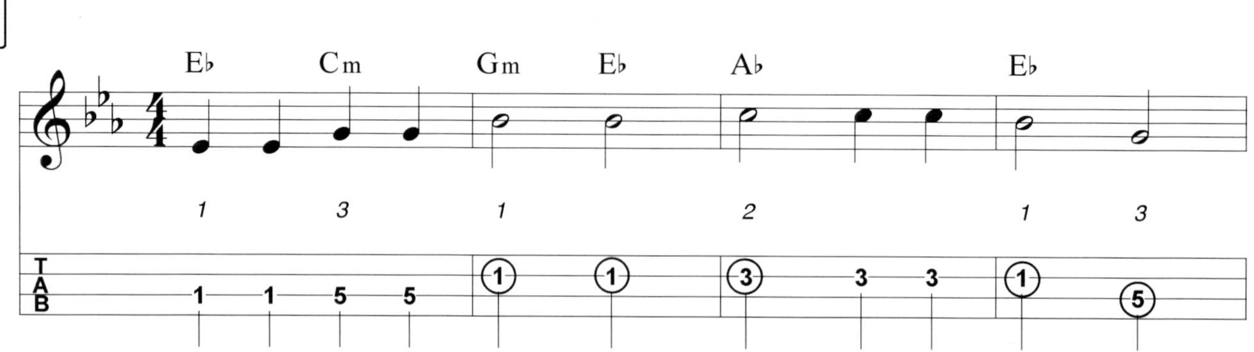

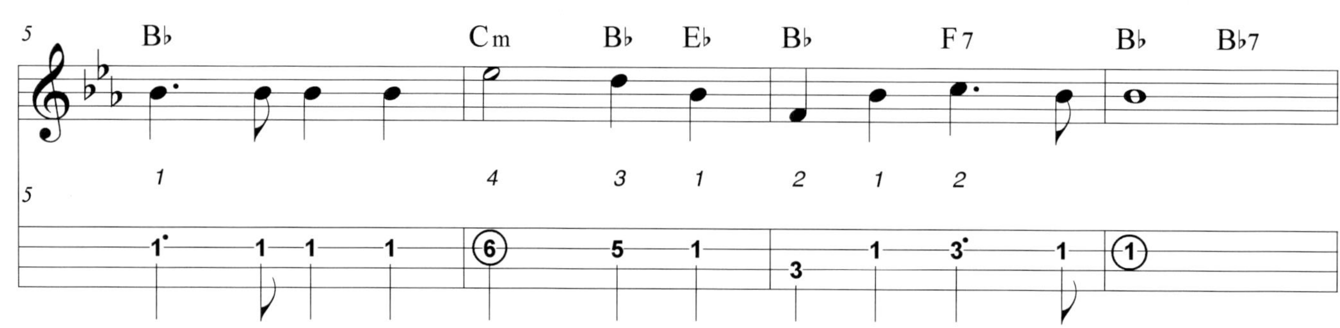

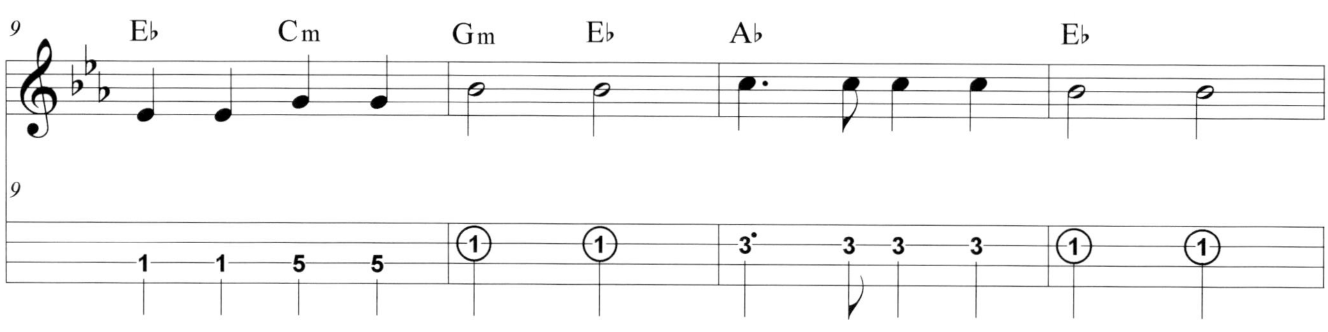

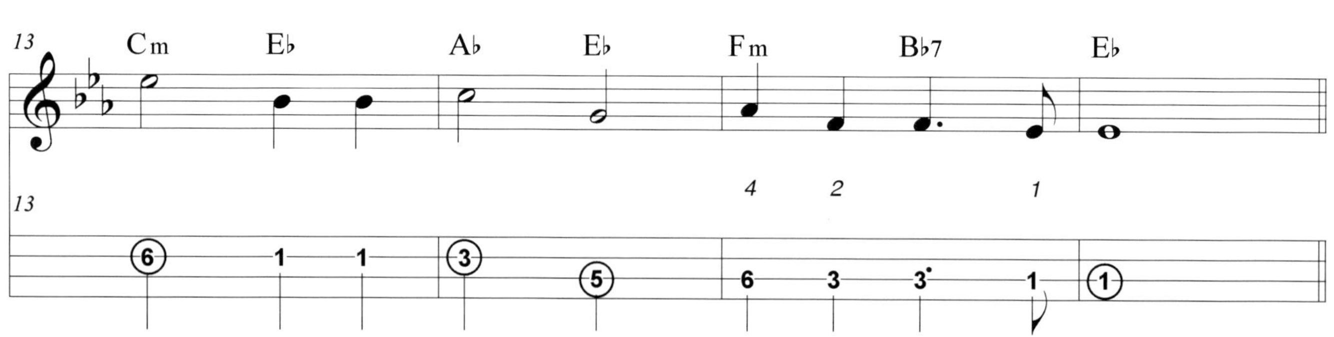

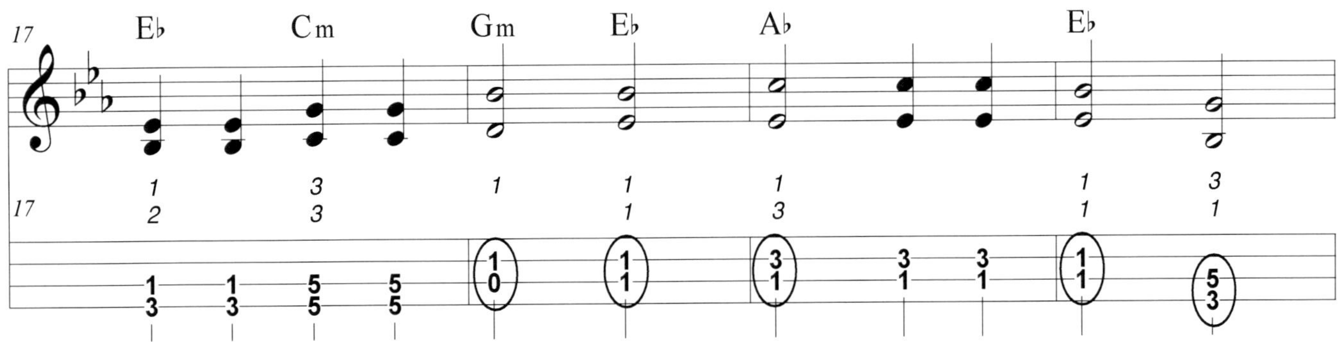
17
E♭
Cm
Gm
E♭
A♭
E♭
17

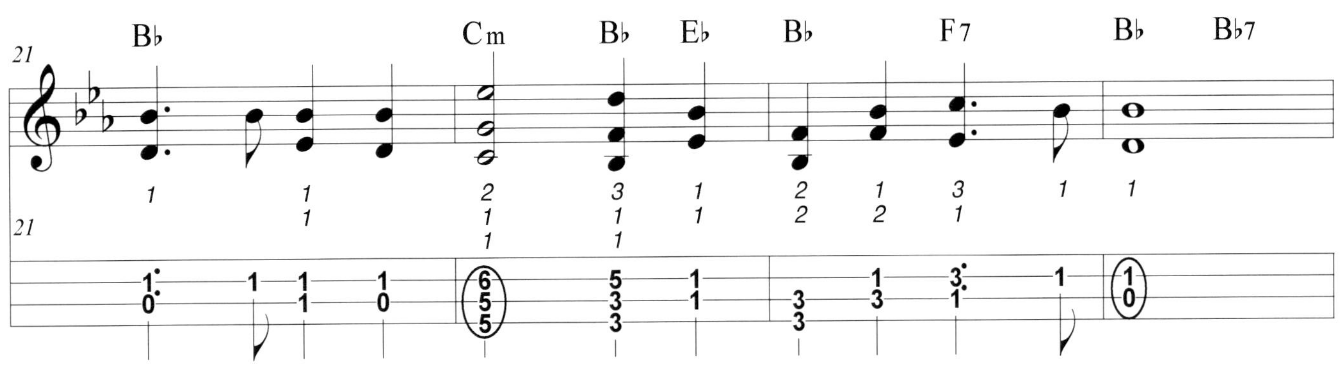
21
B♭
Cm
B♭
E♭
B♭
F7
B♭
B♭7
21

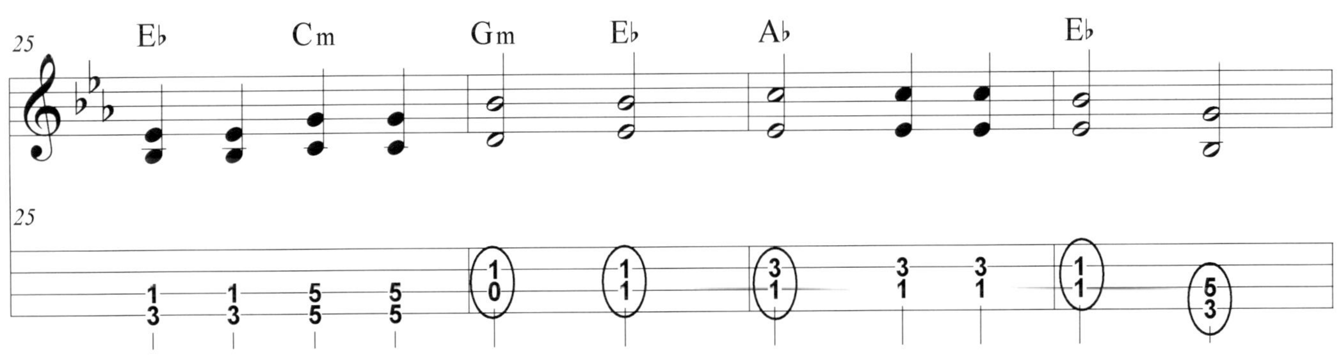
25
E♭
Cm
Gm
E♭
A♭
E♭
25

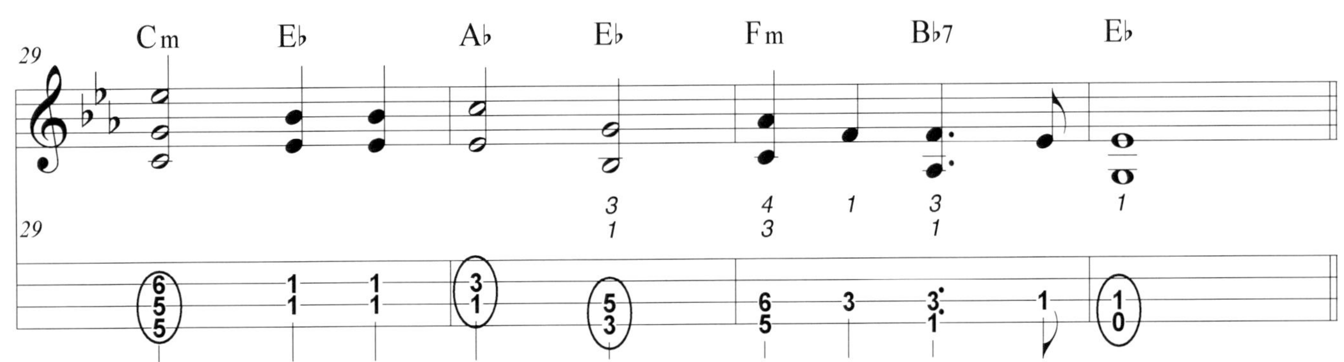
29
Cm
E♭
A♭
E♭
Fm
B♭7
E♭
29

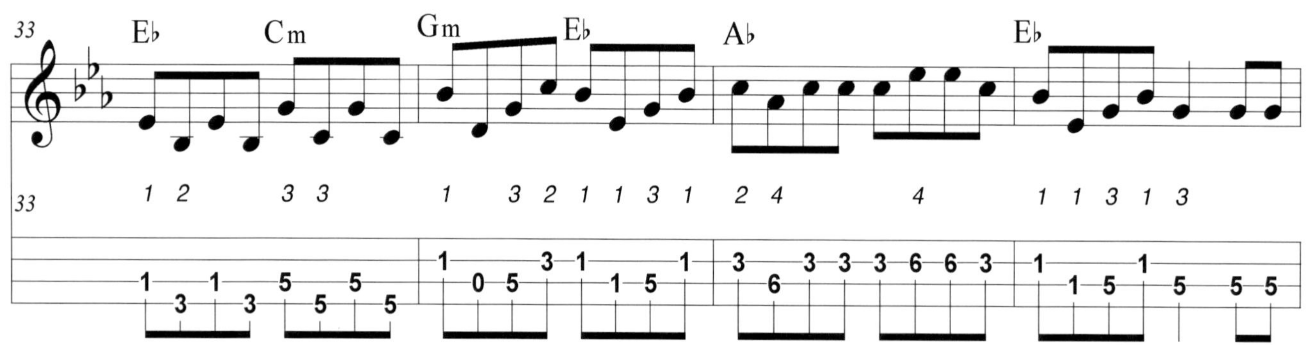
33
E♭
Cm
Gm
E♭
A♭
E♭

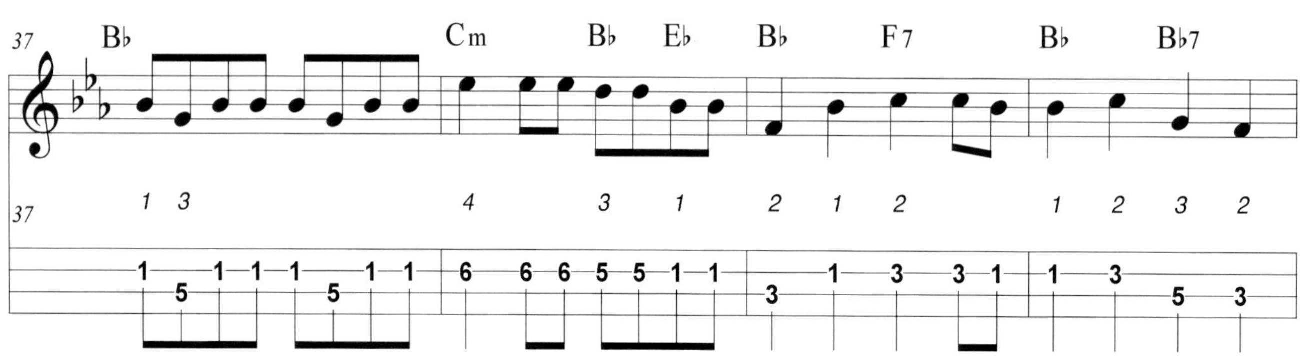
37
B♭
Cm
B♭
E♭
B♭
F7
B♭
B♭7

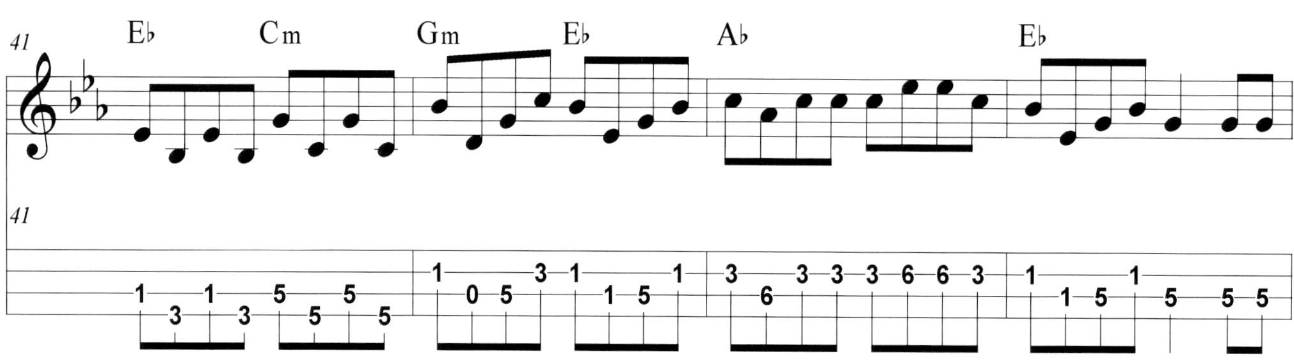
41
E♭
Cm
Gm
E♭
A♭
E♭

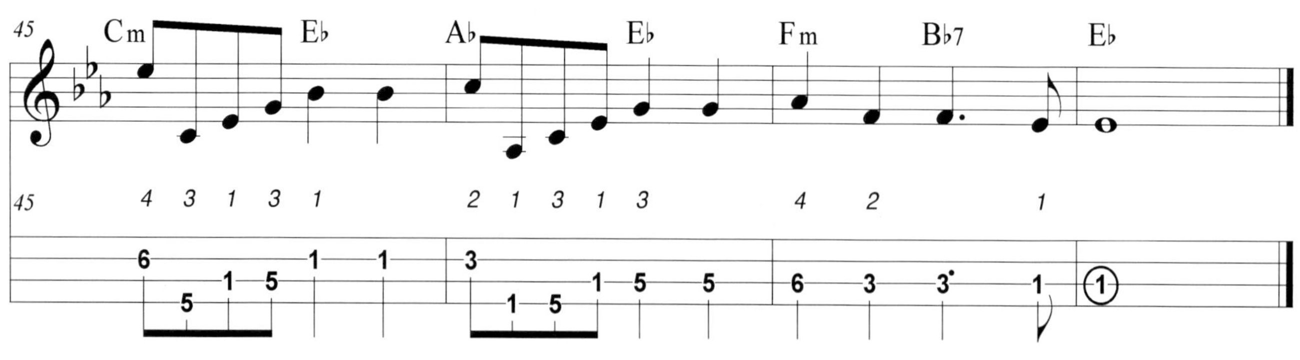
45
Cm
E♭
A♭
E♭
Fm
B♭7
E♭

O Store Gud

Carl Boberg-ca. mid - 1880s
Arr. by Dix Bruce

Introductory note p. 11

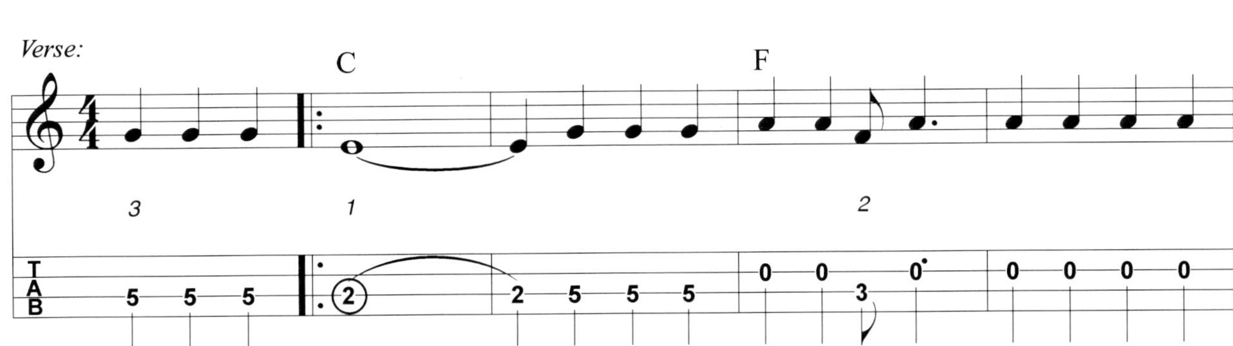

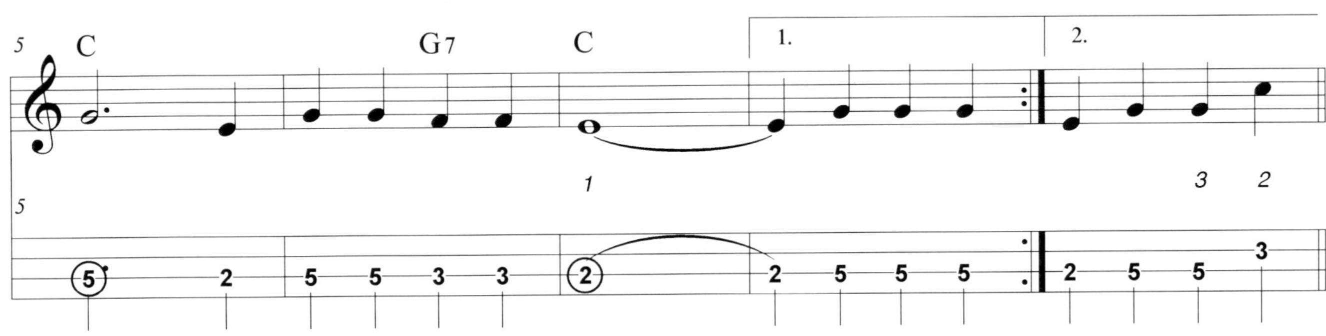

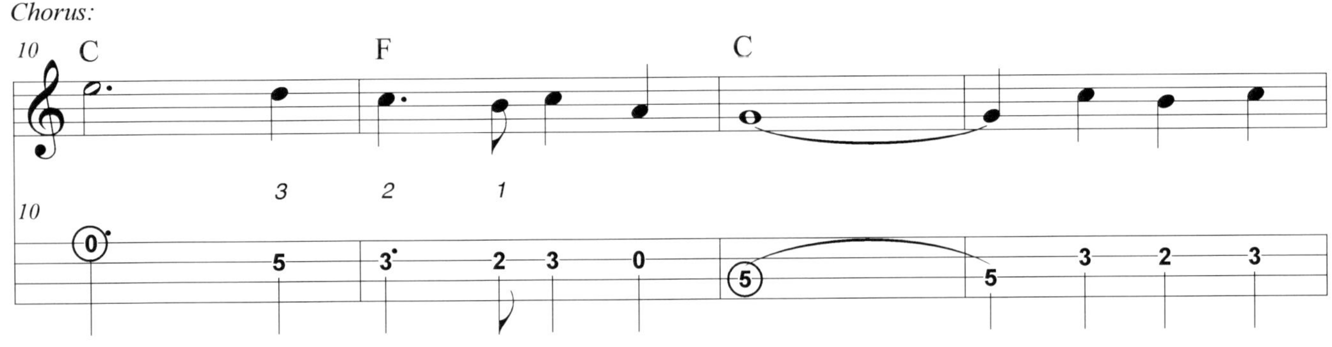

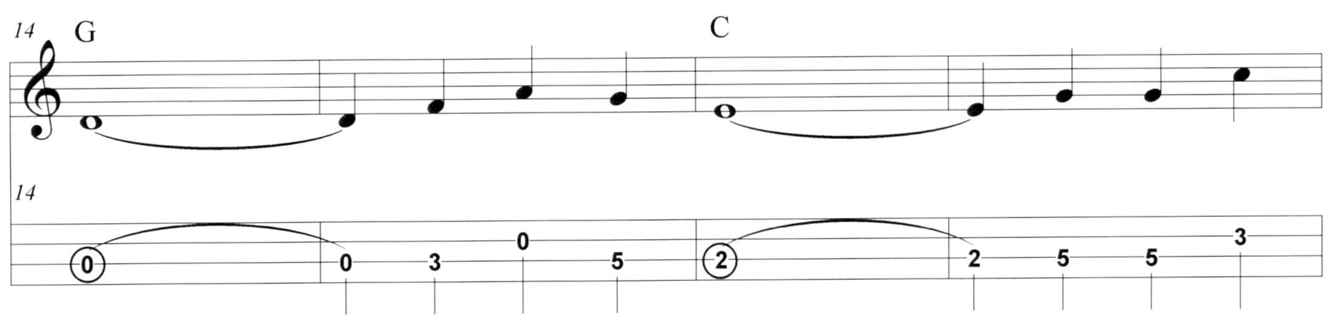

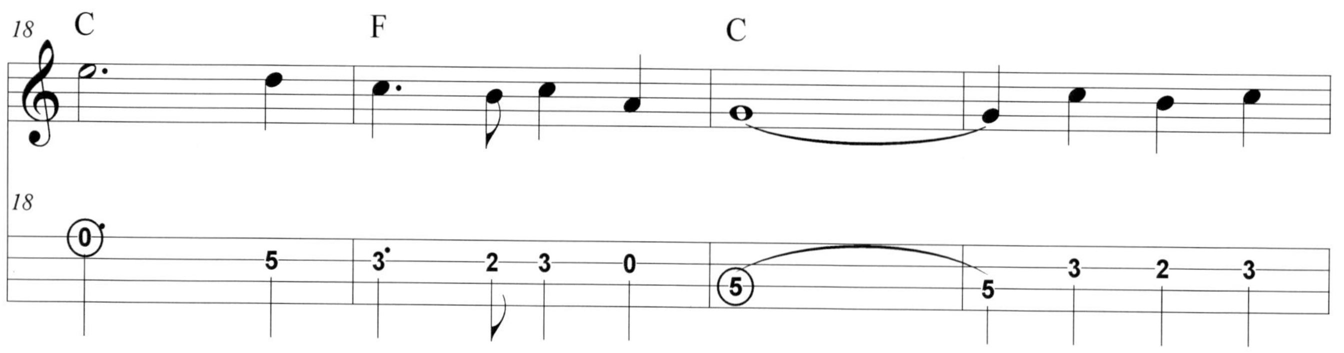
18
C
F
C
18

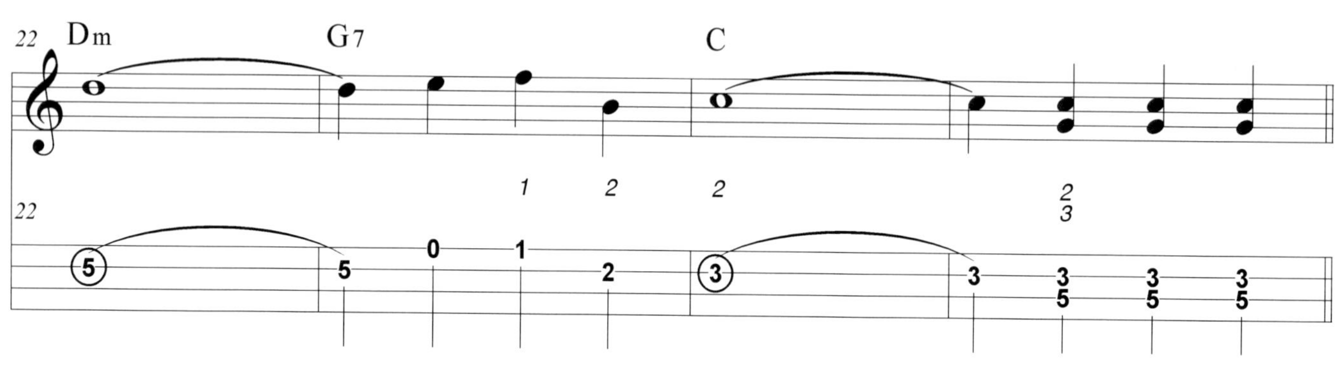
22
Dm
G7
C
22

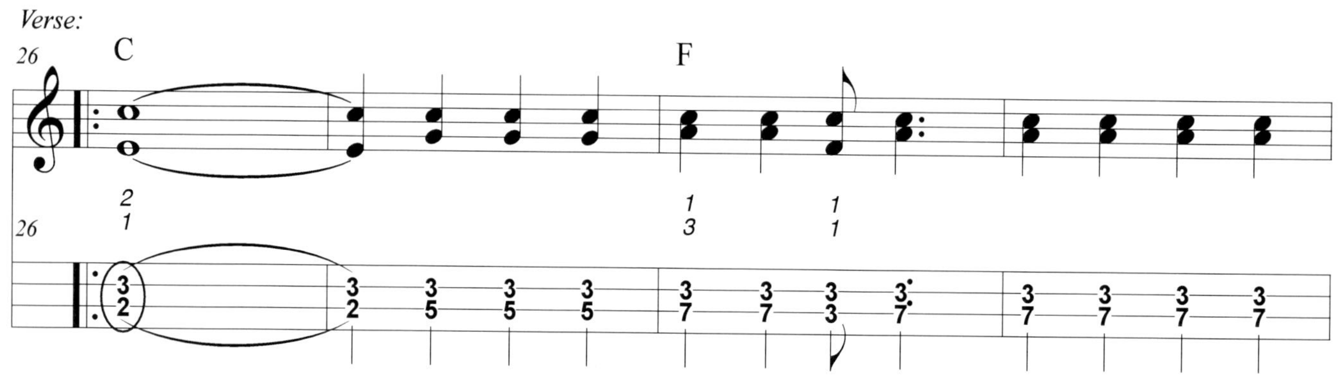
Verse:
26
C
F
26

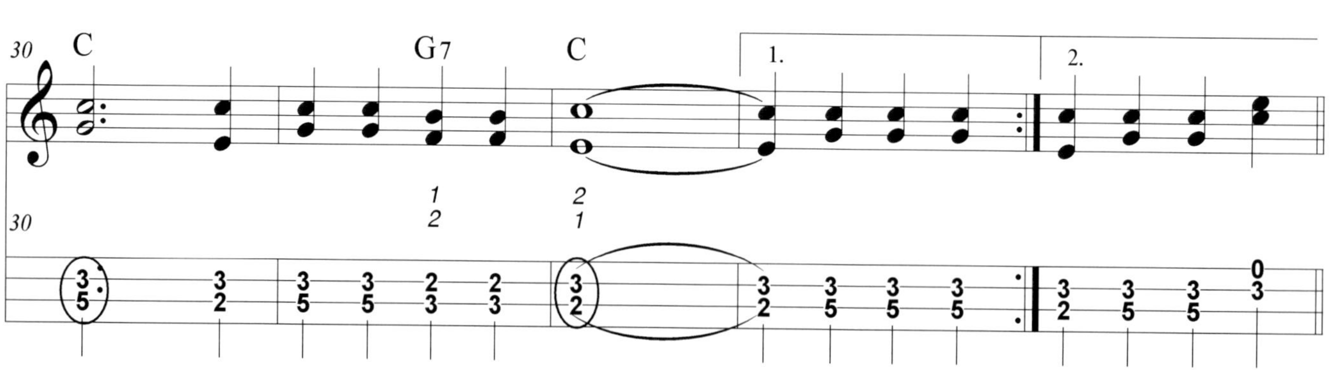
30
C
G7
C
1.
2.
30

Chorus:

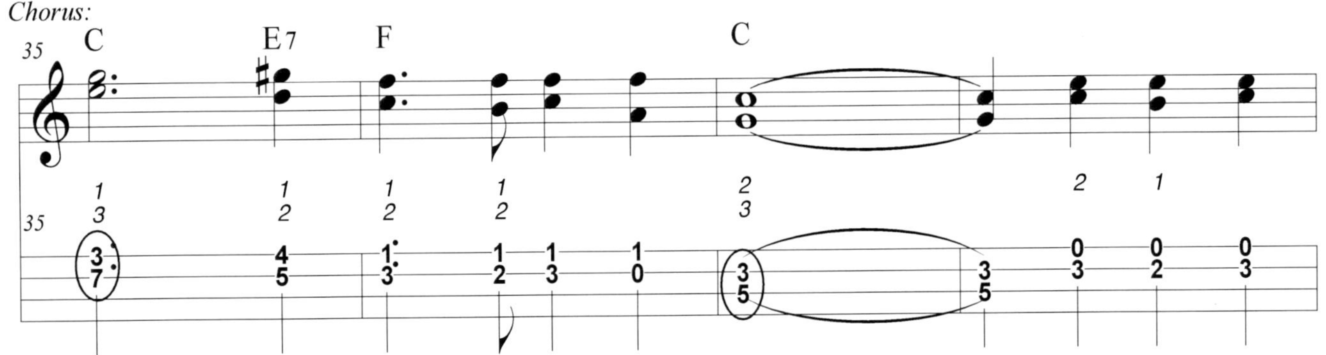

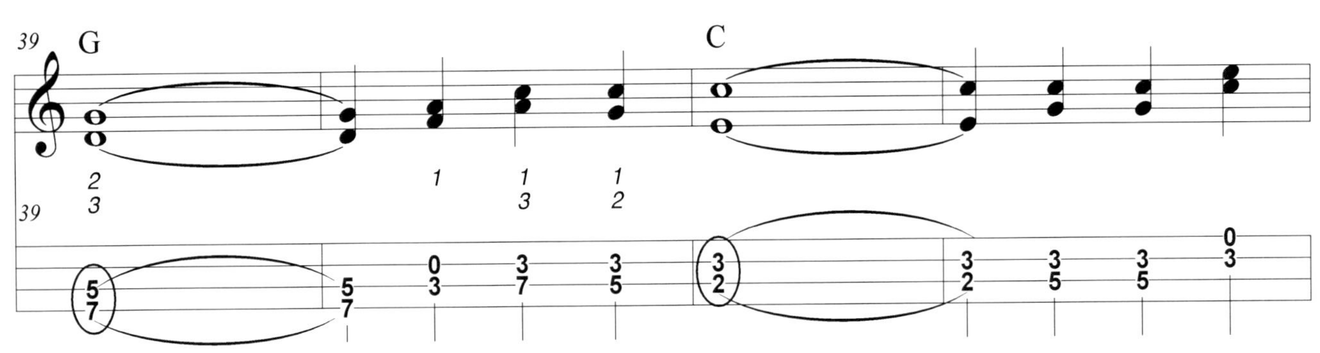

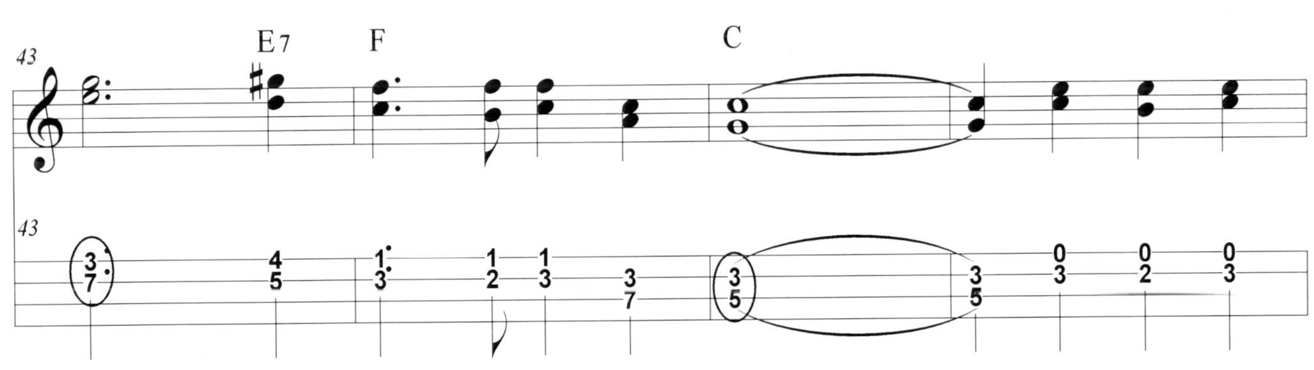

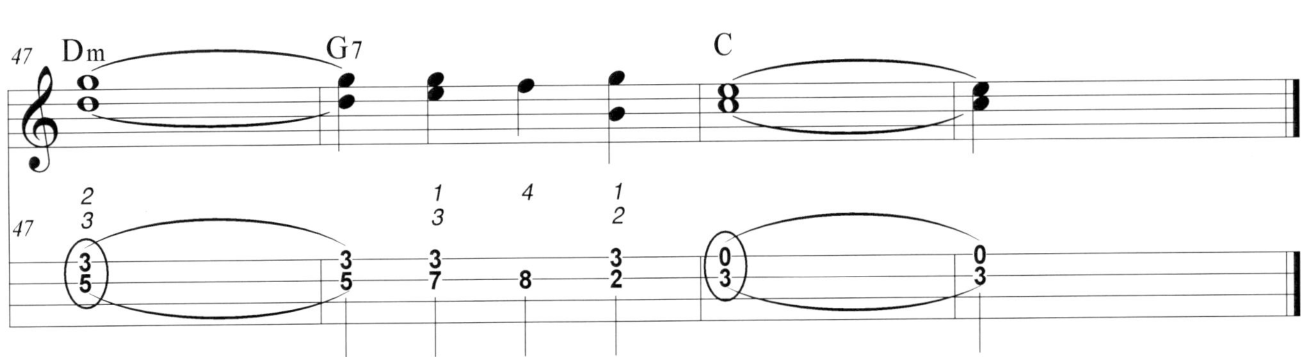

Jesus Loves Me

Introductory note p. 11

A.B. Warner - 1859
Arr. by Dix Bruce

21

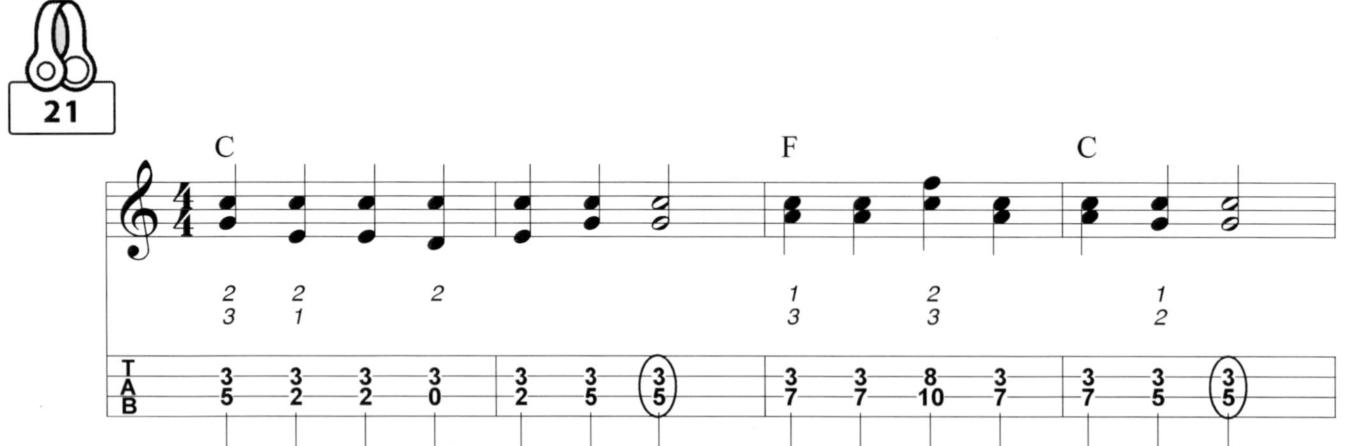

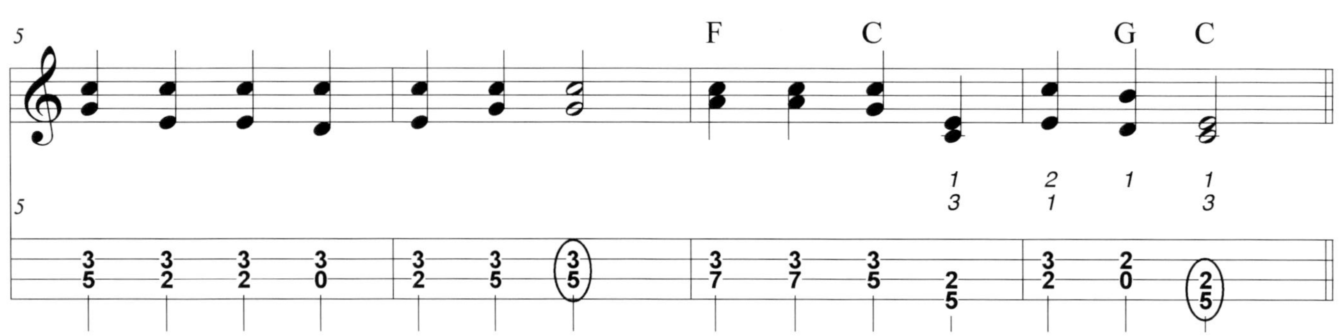

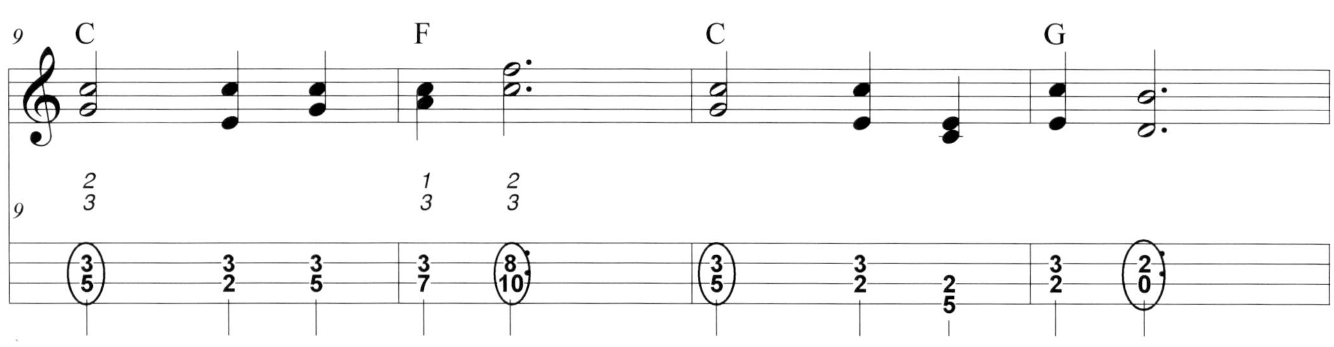

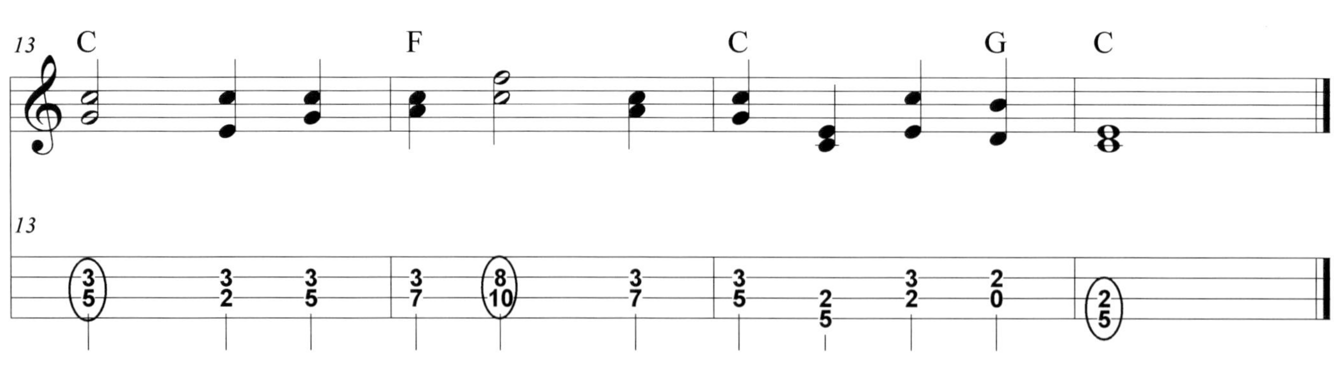

Old Time Religion

Traditional
Arr. by Dix Bruce

Introductory note p. 11

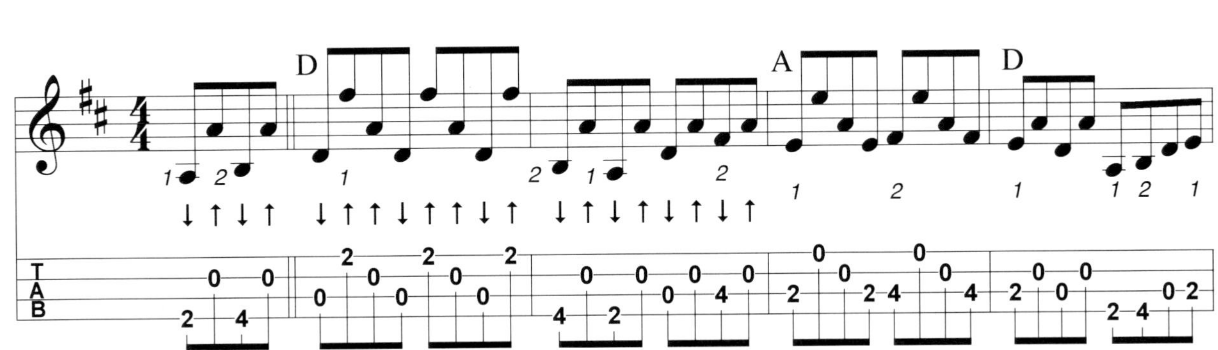

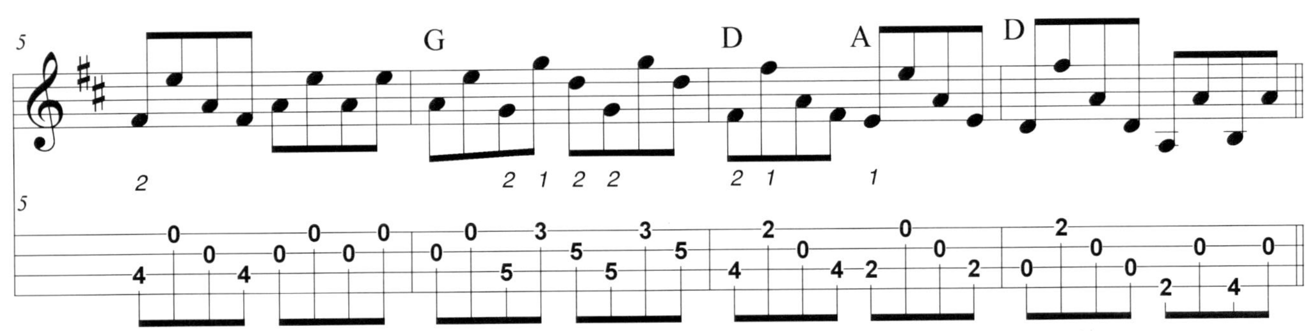

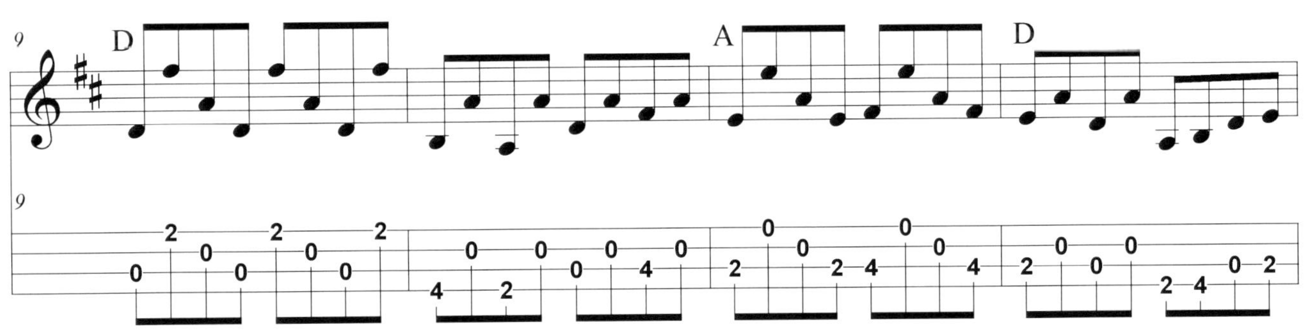

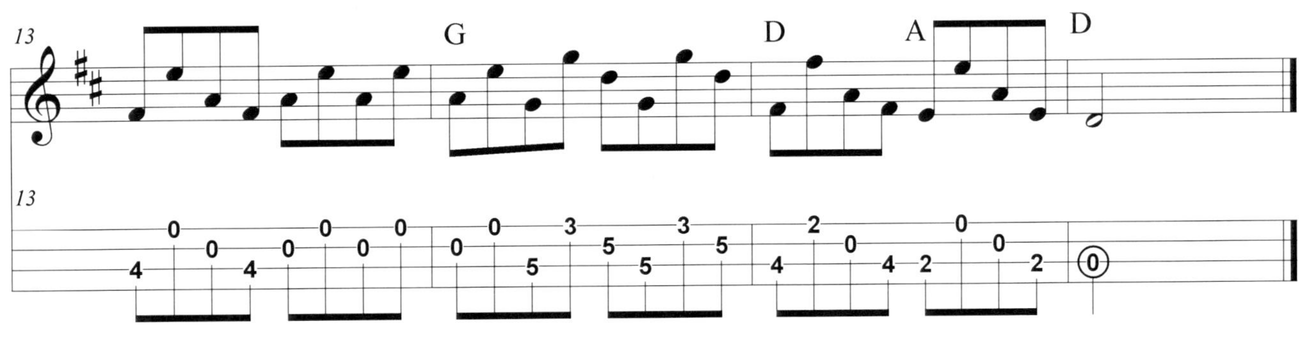

I Love to Tell the Story

Introductory note p. 11

C. Hankey, W.G. Fischer - 1867
Arr. by Dix Bruce

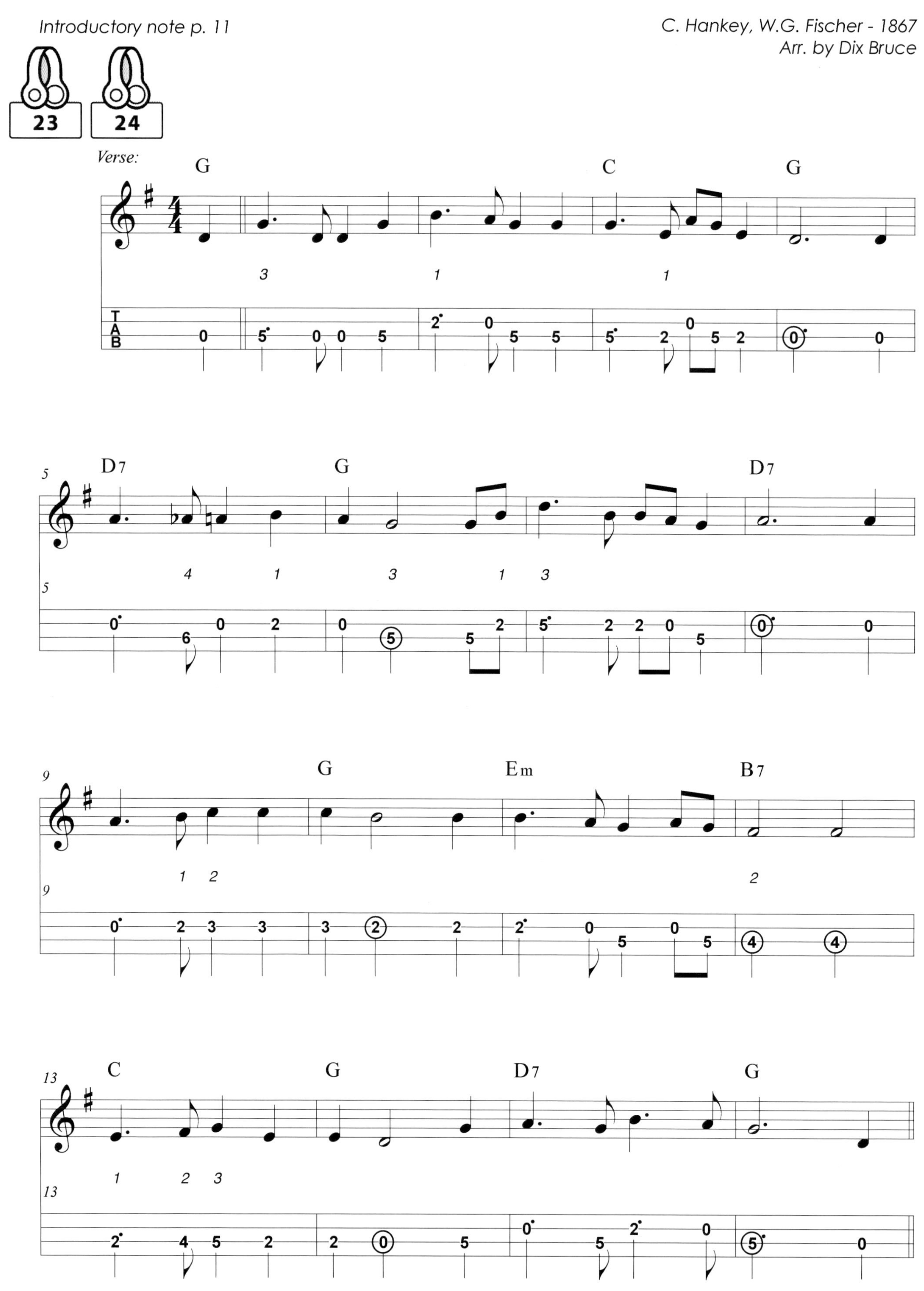

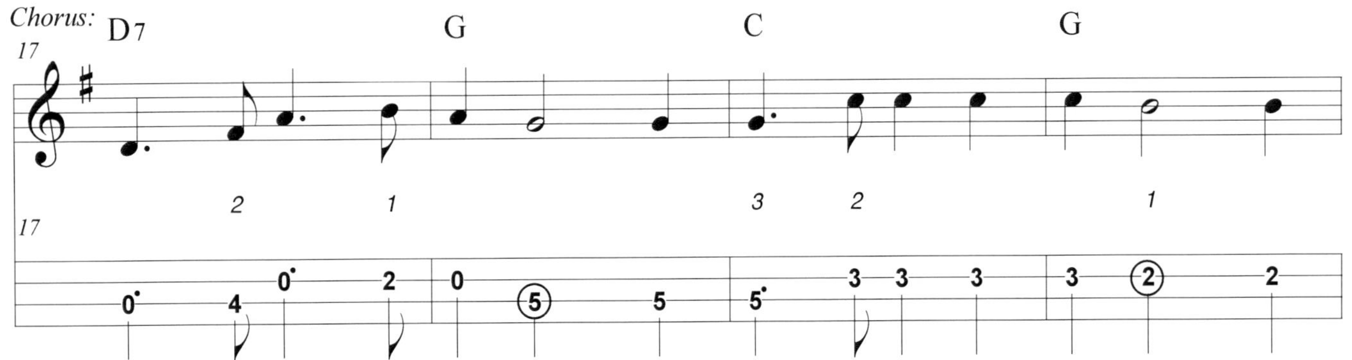

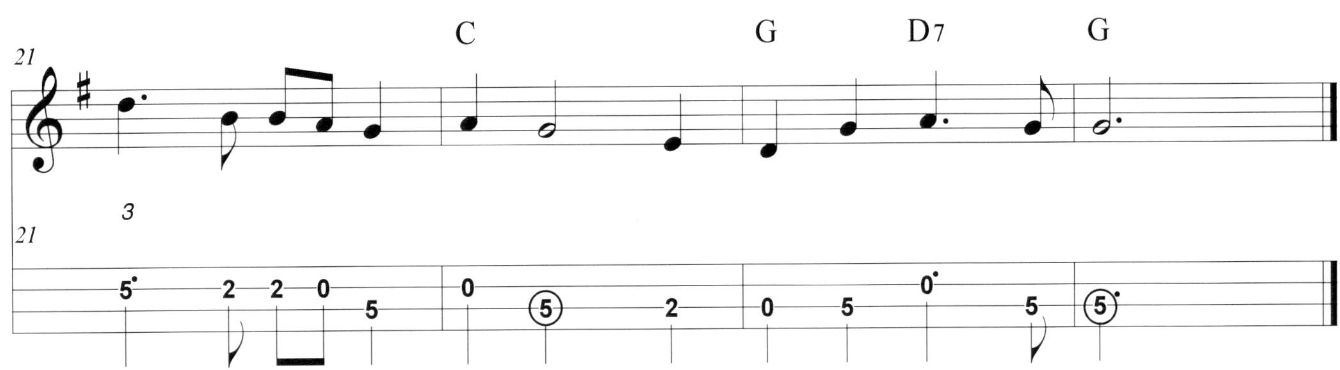

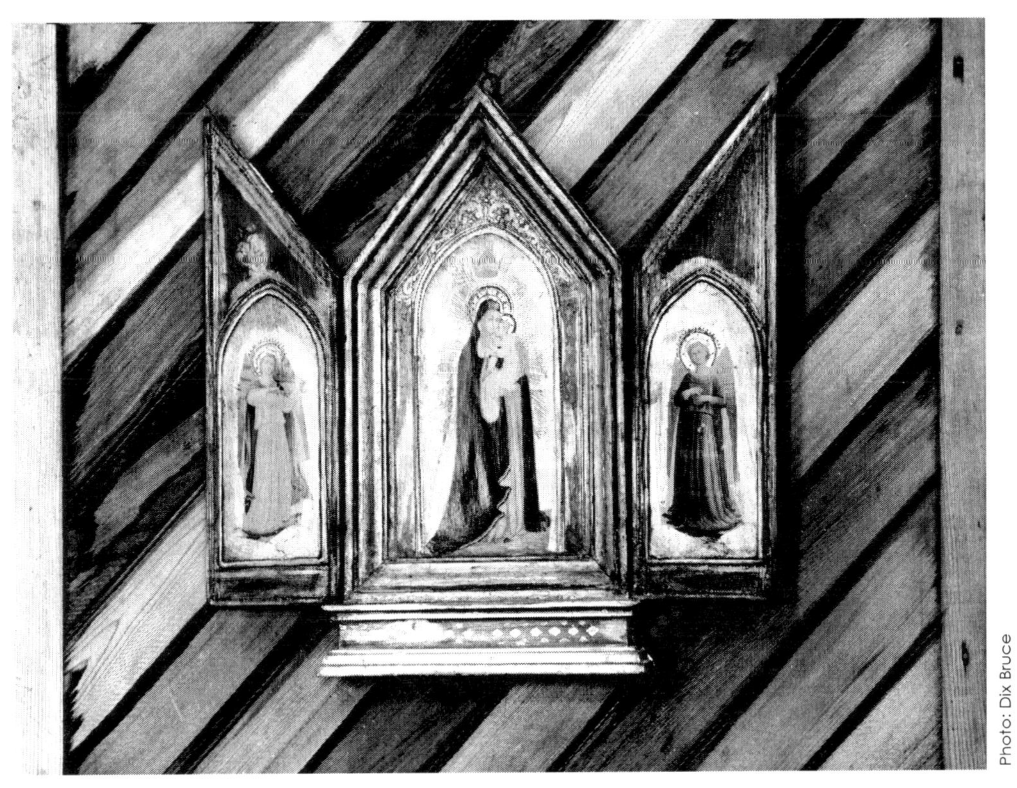

Photo: Dix Bruce

I'm Working on a Building

Traditional
Arr. by Dix Bruce

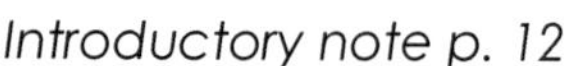
Introductory note p. 12

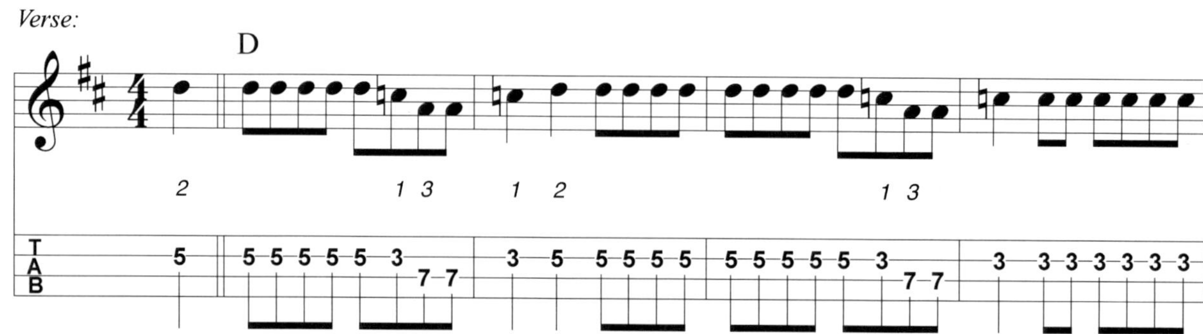

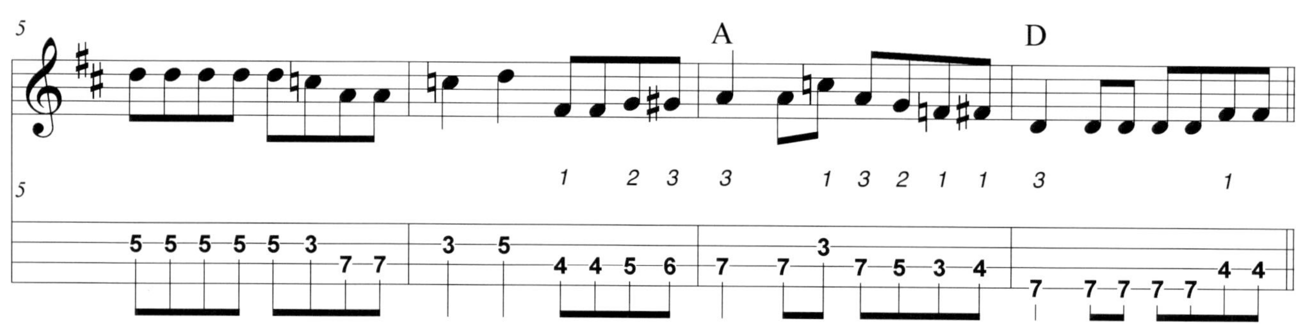

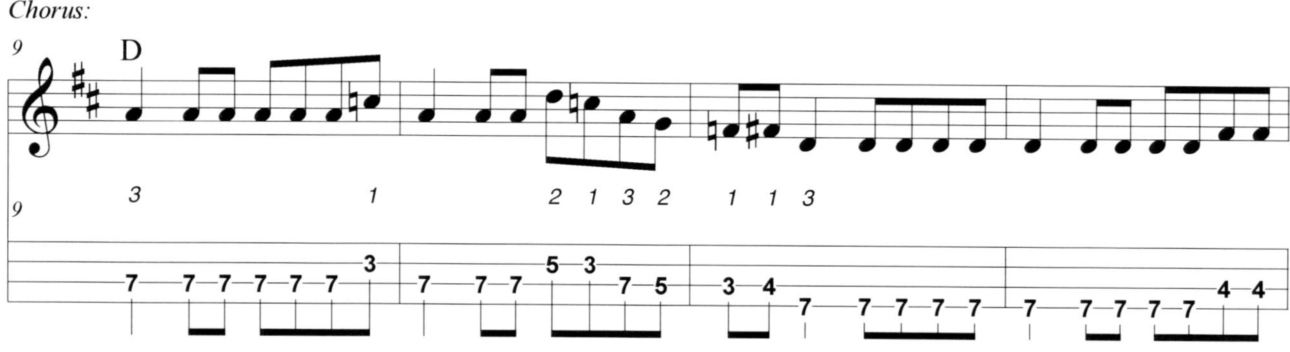

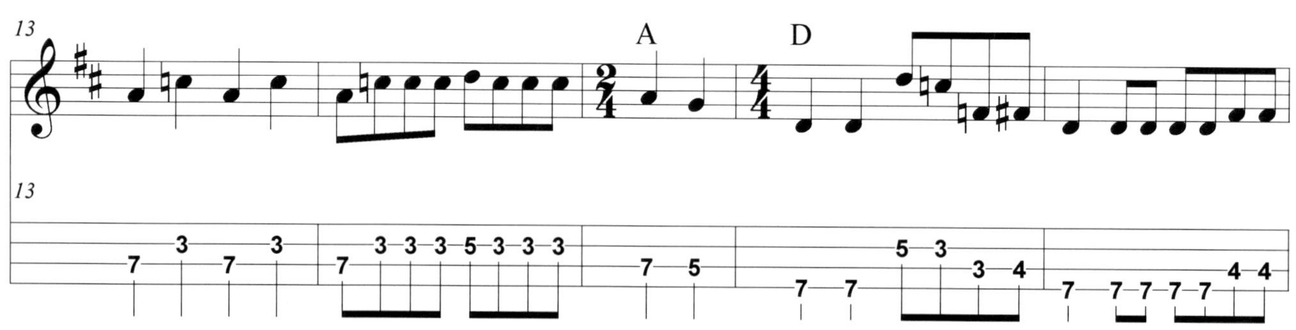

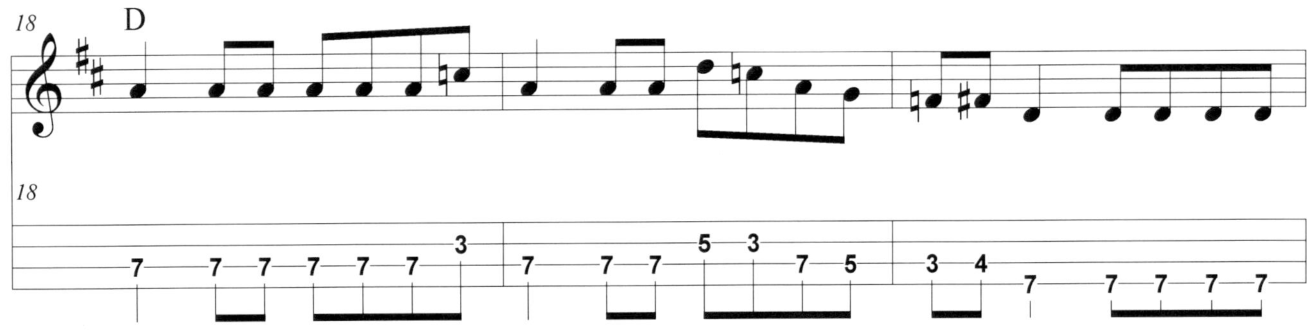

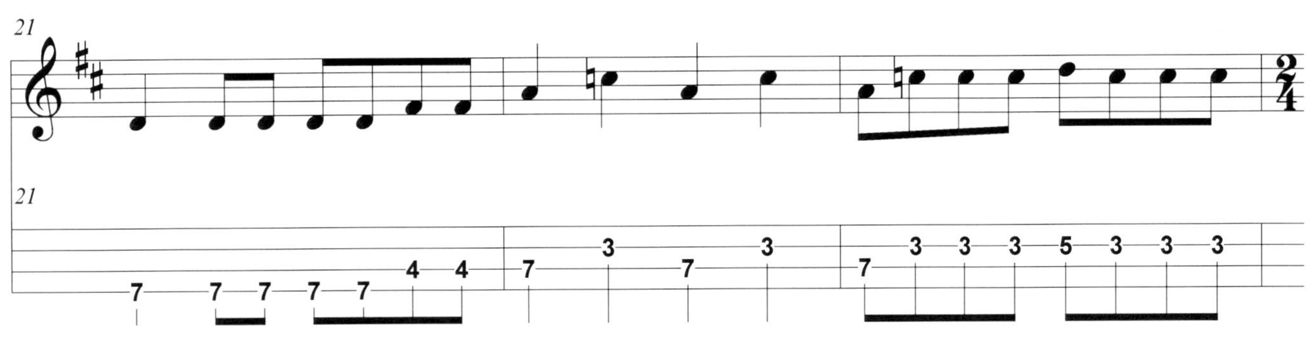

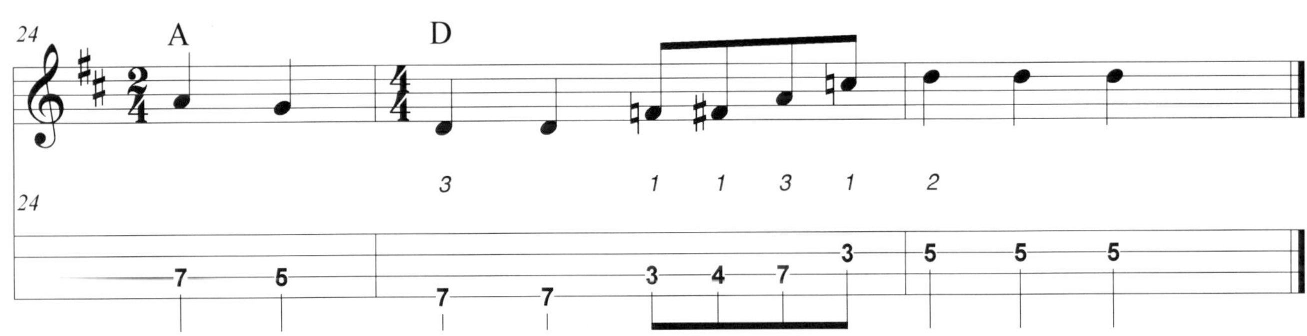

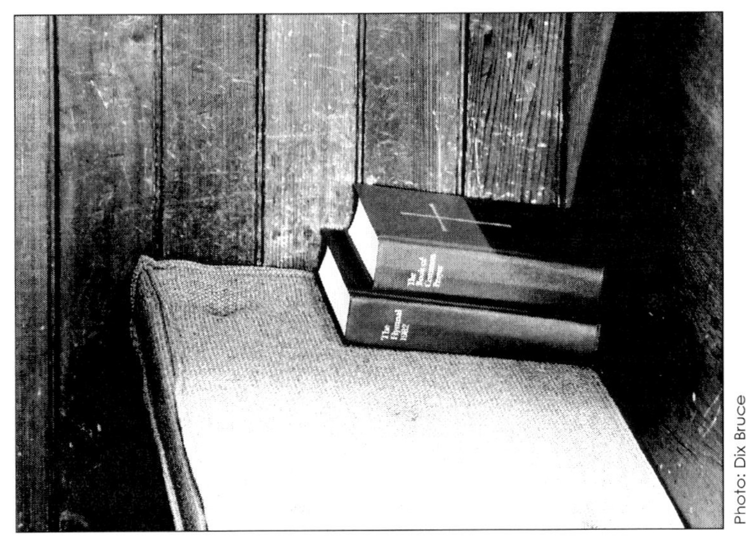
Photo: Dix Bruce

Lord, I'm Coming Home

W.J. Kirkpatrick - 1892
Arr. by Dix Bruce

Introductory note p. 12

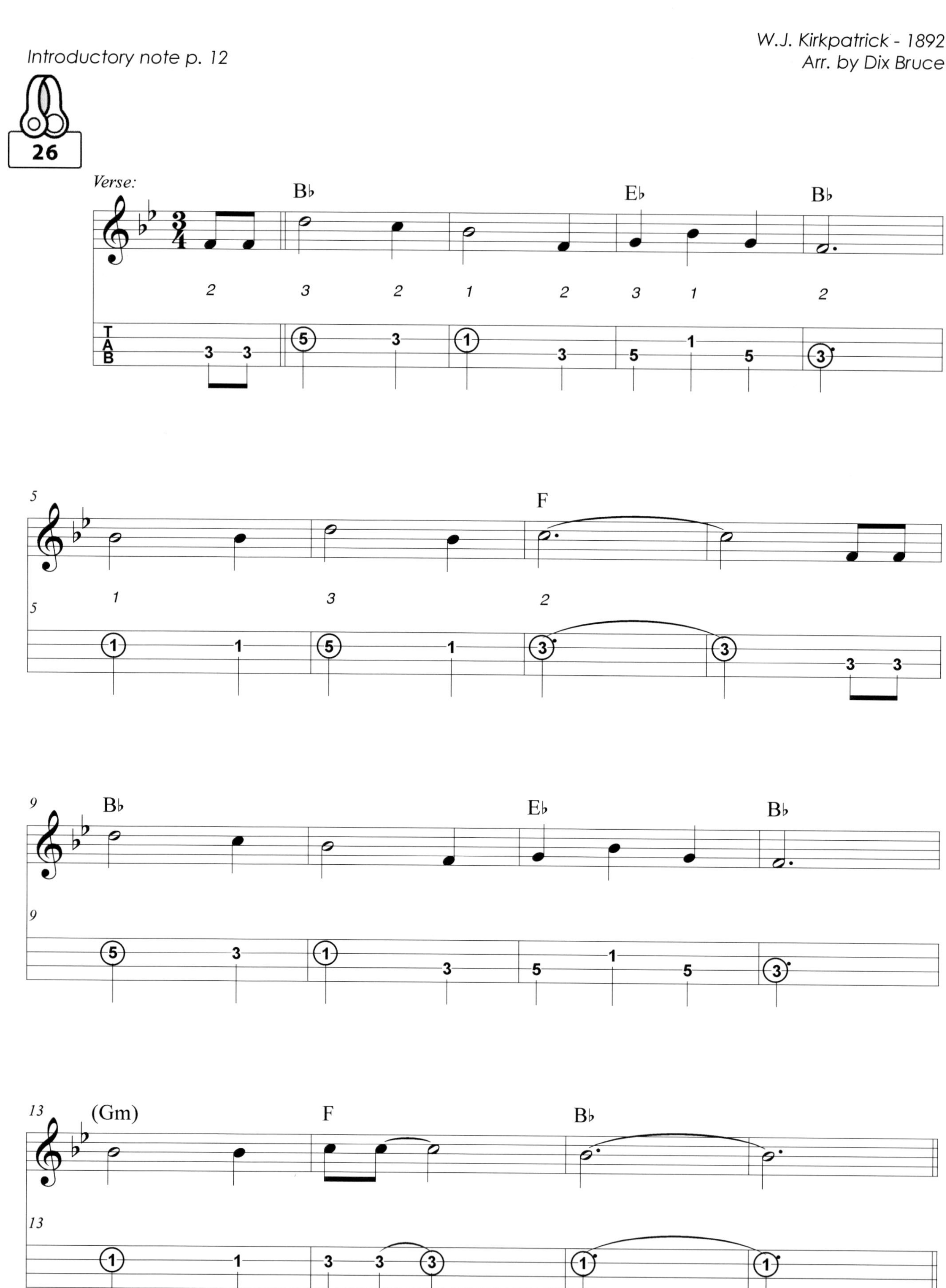

Chorus:

17
B♭
E♭
3
1
3
17
5
5
5
1
1
1
1
5

21
B♭
F
2
1
3
1
2
21
3
1
5
1
3
3

25
B♭
E♭
B♭
25
5
3
1
3
5
1
5
3

29
(Gm)
F
B♭
29
1
1
3
3
3
1
1
1
3

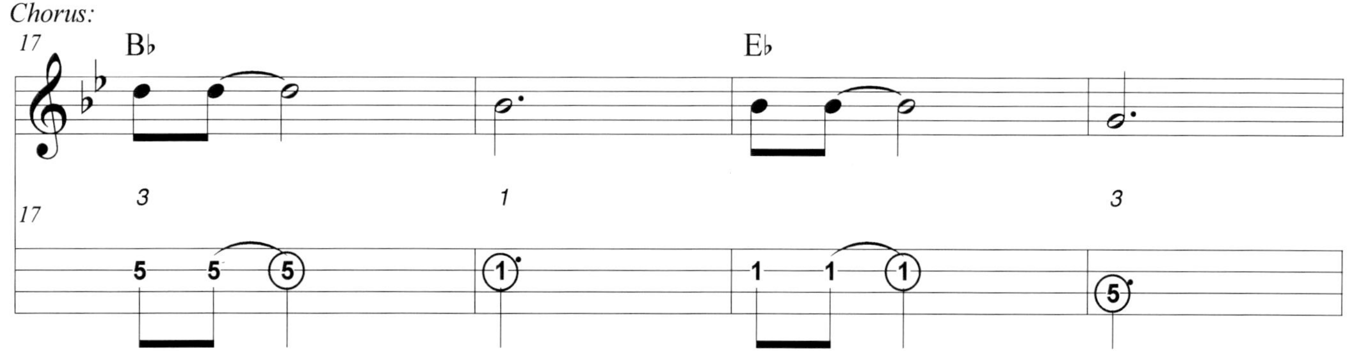

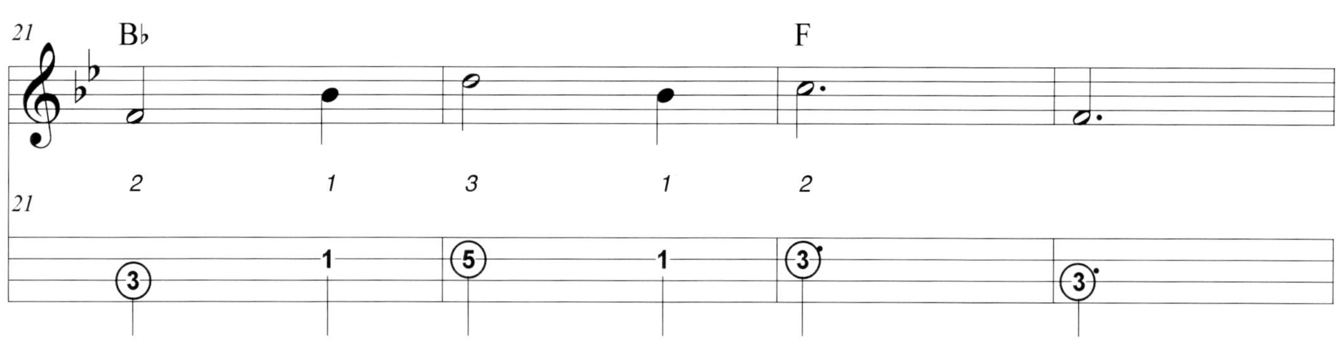

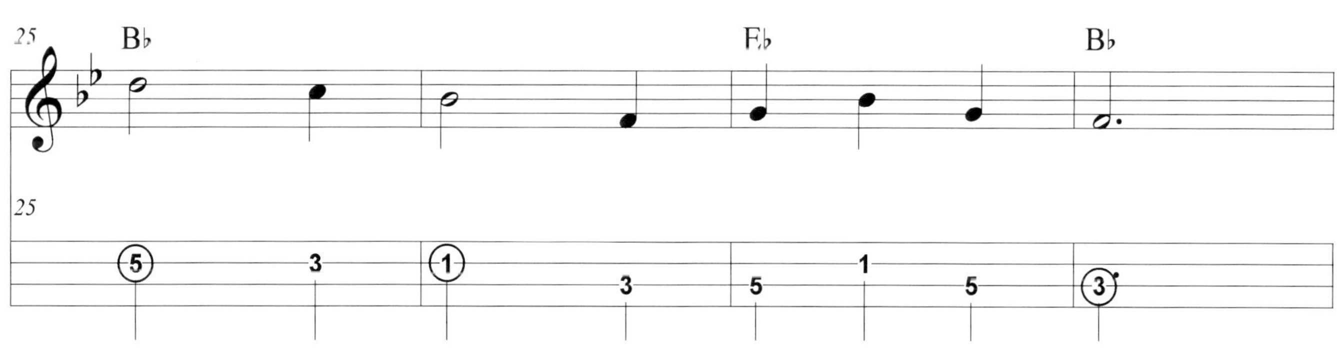

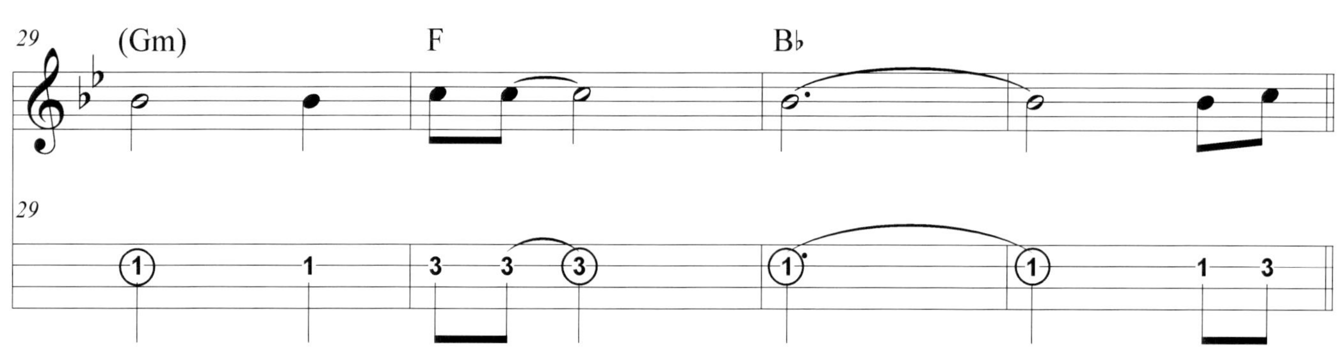

Verse:

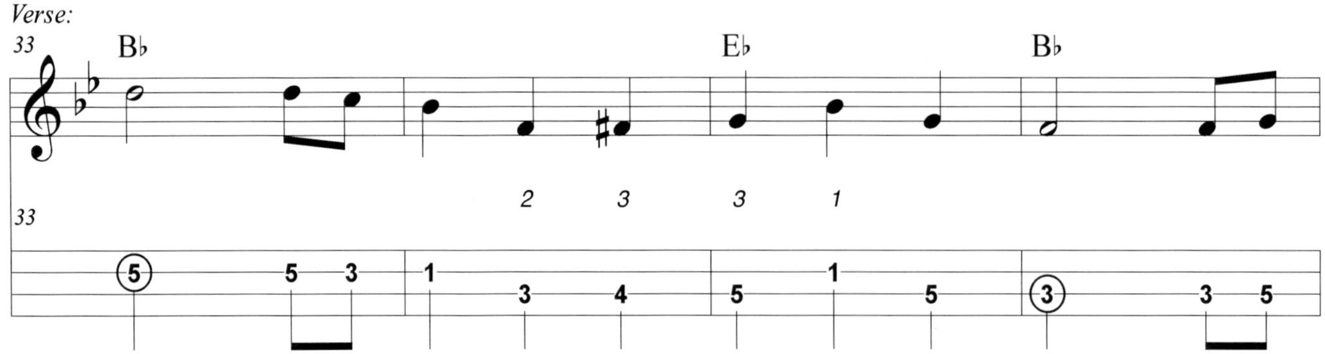

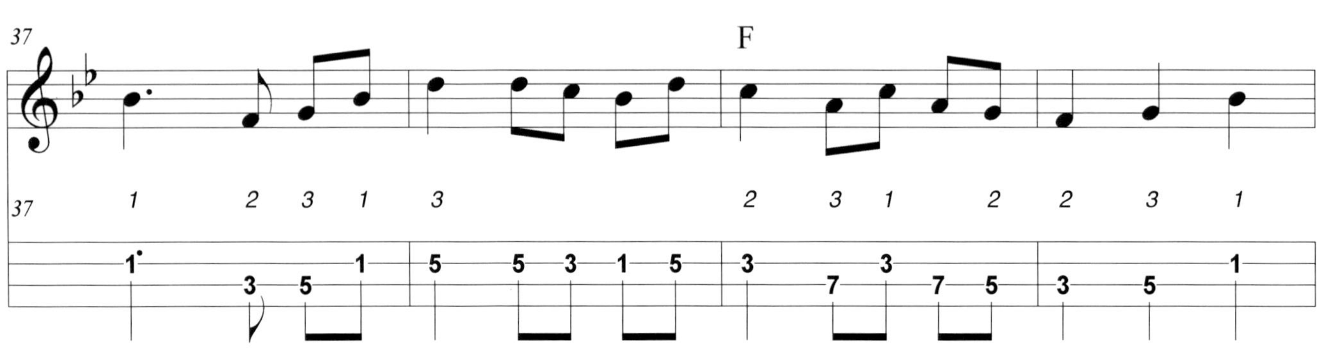

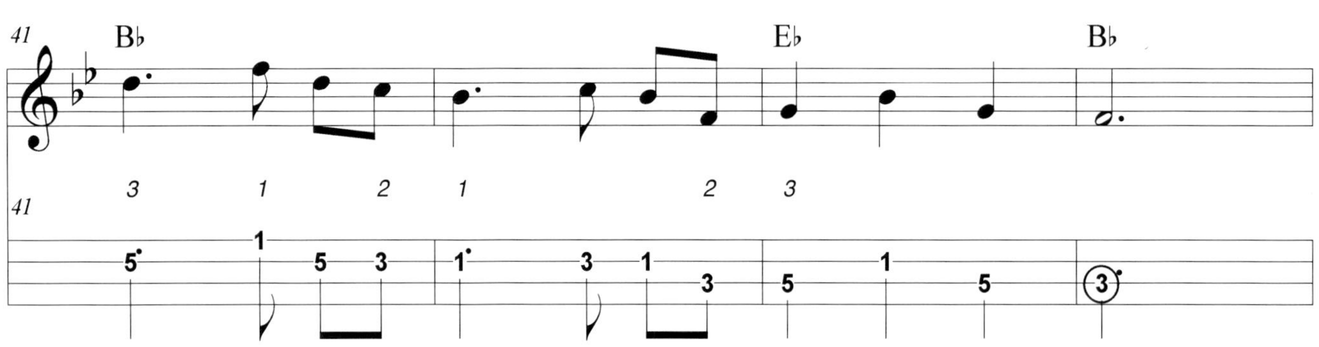

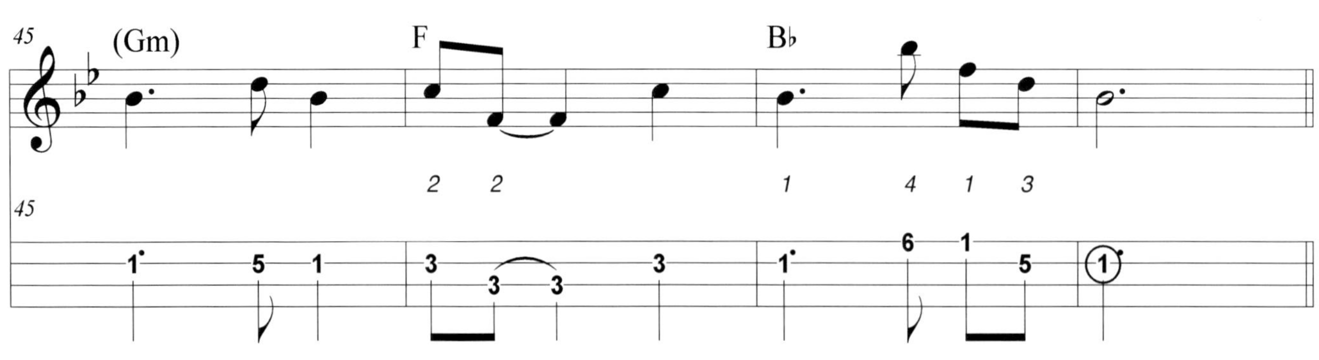

Chorus:

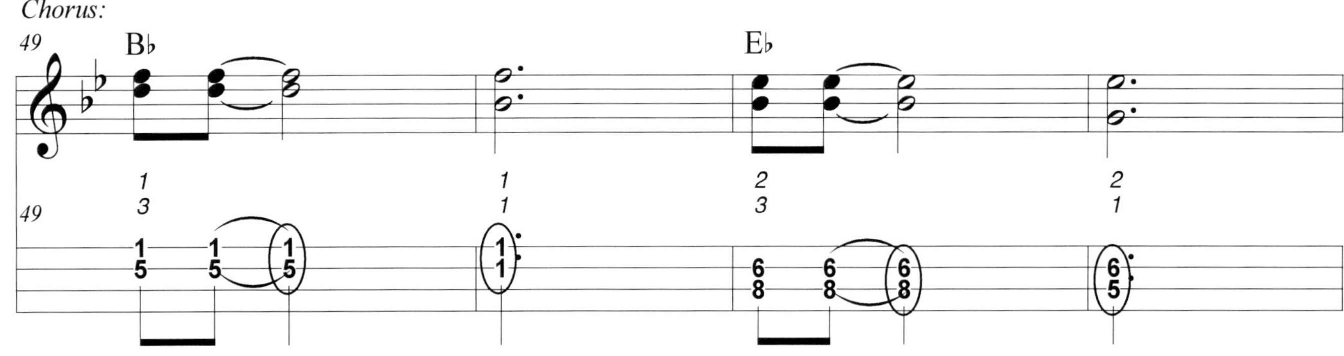

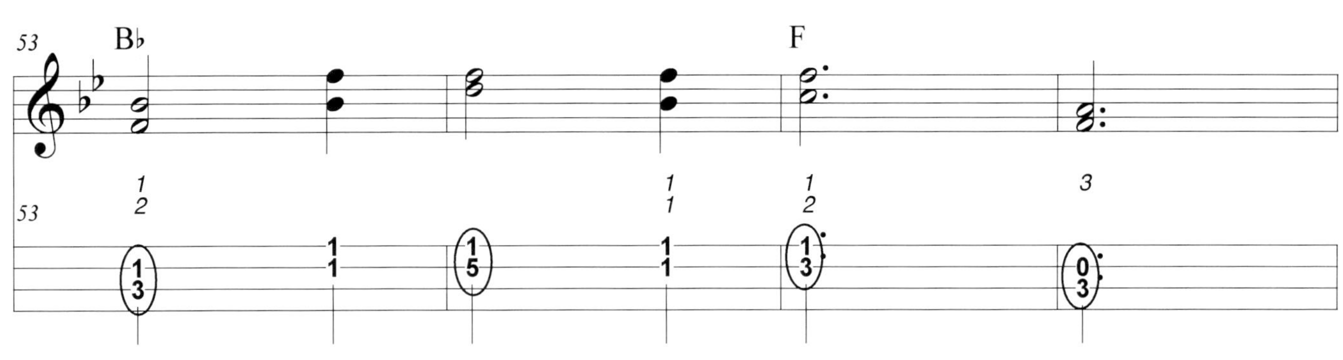

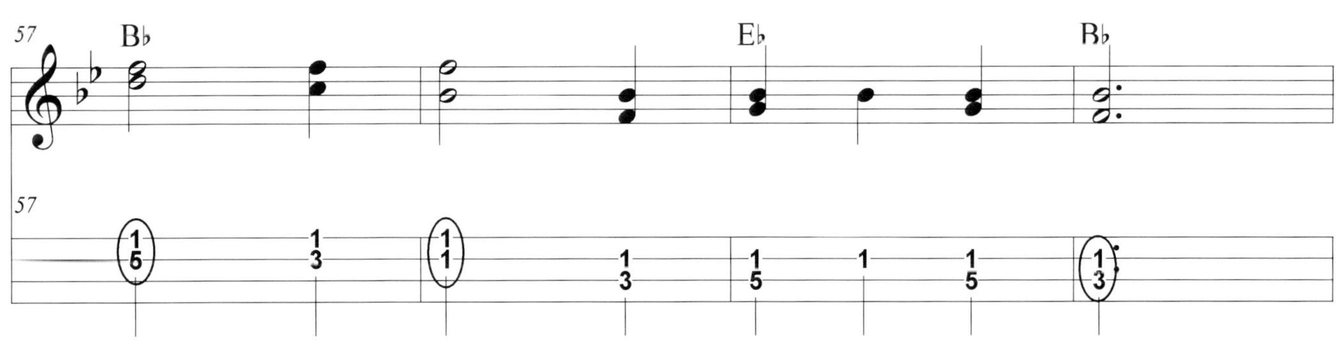

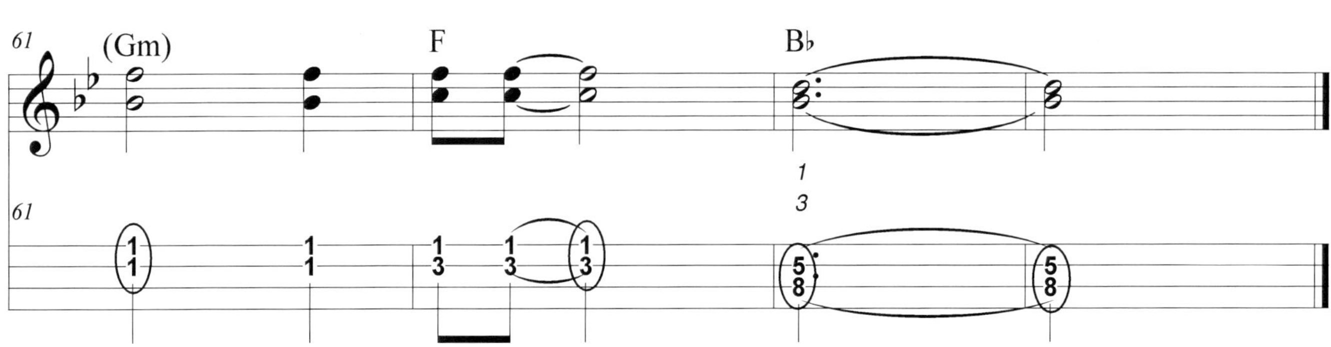

Just a Closer Walk With Thee

Introductory note p. 12

Traditional
Arr. by Dix Bruce

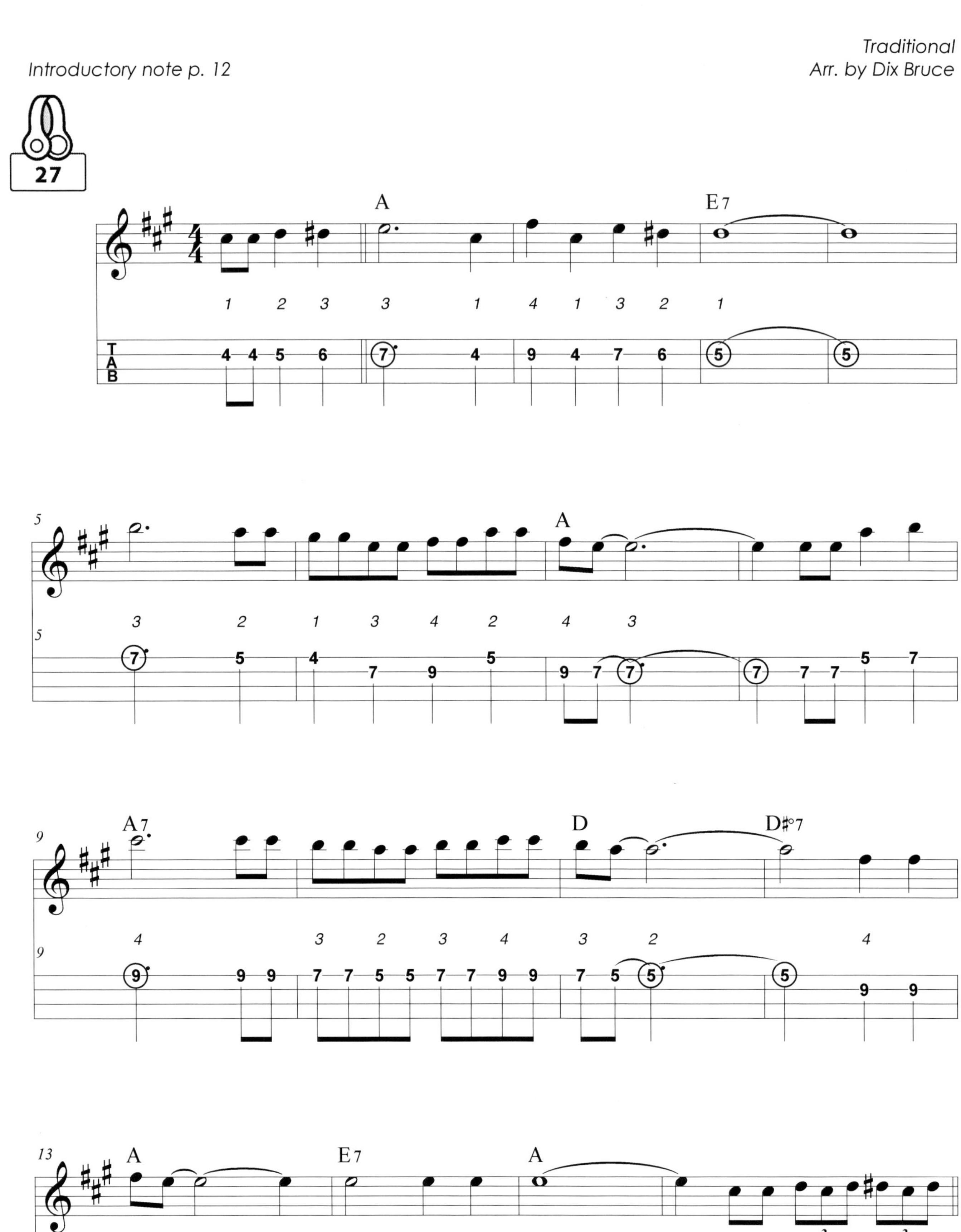

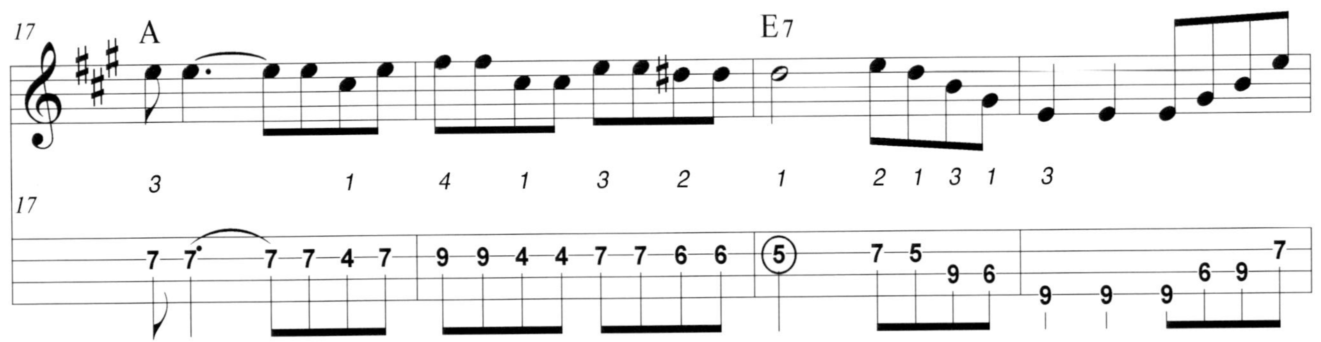
17
A
E7

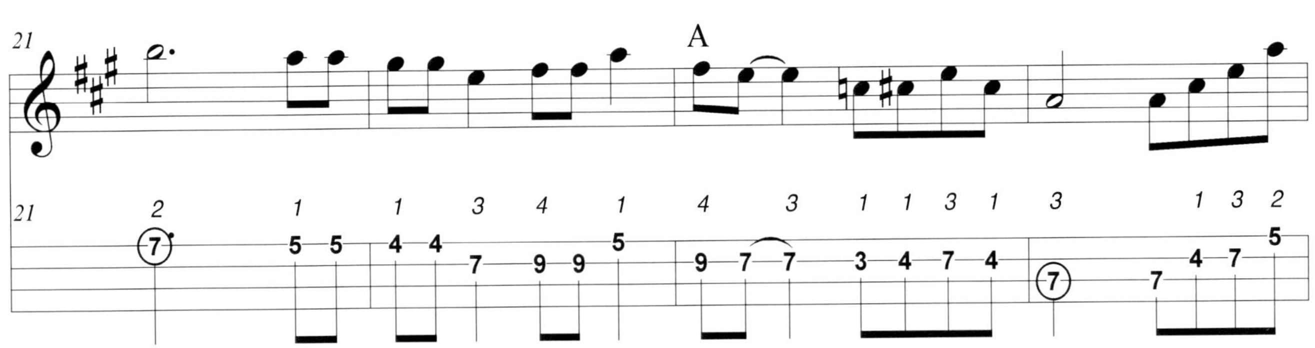
21
A

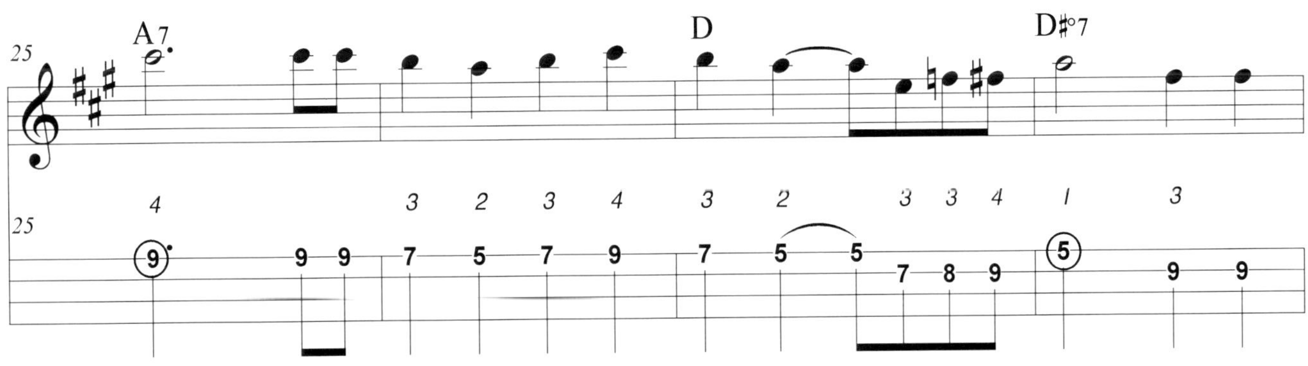
25
A7
D
D♯°7

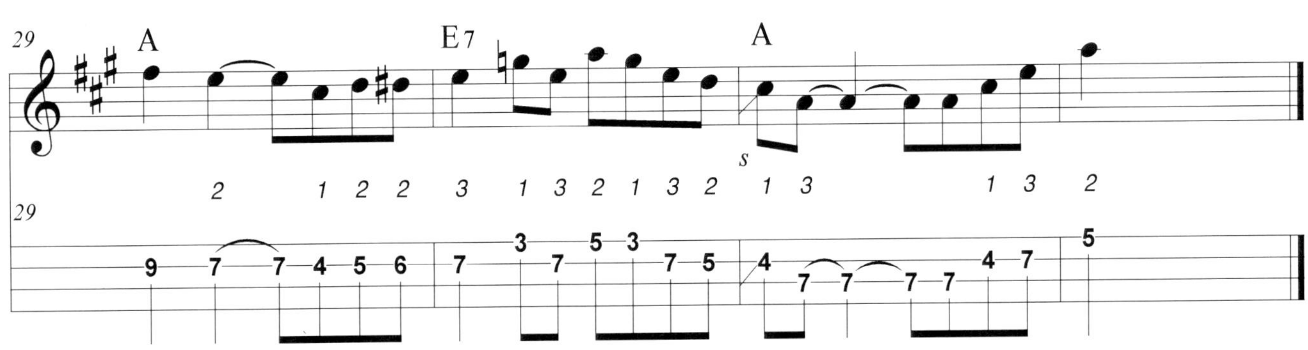
29
A
E7
A

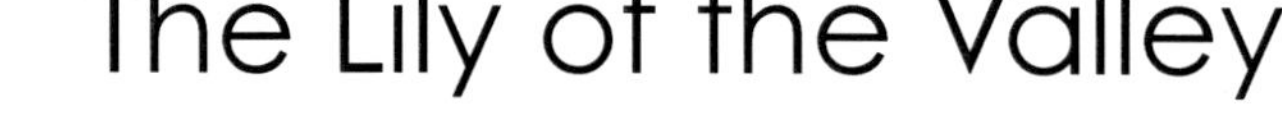

The Lily of the Valley

Introductory note p. 12

C.W. Fry - 1881
Arr. by Dix Bruce

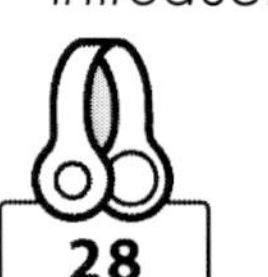

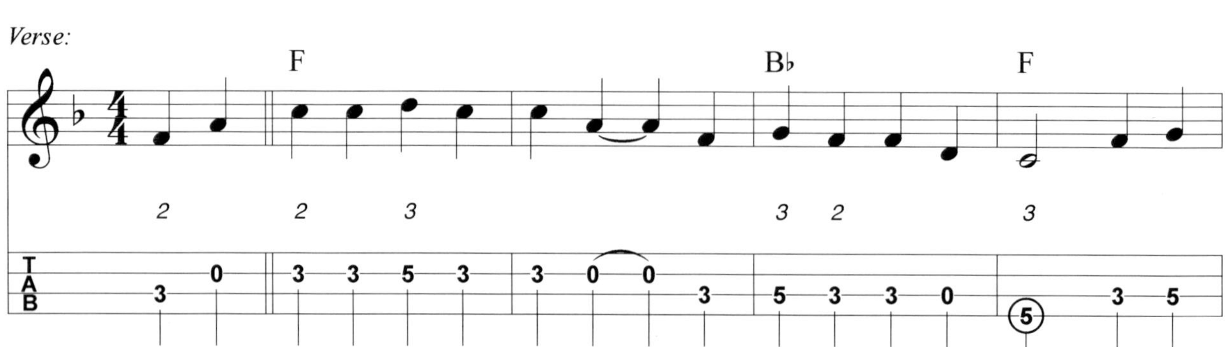

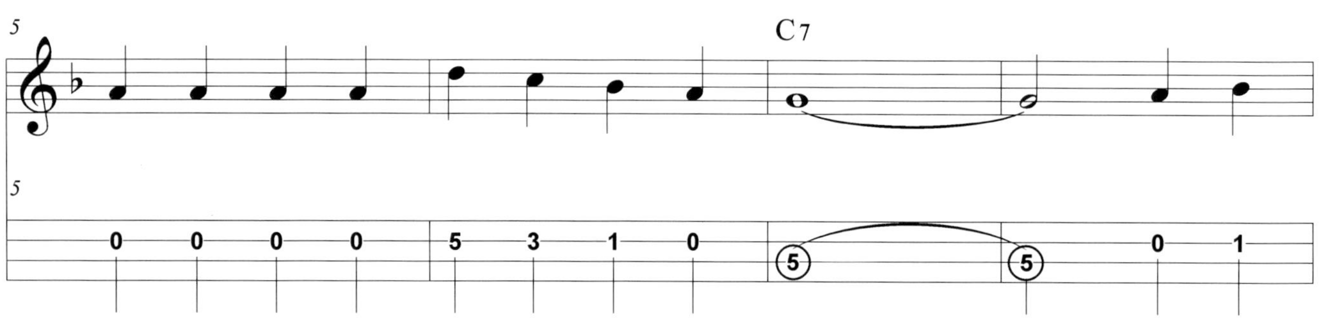

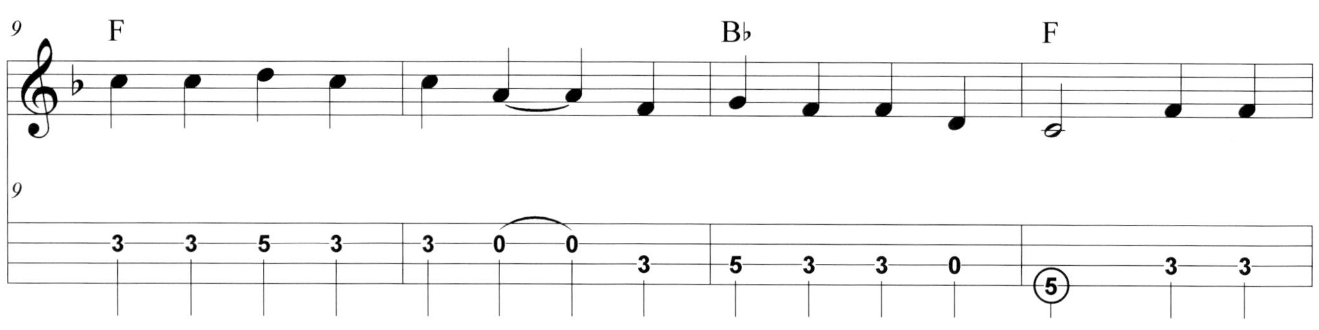

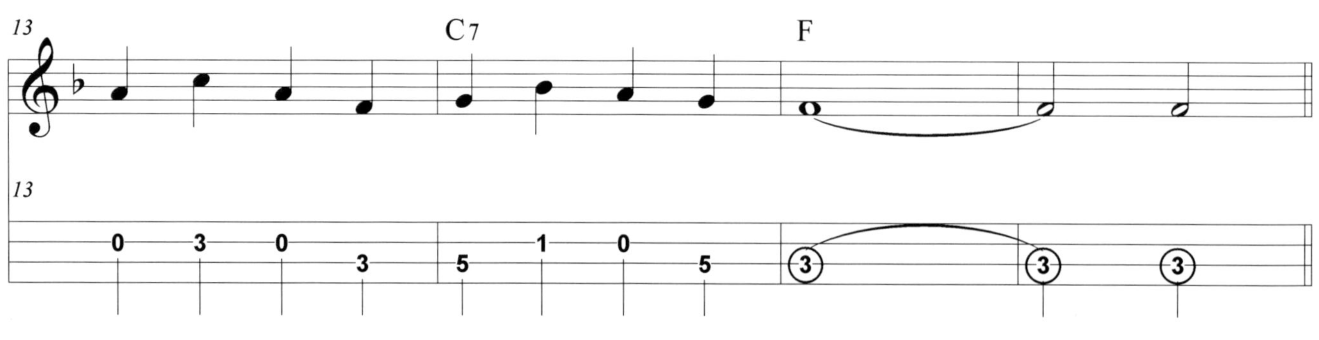

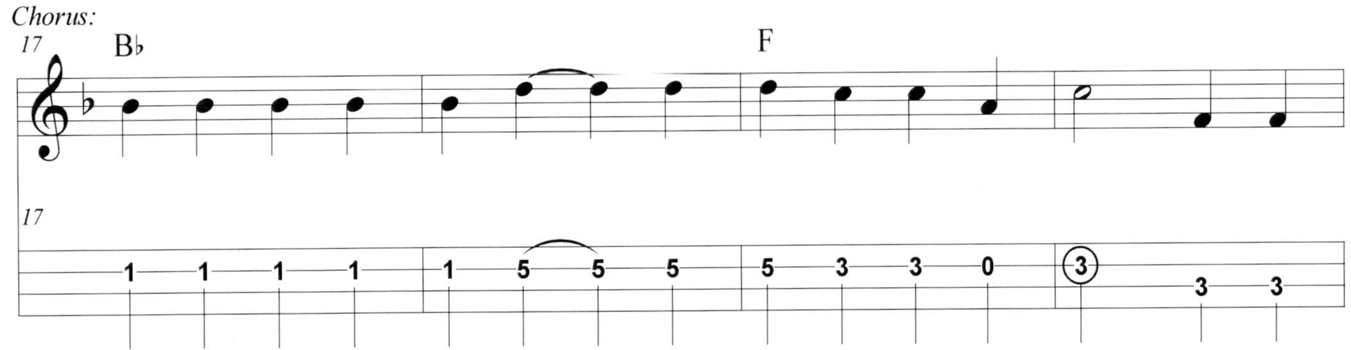
Chorus:
17
B♭
F
17

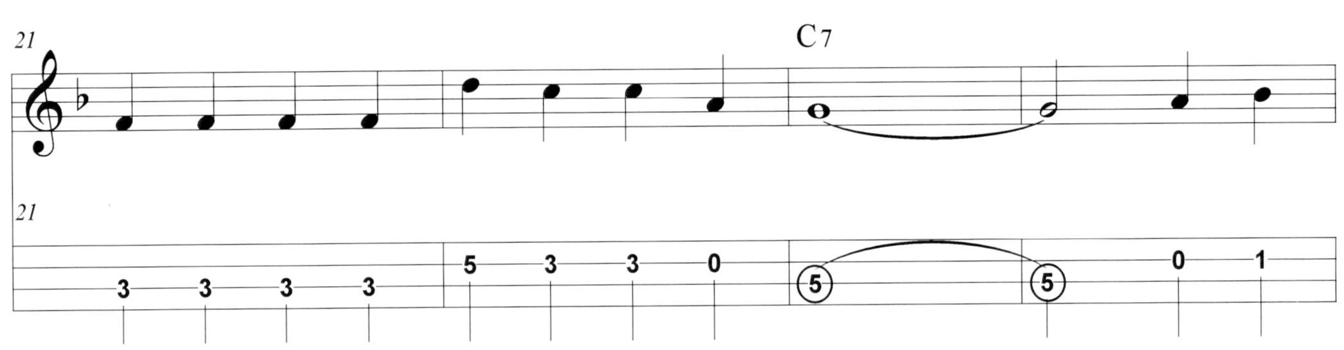
21
C7
21

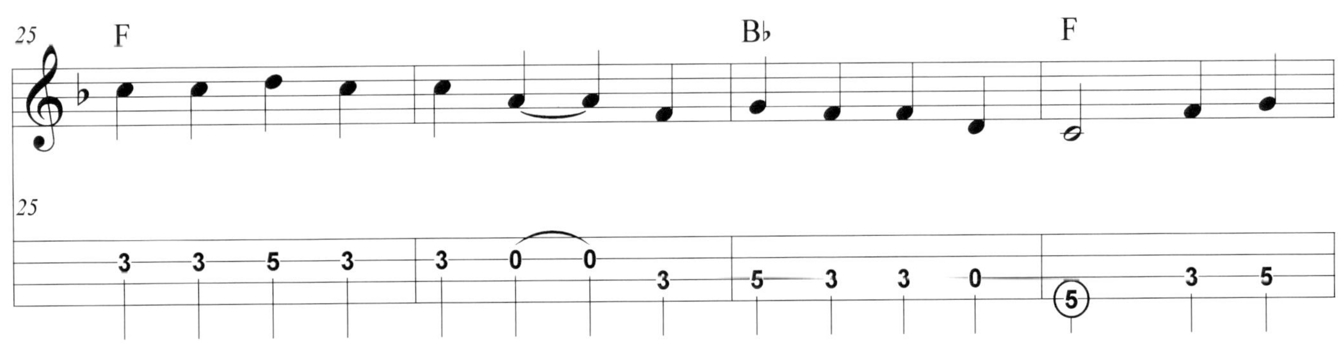
25
F
B♭
F
25

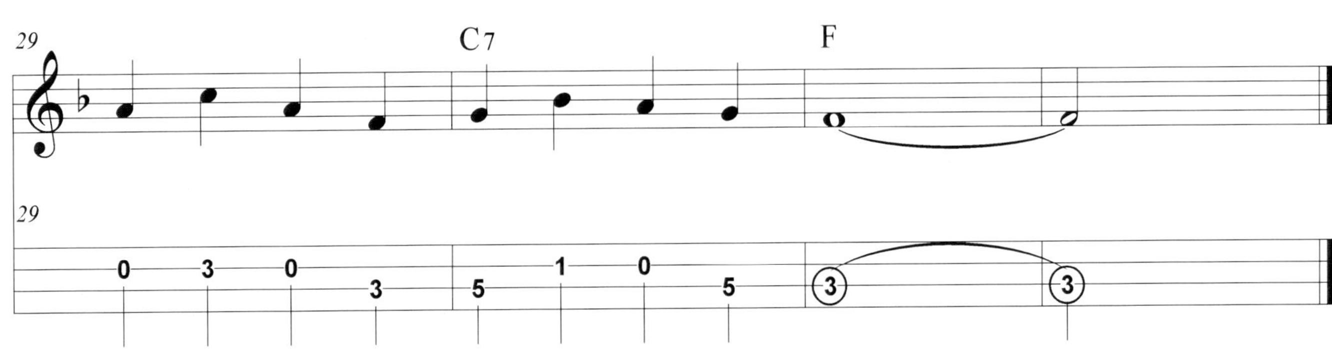
29
C7
F
29

Come, Ye Thankful People Come

Introductory note p. 13

H. Alford - 1849
Arr. by Dix Bruce

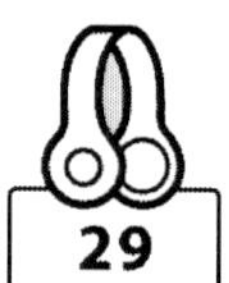

G Em D G Em Am B7

5 Em Am D G A7 D G D A7 D

9 D G D7 G C G7 C E Am

14 D G C Em G D G

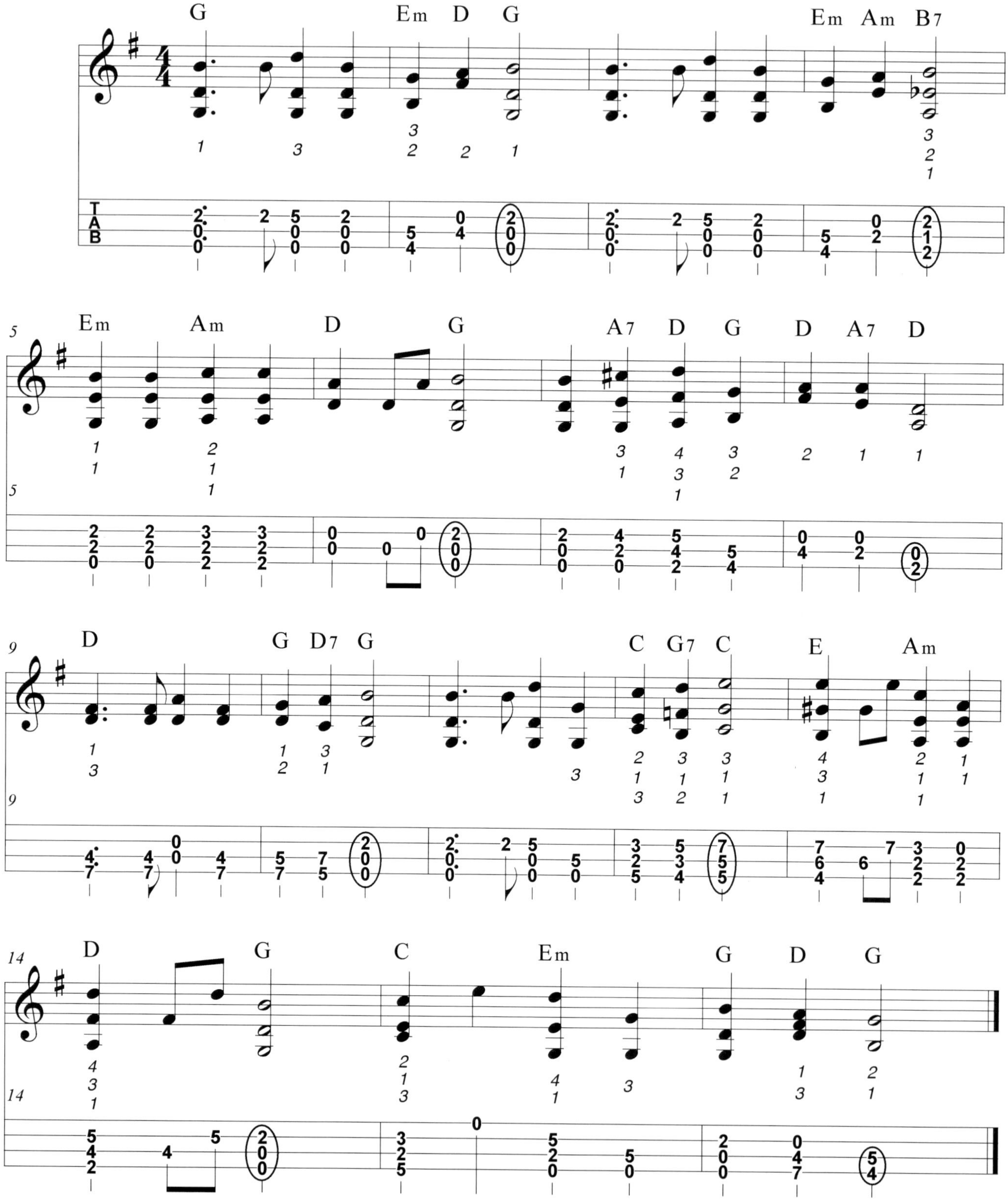

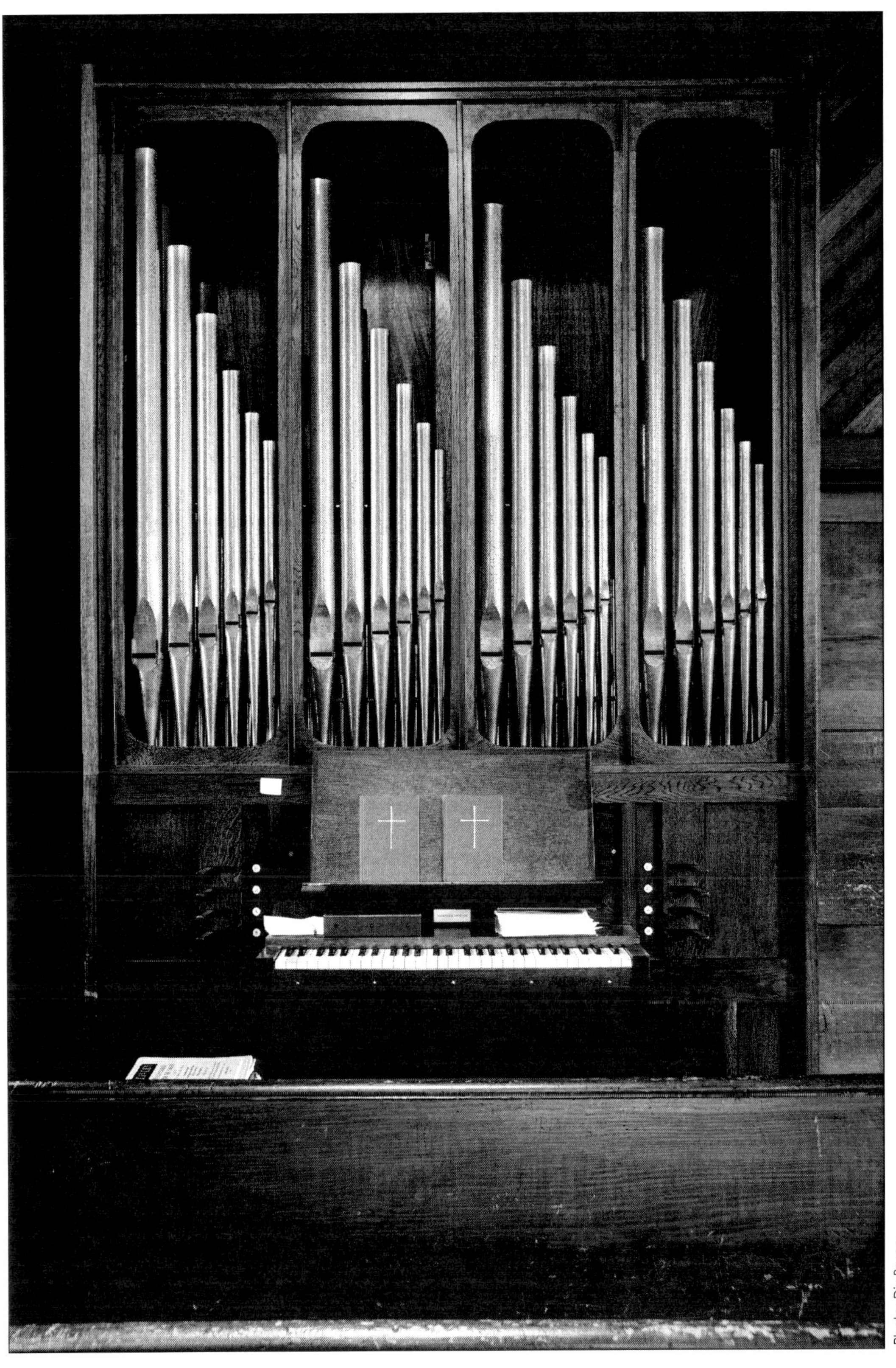

Photo: Dix Bruce

Oh, How I Love Jesus

Introductory note p. 13

F. Whitfield
Arr. by Dix Bruce

30

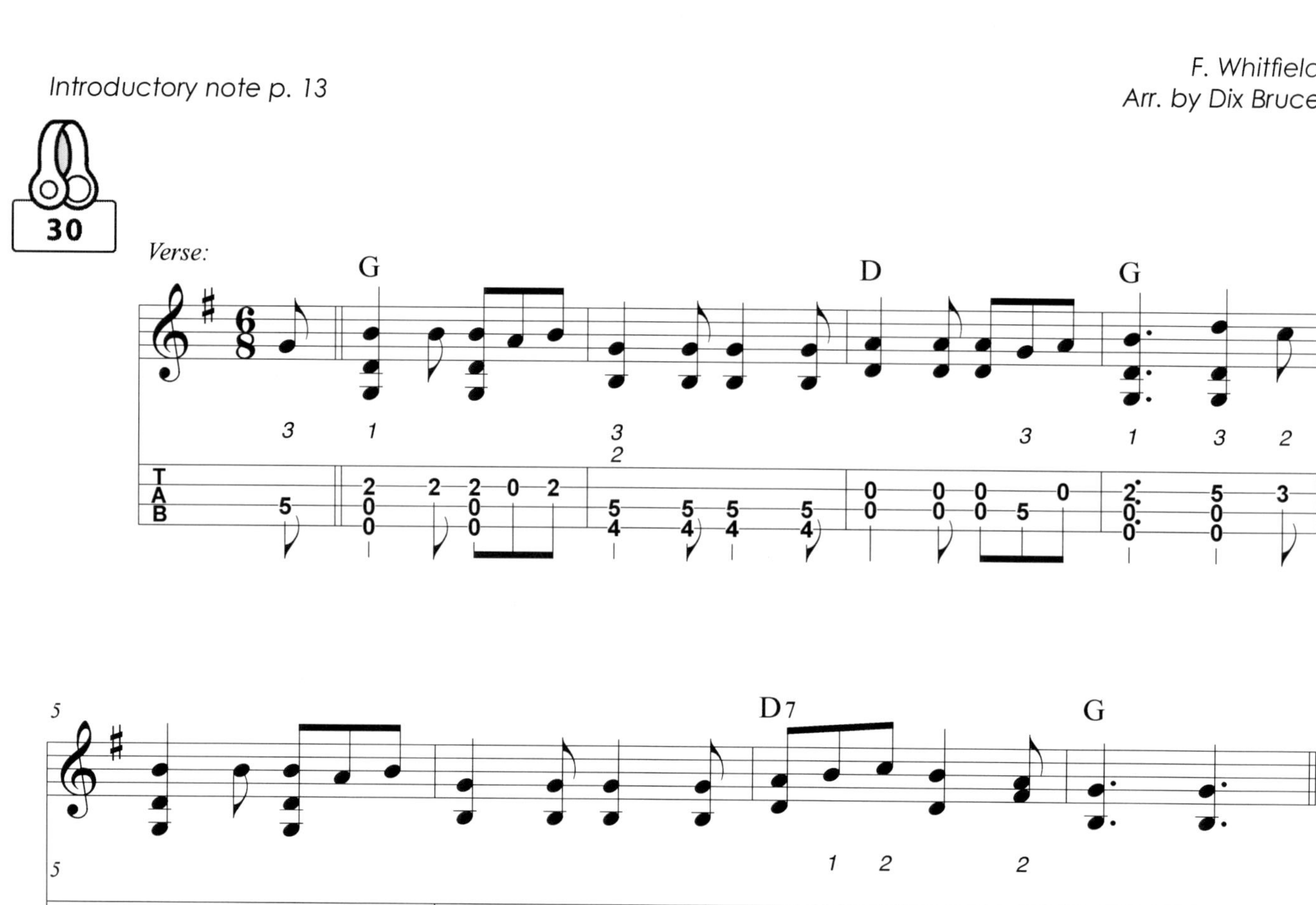

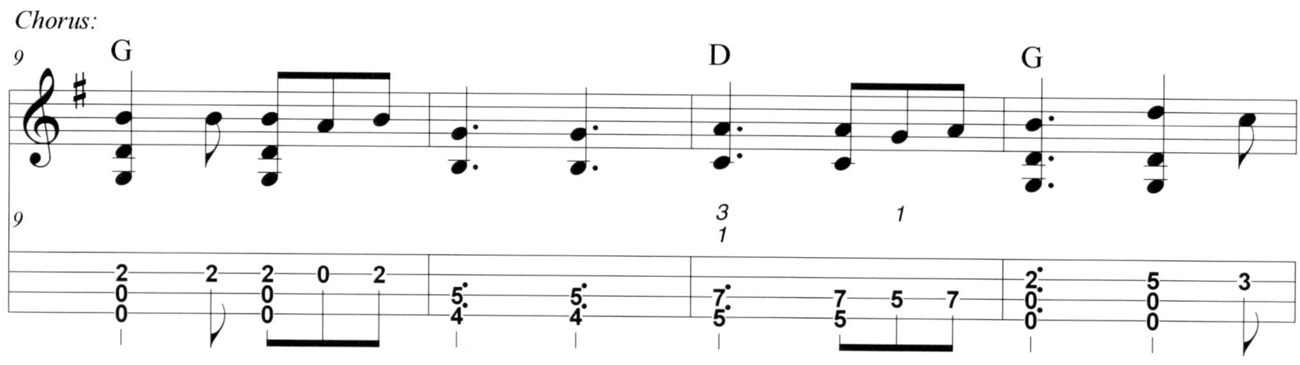

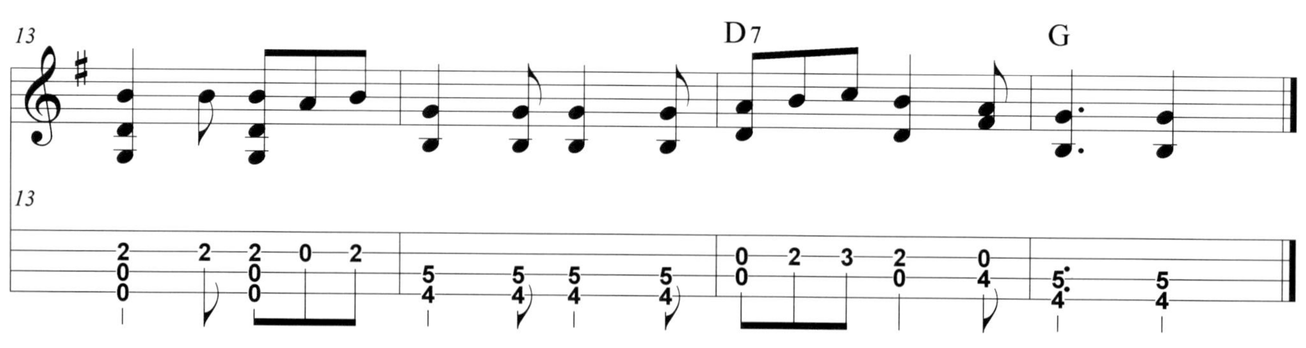

Sweet Hour of Prayer

Introductory note p. 13

W. W. Walford - 1845
Arr. by Dix Bruce

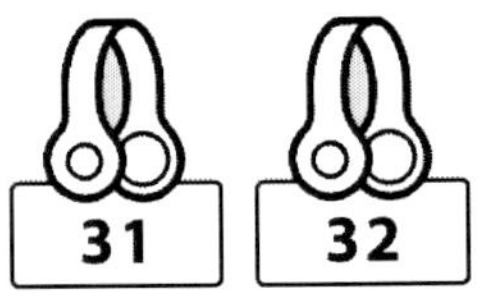

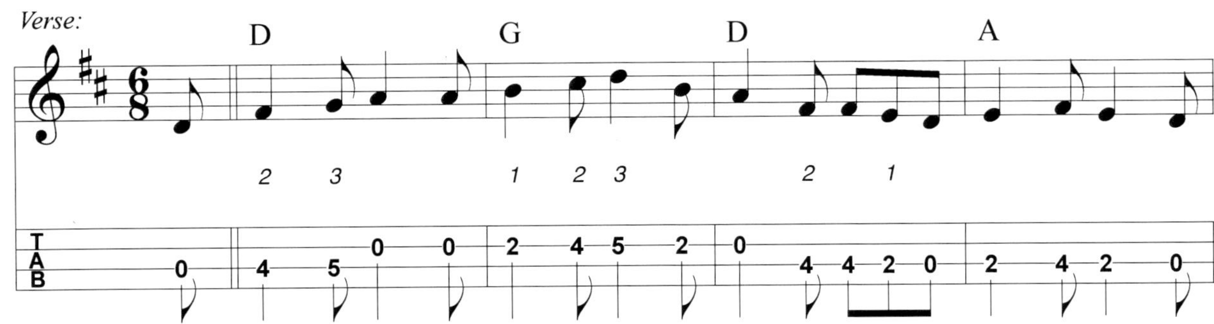

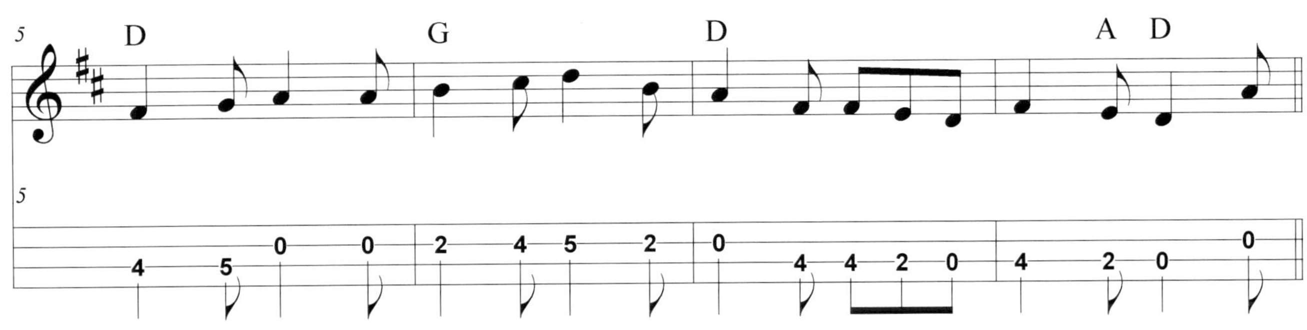

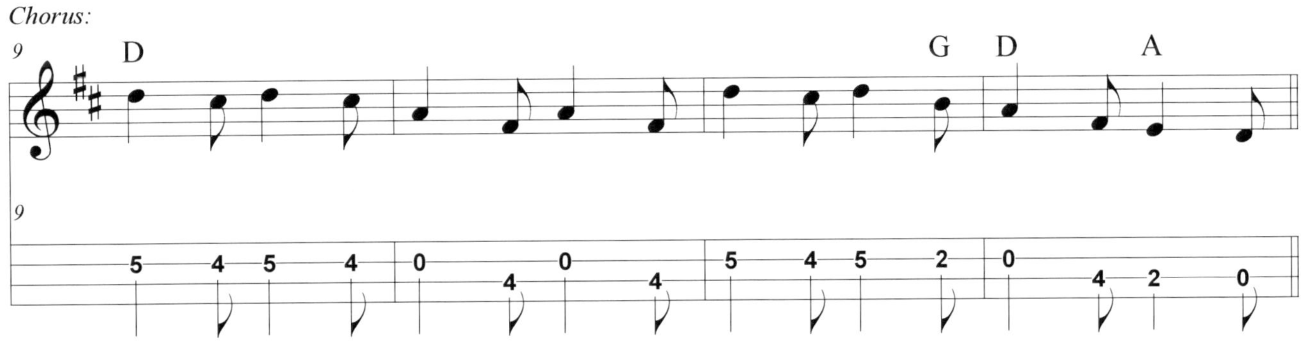

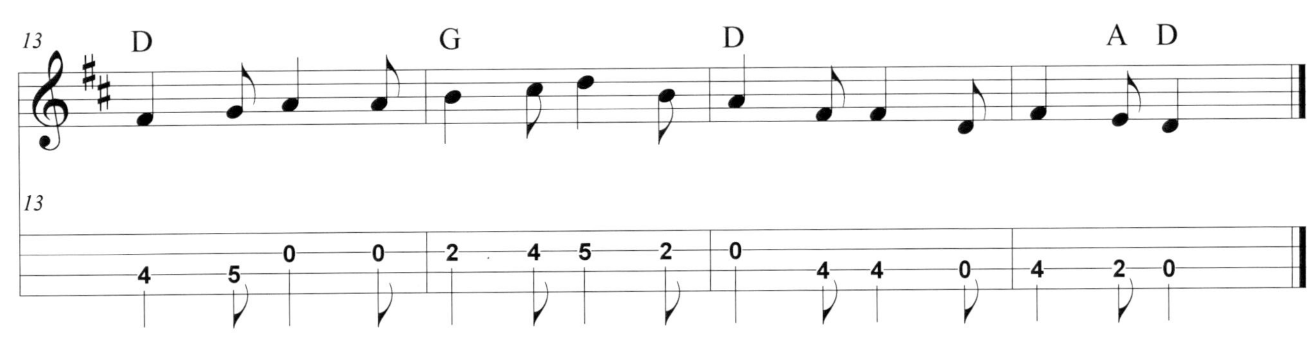

The Old Rugged Cross

Introductory note p. 13

G. Bennard - 1912
Arr. by Dix Bruce

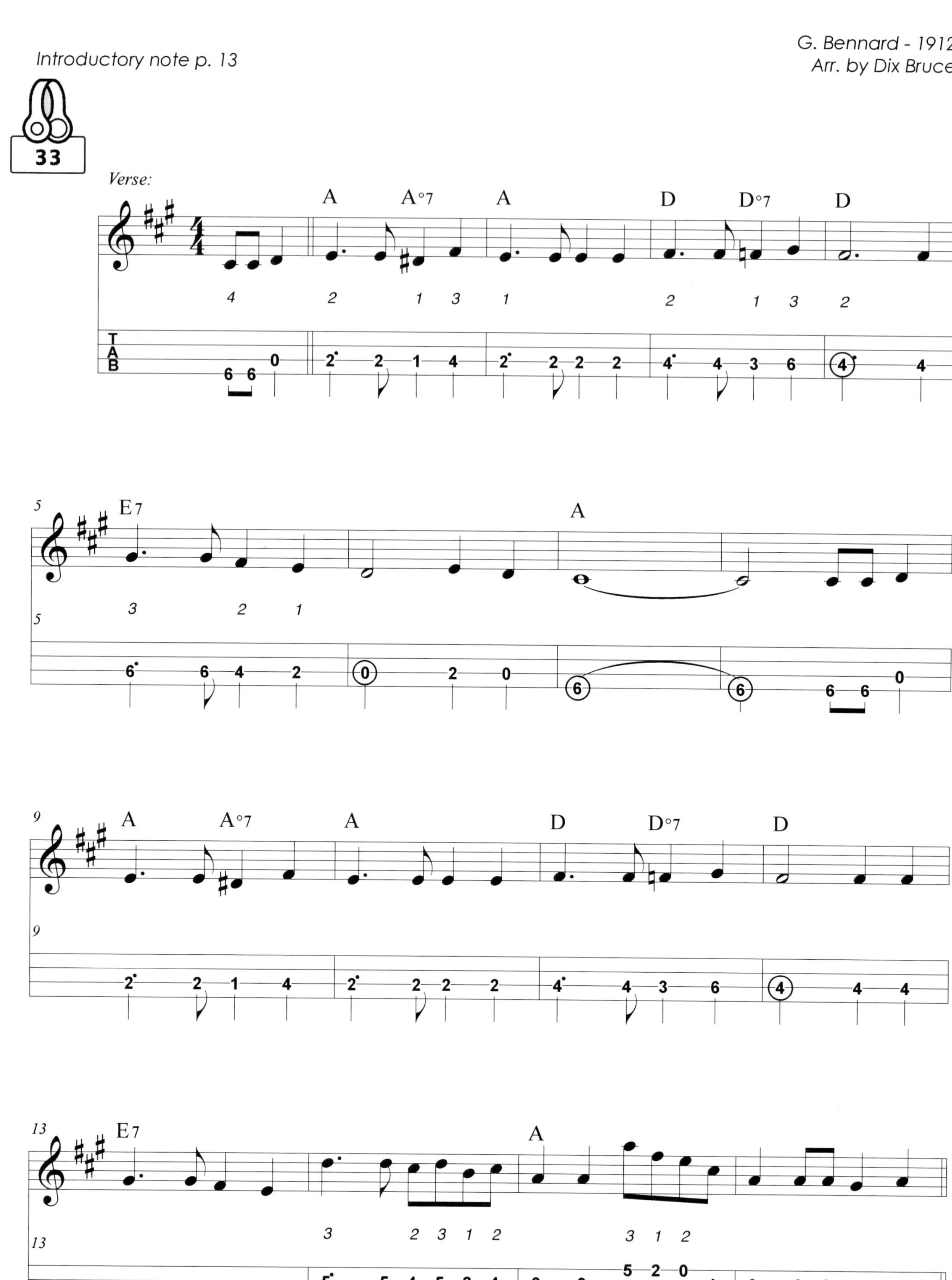

Chorus:

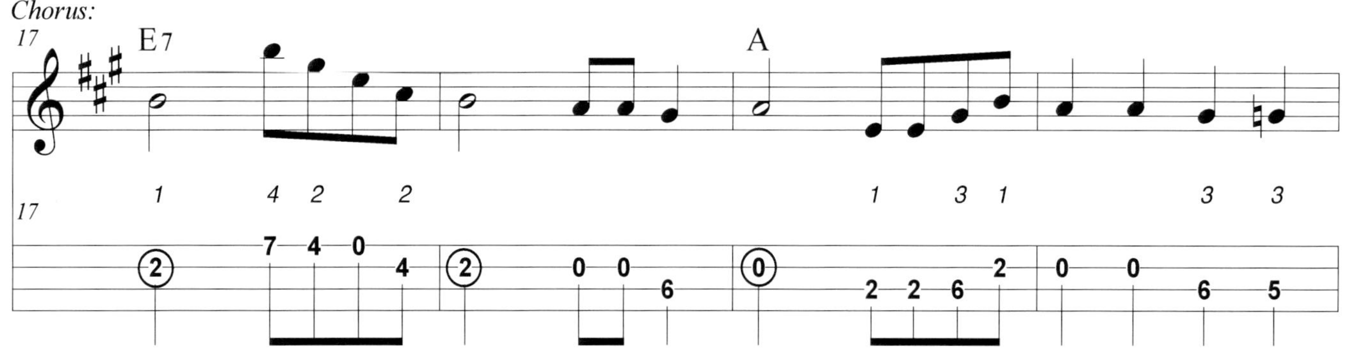

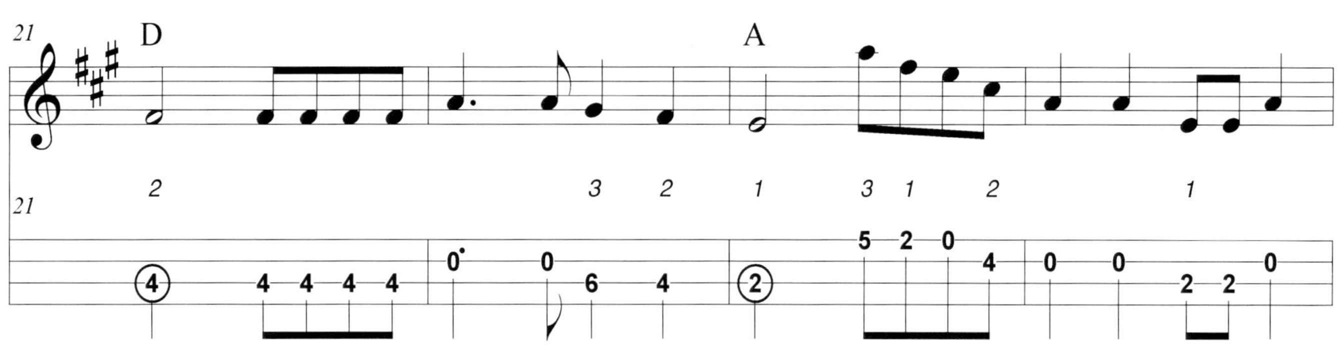

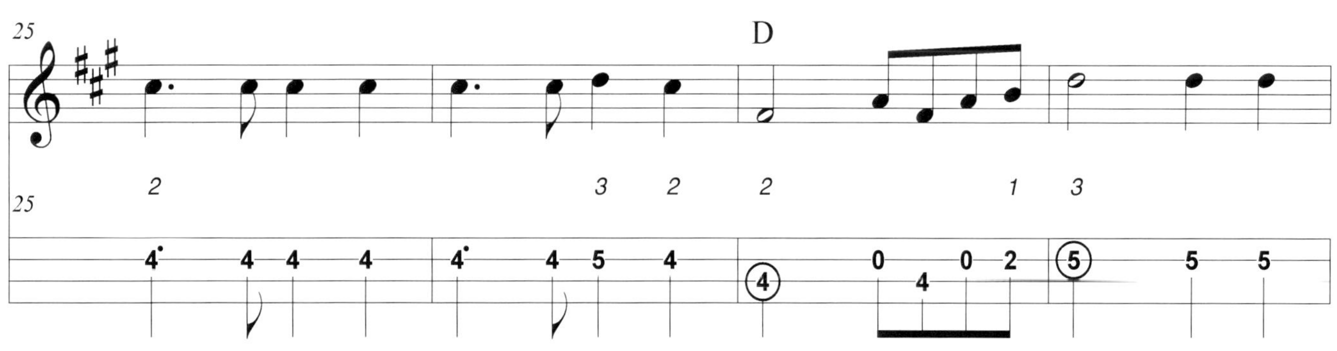

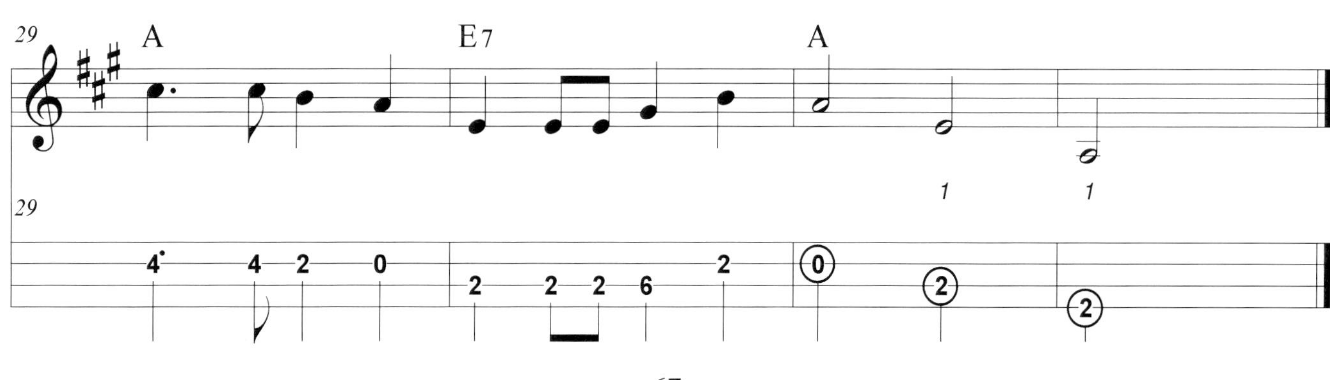

Just as I Am

C. Elliott - 1835
Arr. by Dix Bruce

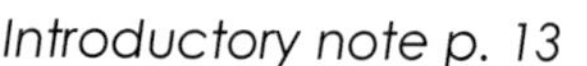
Introductory note p. 13

34

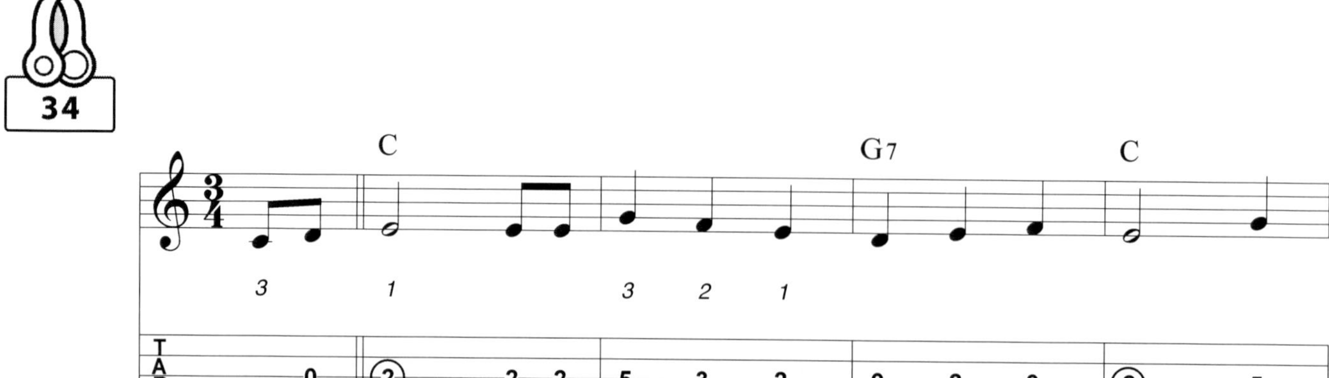

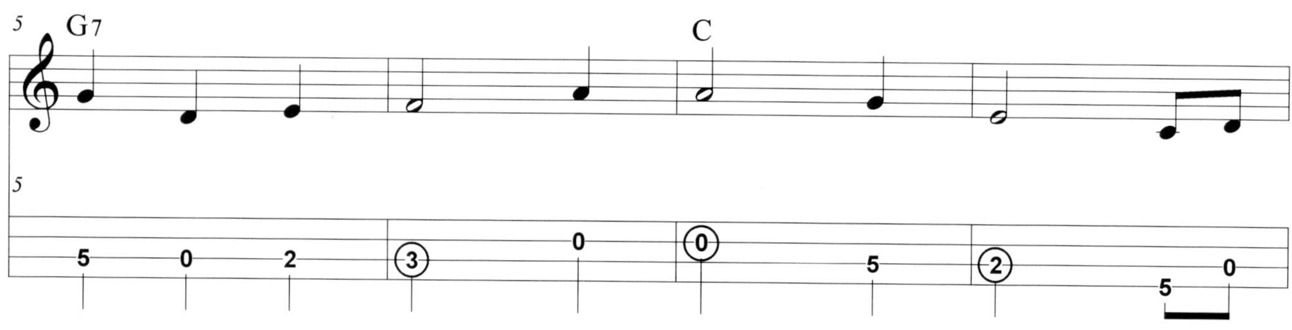

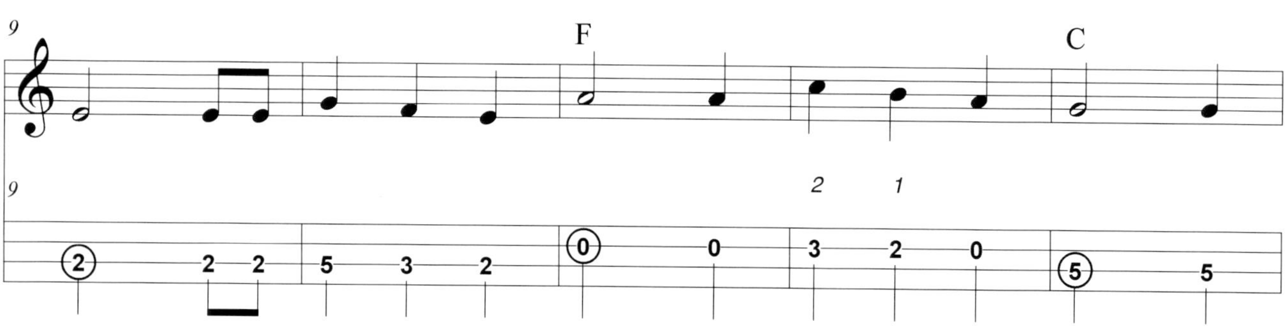

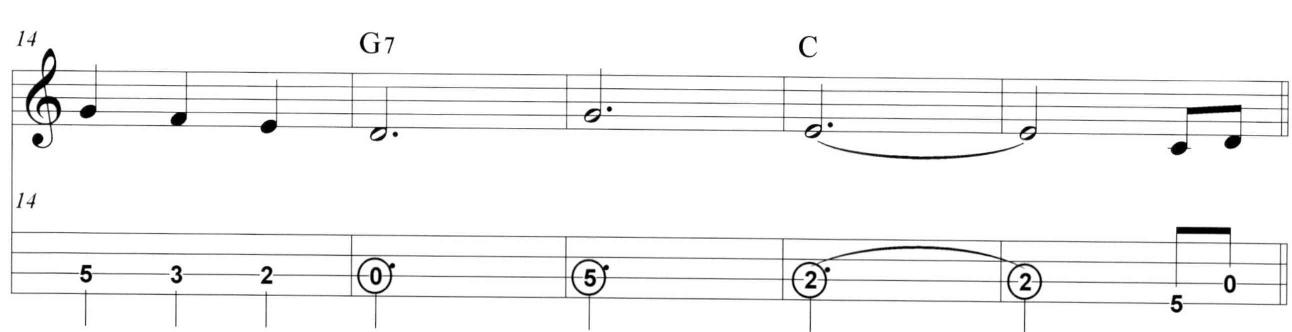

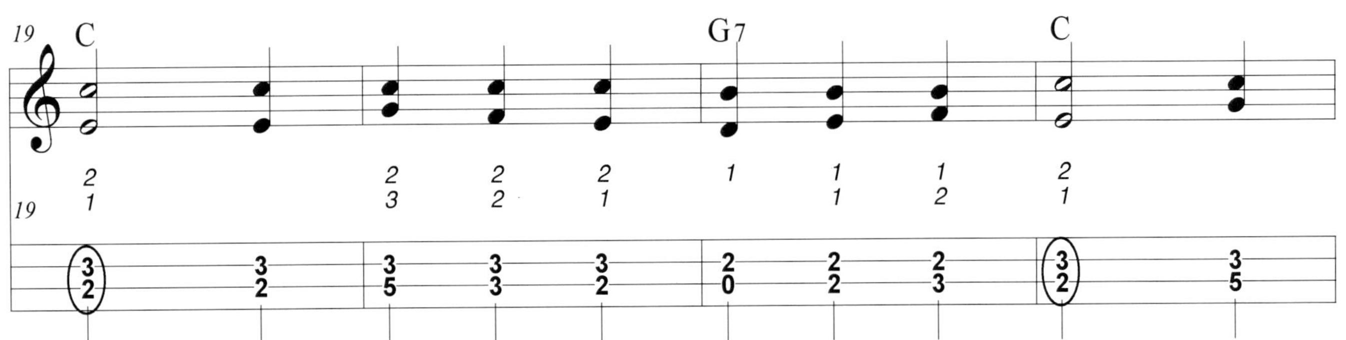
C
G7
C

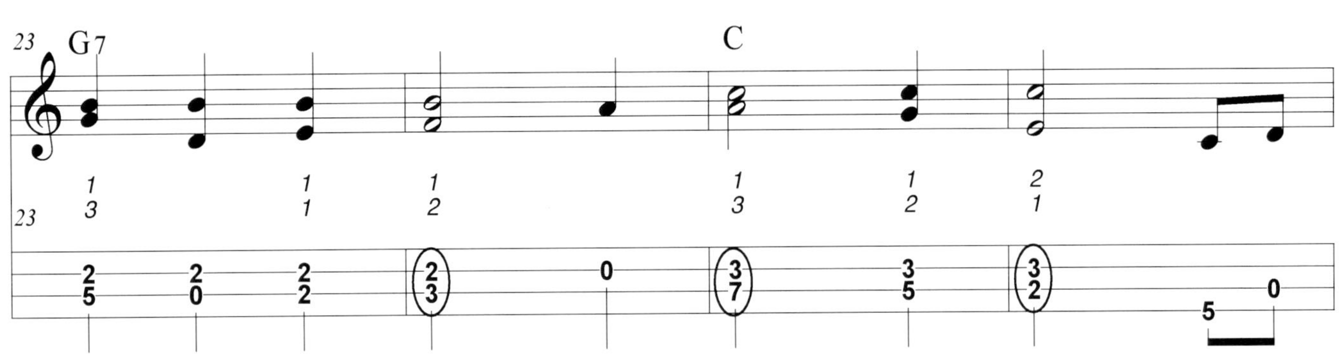
G7
C

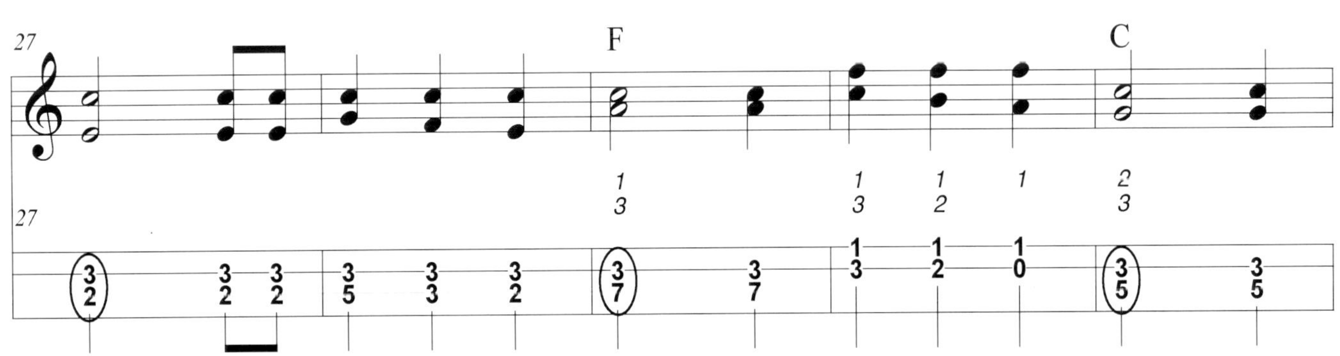
F
C

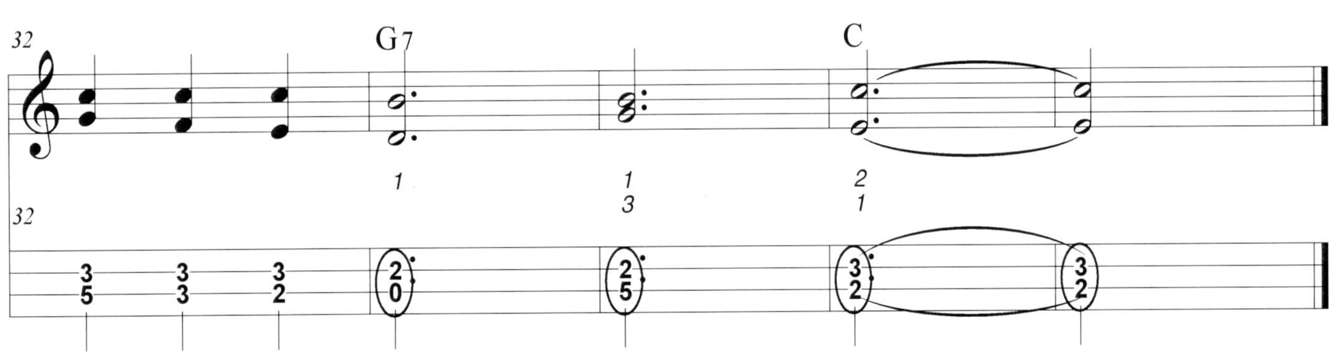
G7
C

Savior, Like a Shepherd Lead Us

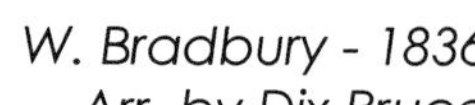
W. Bradbury - 1836
Arr. by Dix Bruce

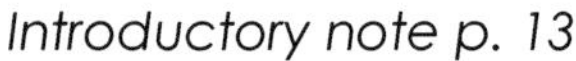
Introductory note p. 13

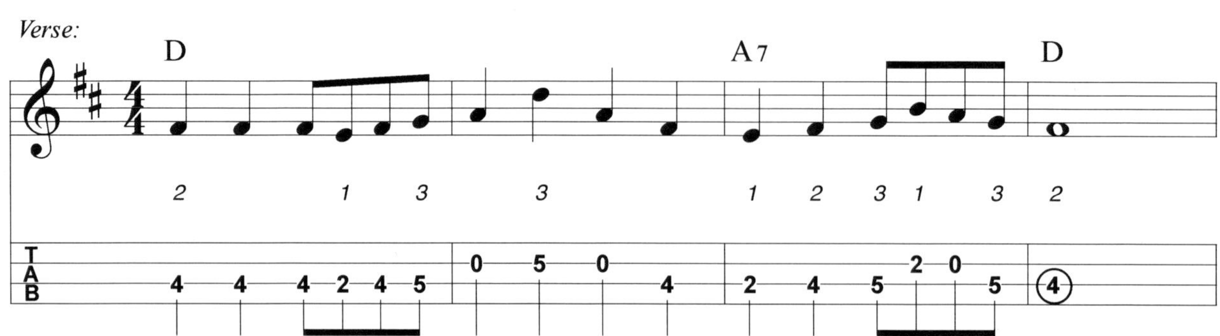

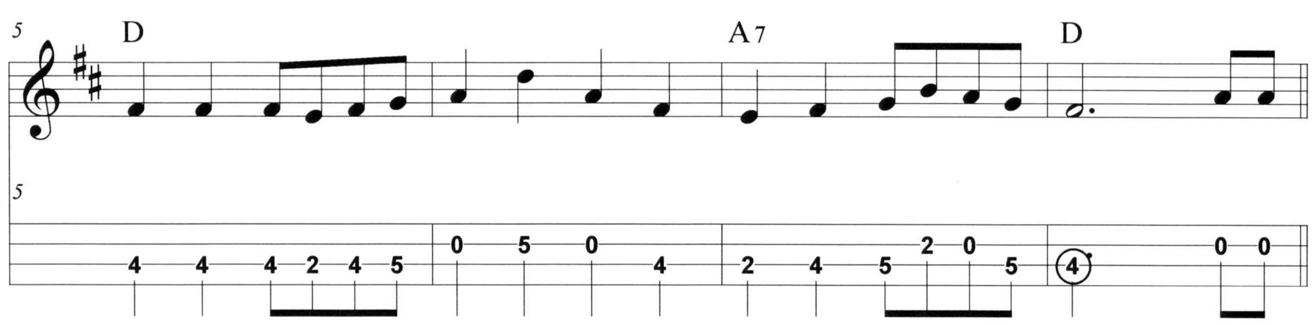

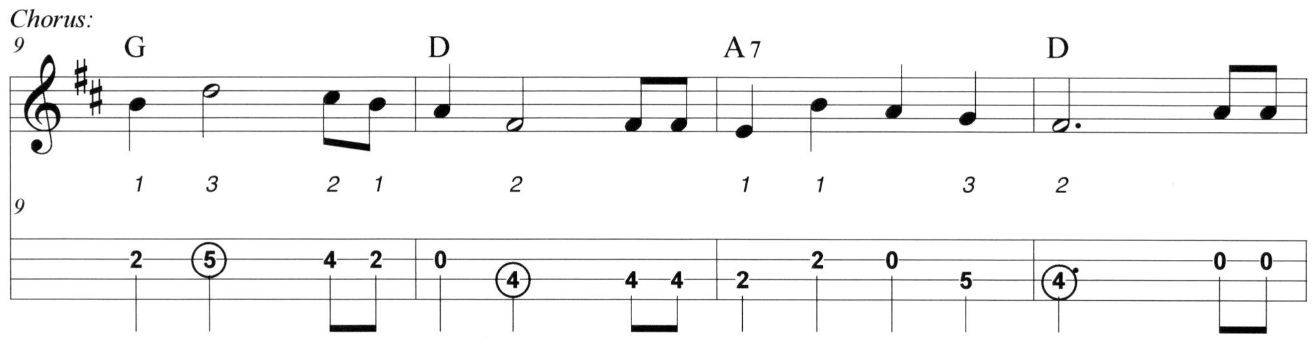

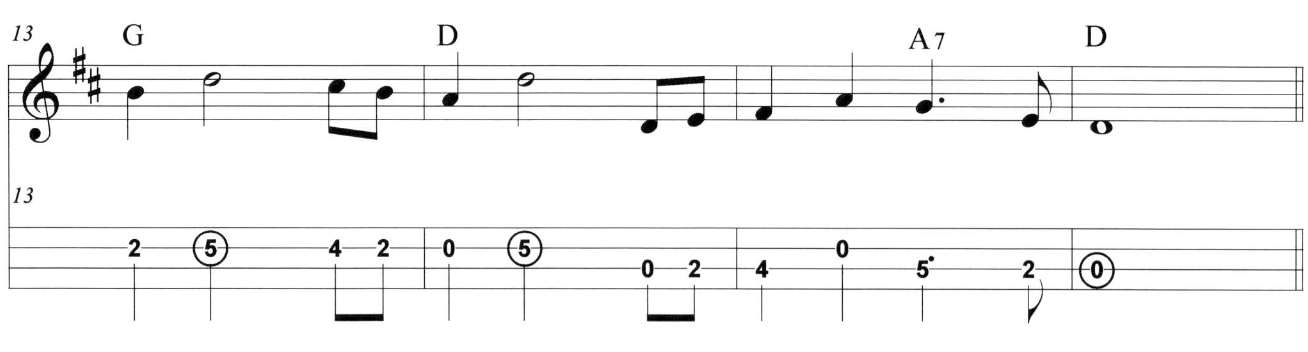

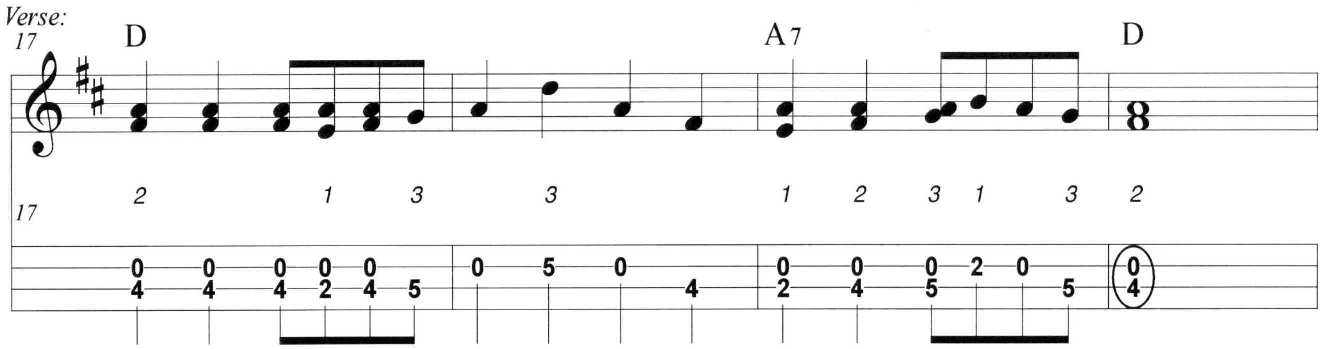
Verse:
17
D
A7
D
2 1 3 3 1 2 3 1 3 2
17
0 0 0 0 0 0 5 0 0 0 0 2 0 0
4 4 4 2 4 5 4 2 4 5 5 4

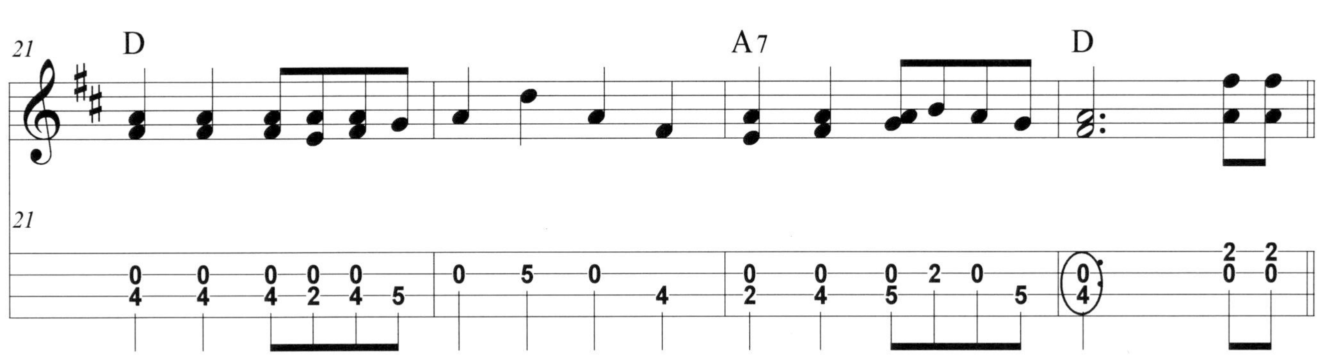
21
D
A7
D
21
0 0 0 0 0 0 5 0 0 0 0 2 0 0 2 2
4 4 4 2 4 5 4 2 4 5 5 4 0 0

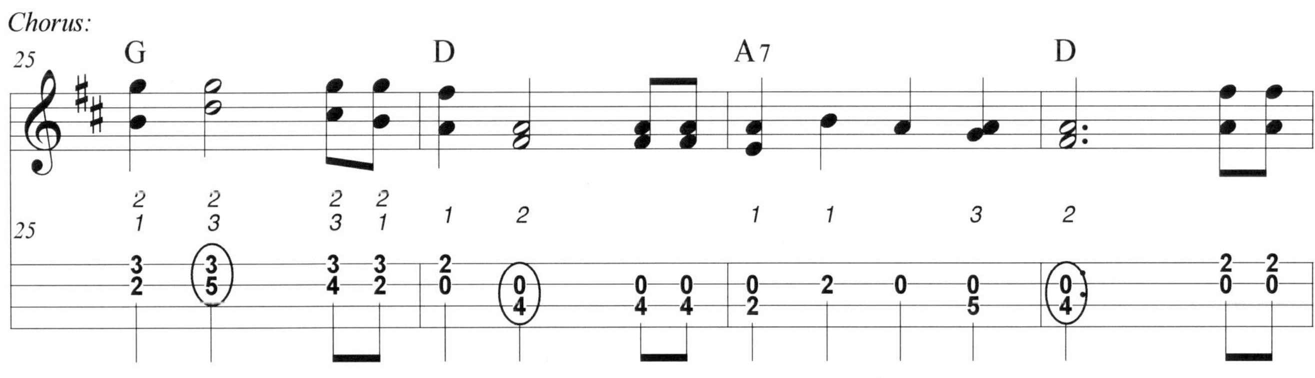
Chorus:
25
G
D
A7
D
2 2 2 2
1 3 3 1 1 2 1 1 3 2
25
3 3 3 3 2 0 0 0 0 2 0 0 0 2 2
2 5 4 2 0 4 4 4 2 5 4 0 0

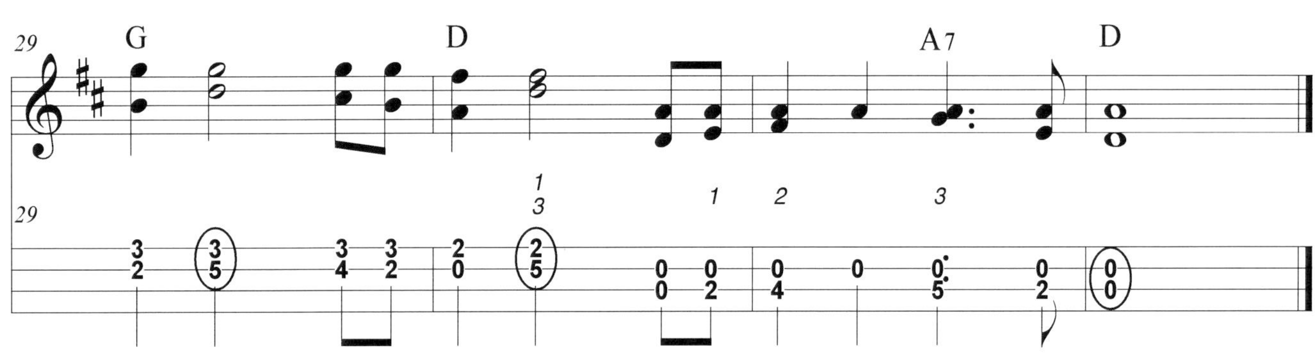
29
G
D
A7
D
1
3 1 2 3
29
3 3 3 3 2 2 0 0 0 0 0 0 0
2 5 4 2 0 5 0 2 4 5 2 0

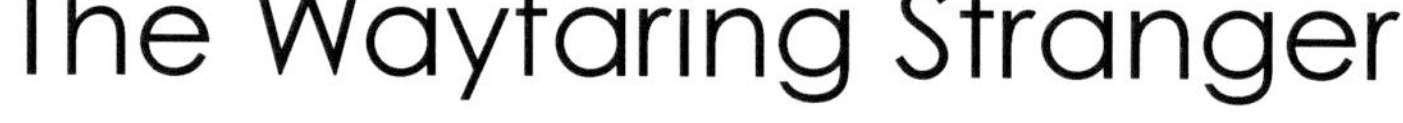

The Wayfaring Stranger

Traditional
Arr. by Dix Bruce

Introductory note p. 13

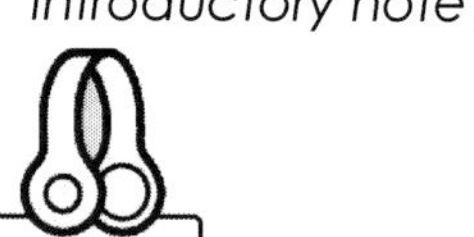

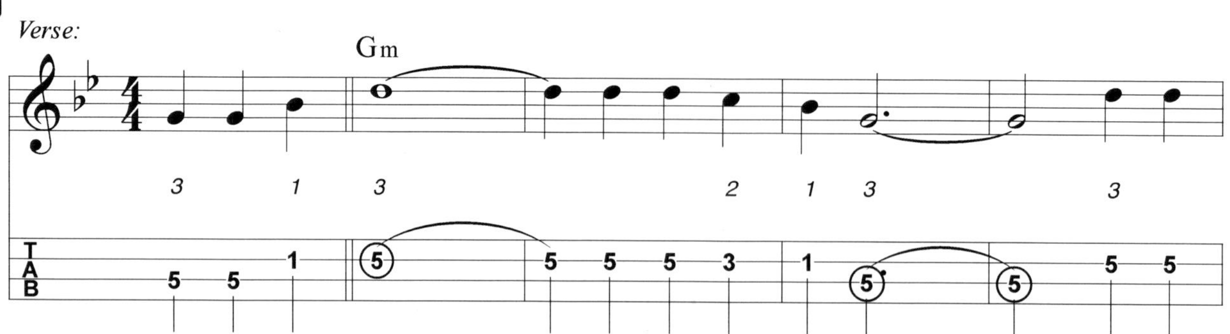

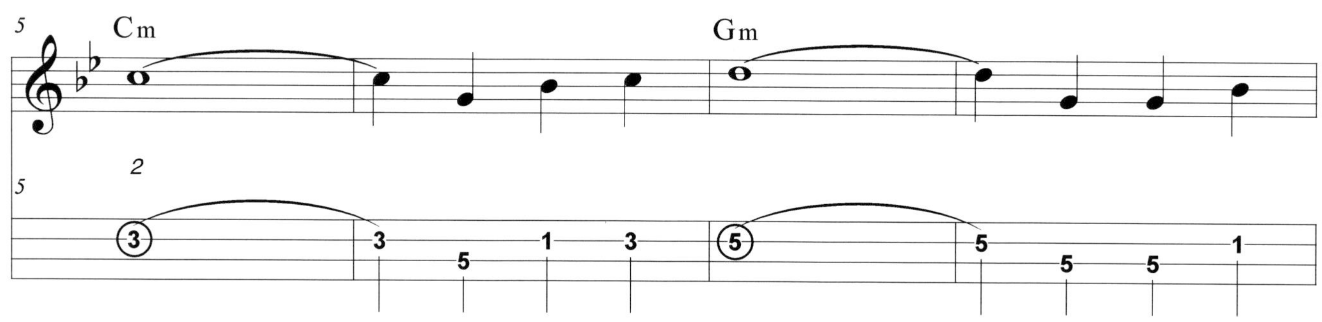

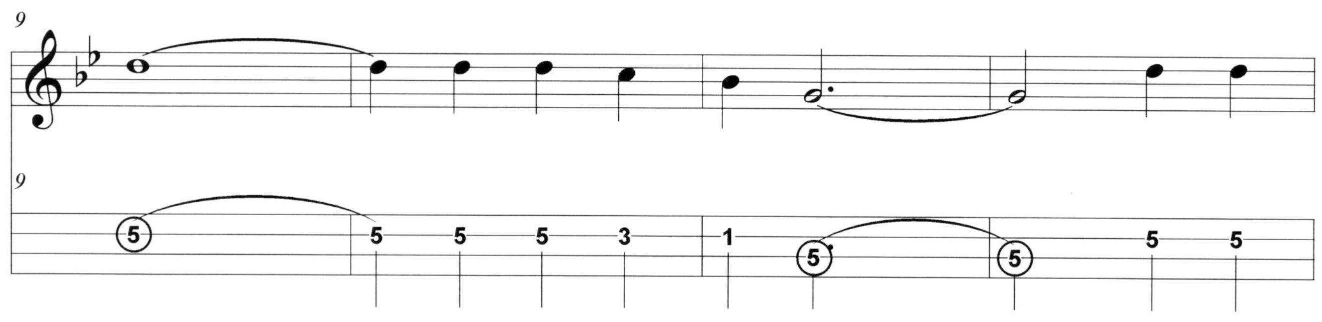

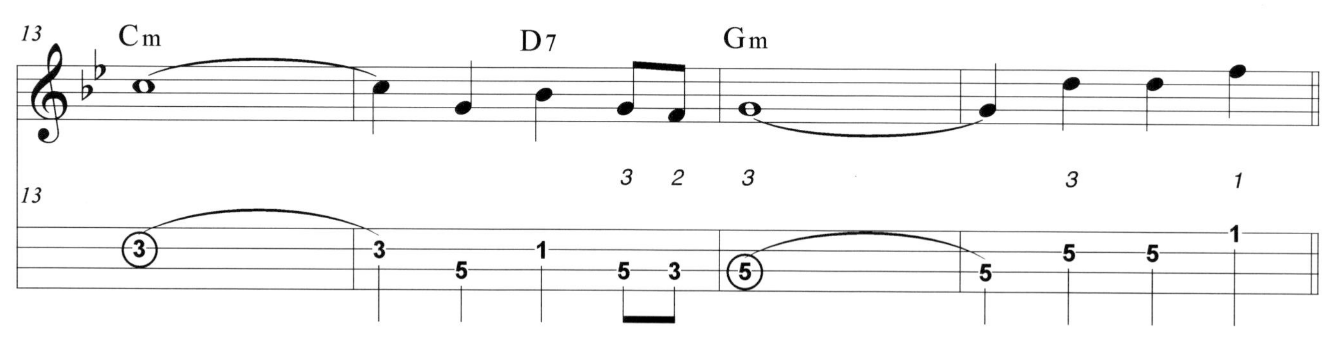

Chorus:

17
E♭
B♭
2
1
2
3
1
17
3
3
1
3
1
5
1
1
1
5
5
1

21
E♭
D7
3
2
1
3
3
1
21
3
3
5
5
3
1
5
5
5
5
1

25
Gm
25
5
5
5
5
3
1
5
5
5
5
5

29
Cm
D7
Gm
3
1
29
3
3
5
1
5
3
5
5
5
5
5
5
1

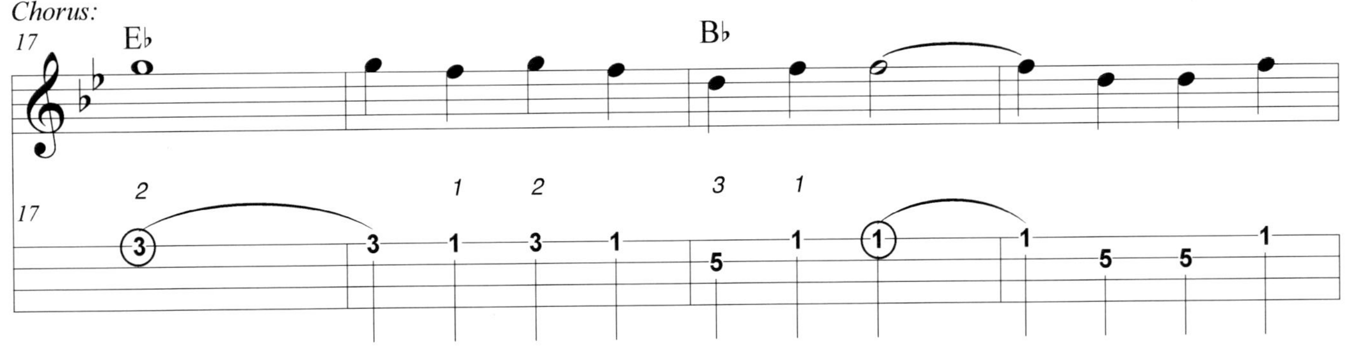

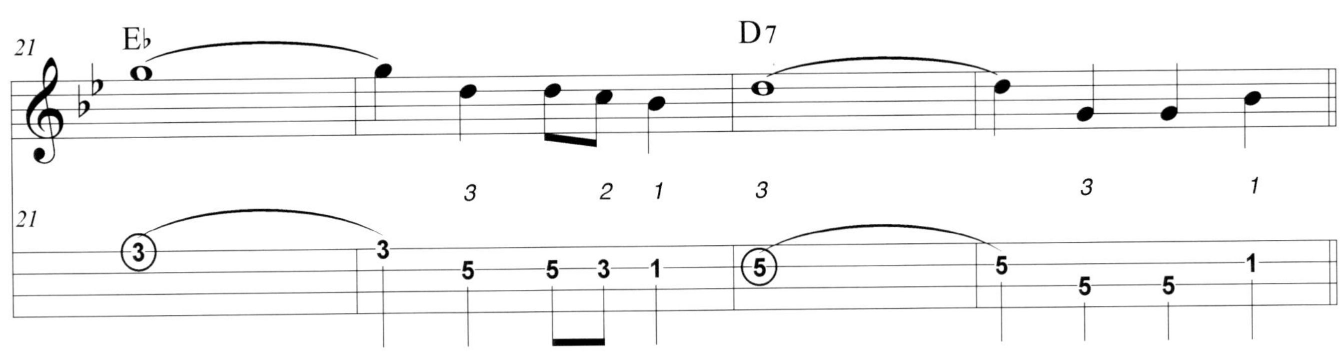

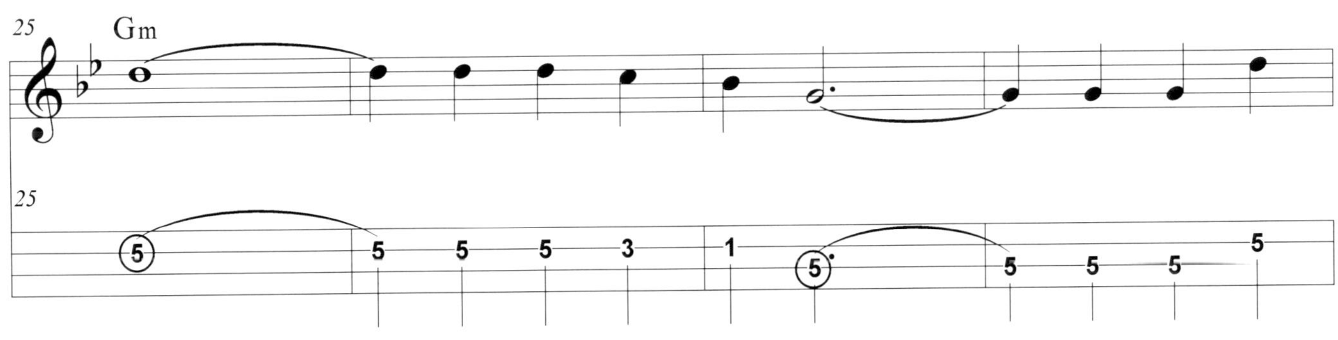

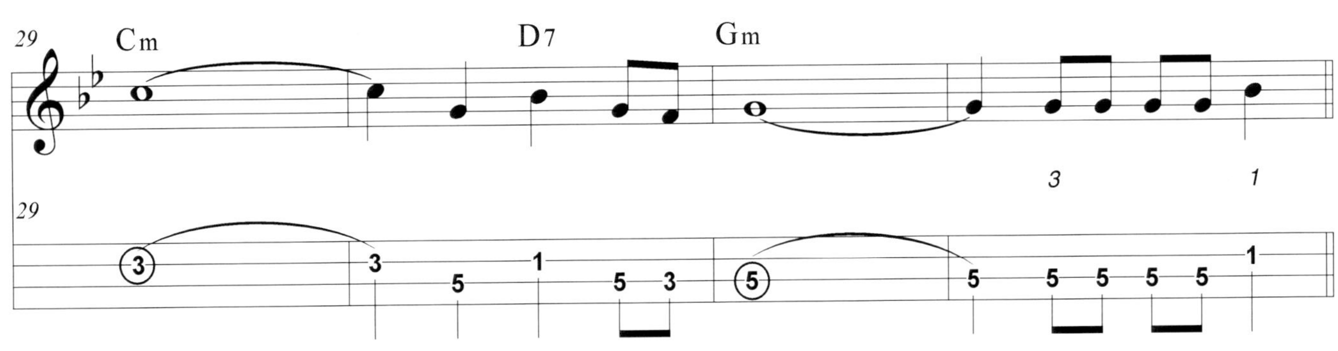

Verse:

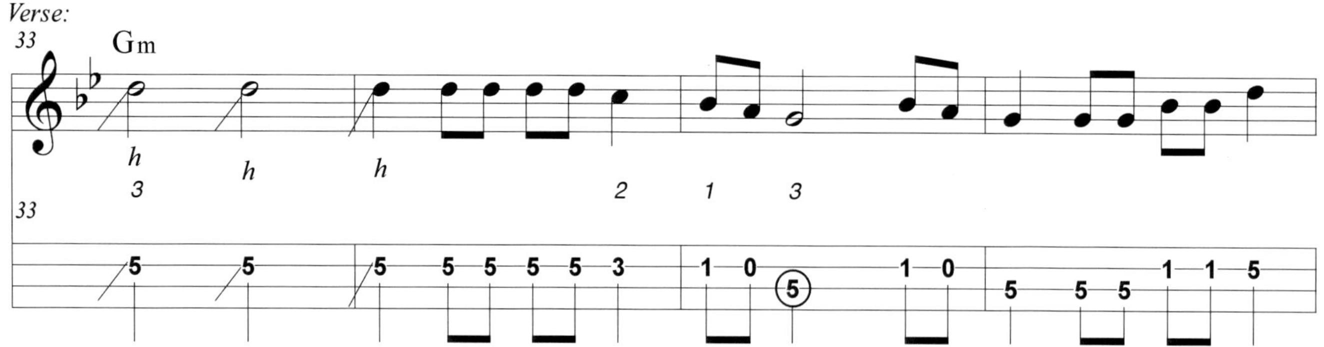

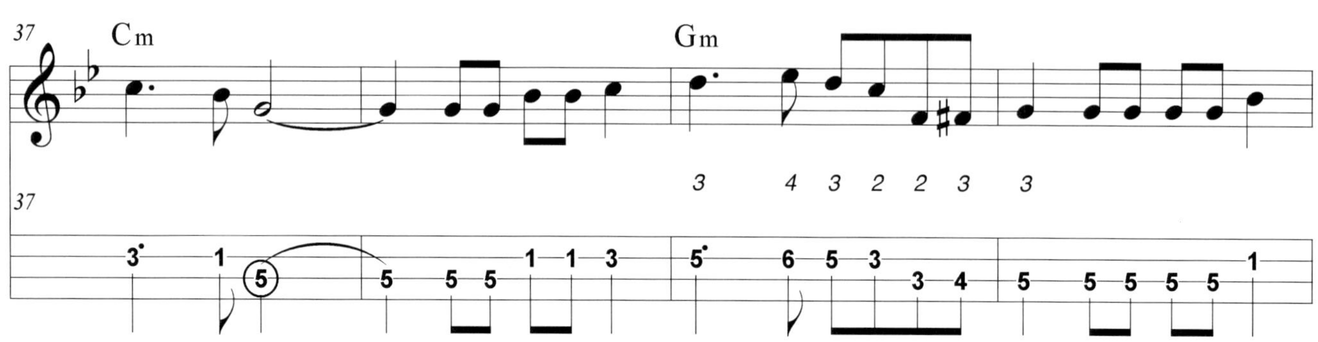

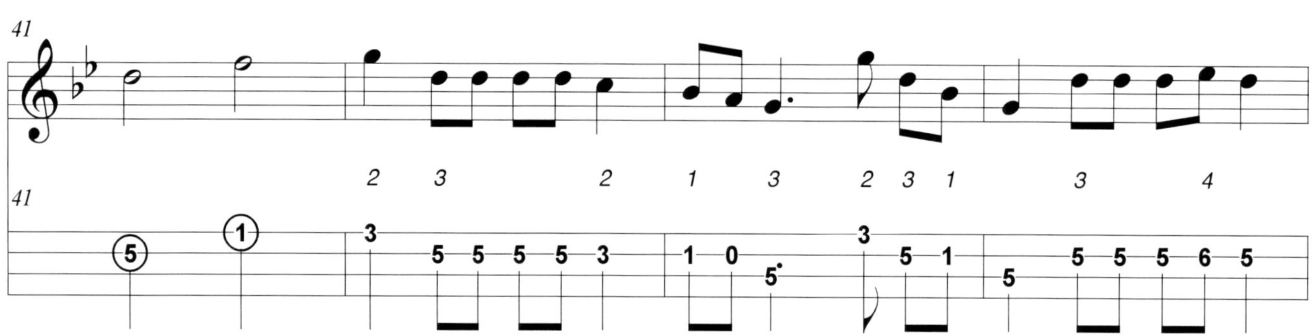

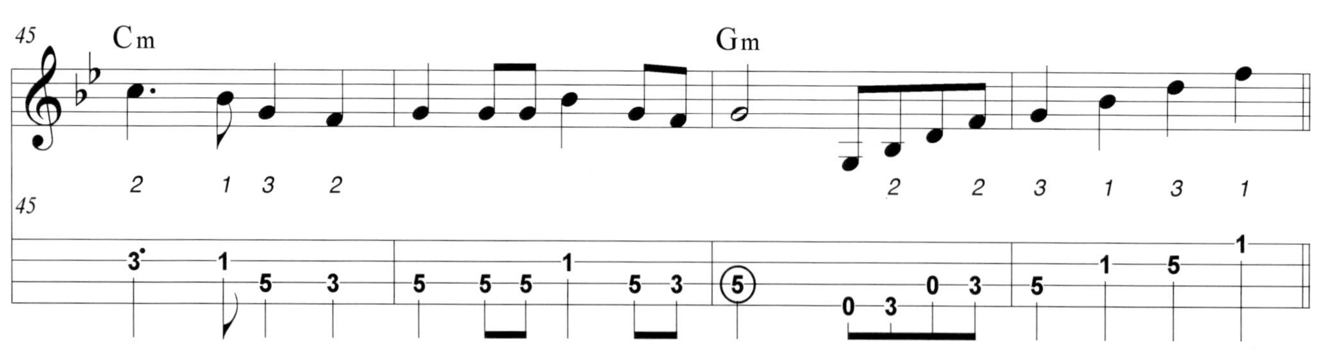

Chorus:

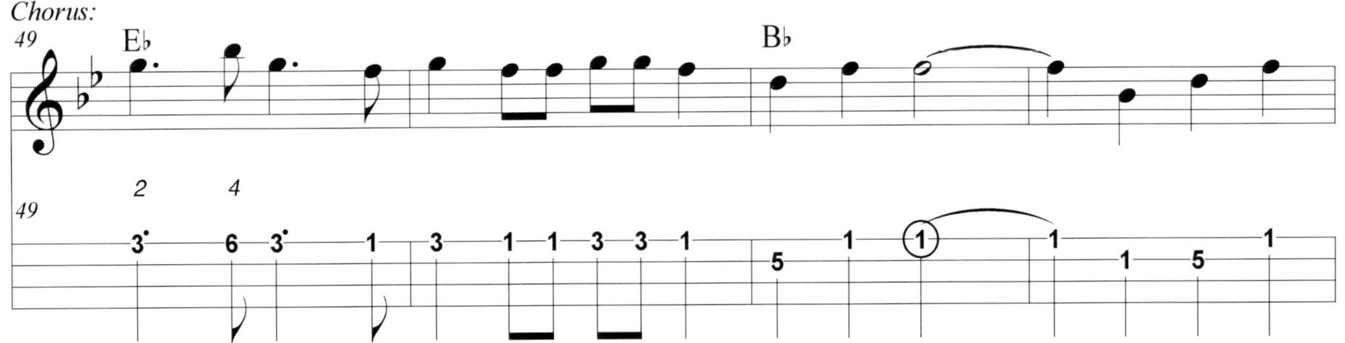

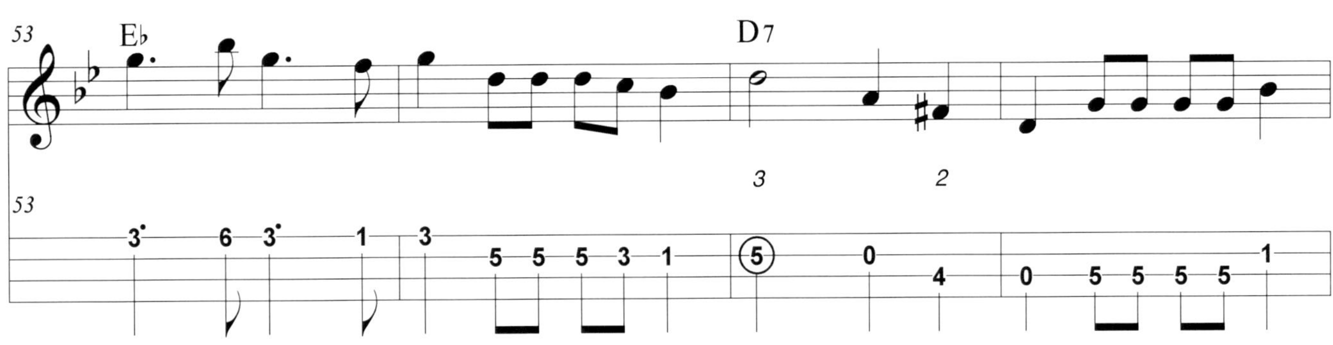

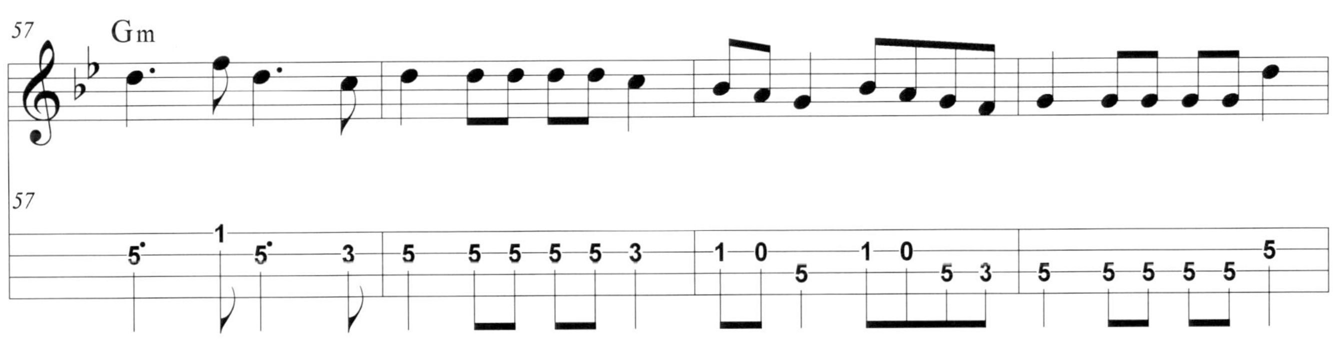

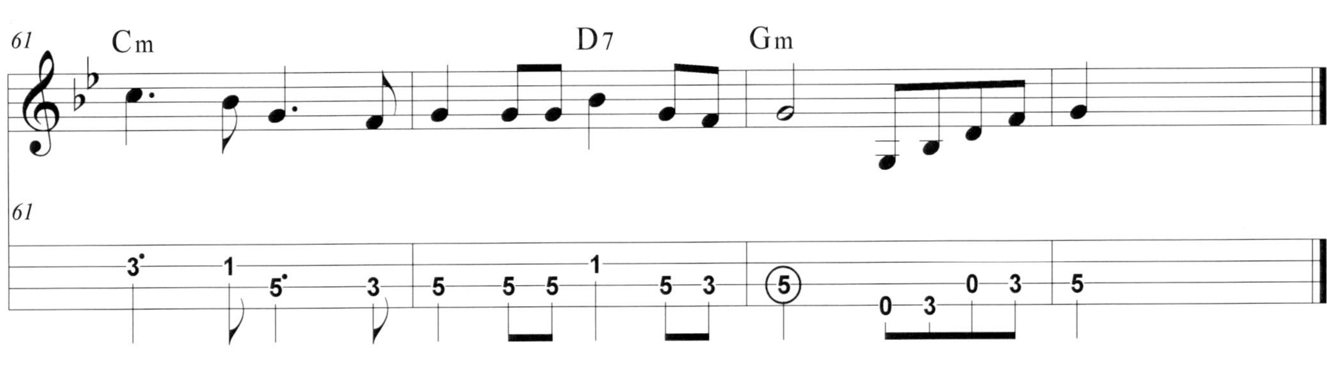

When I Lay My Burden Down

Introductory note p. 13

Traditional
Arr. by Dix Bruce

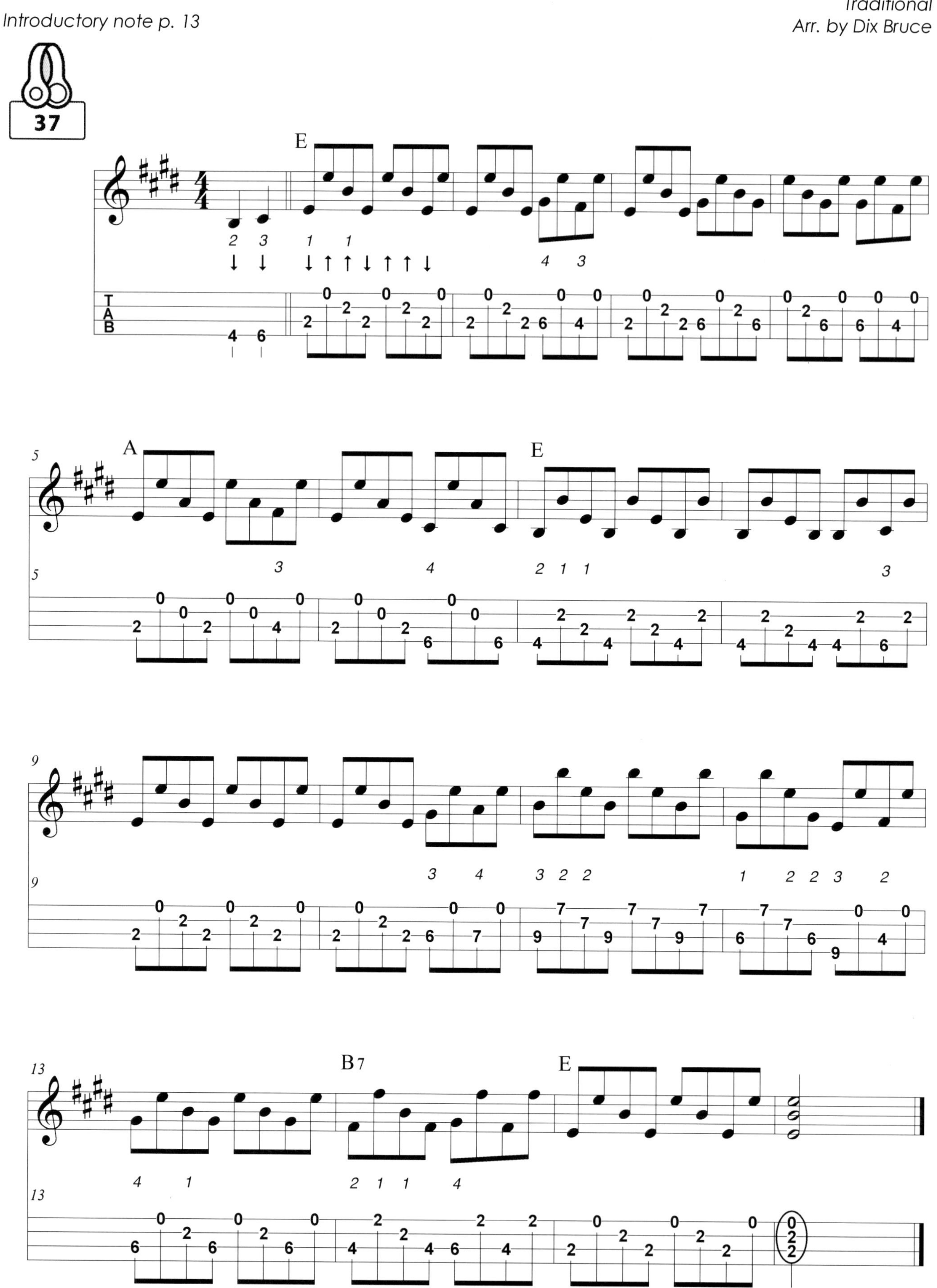

Index

*The first page number below shows the location of the introductory note on the song.
The second is the location of the song.*

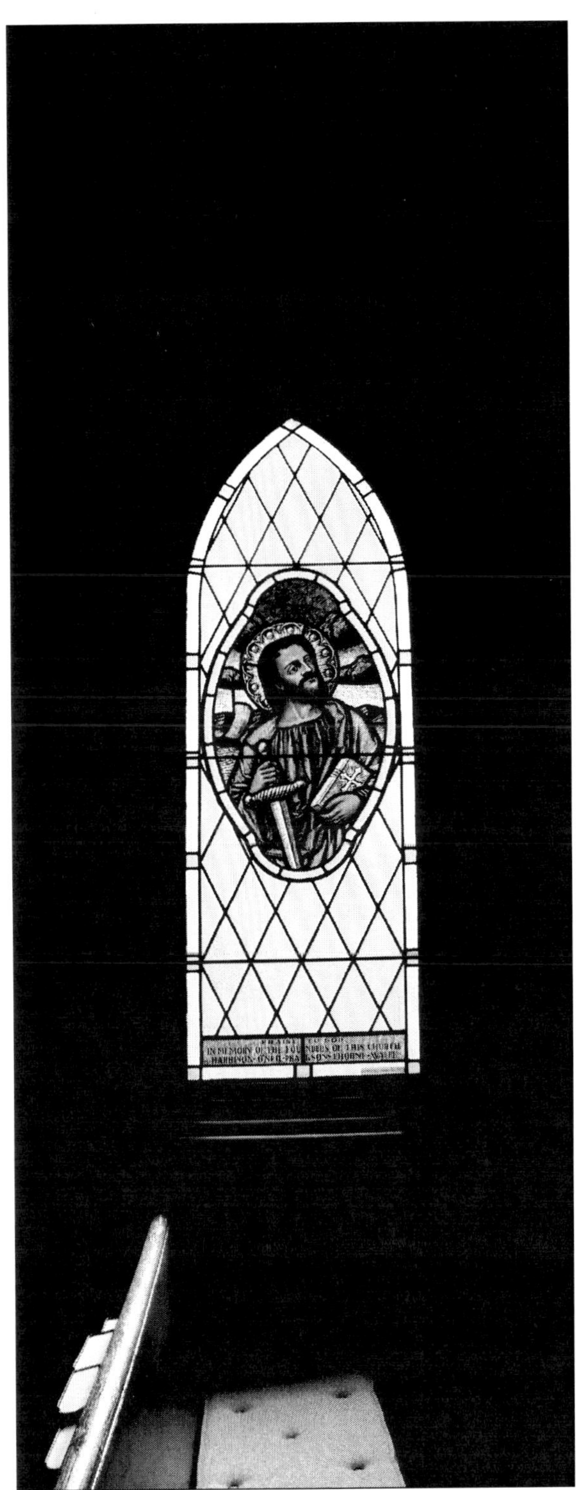

Photo: Dix Bruce

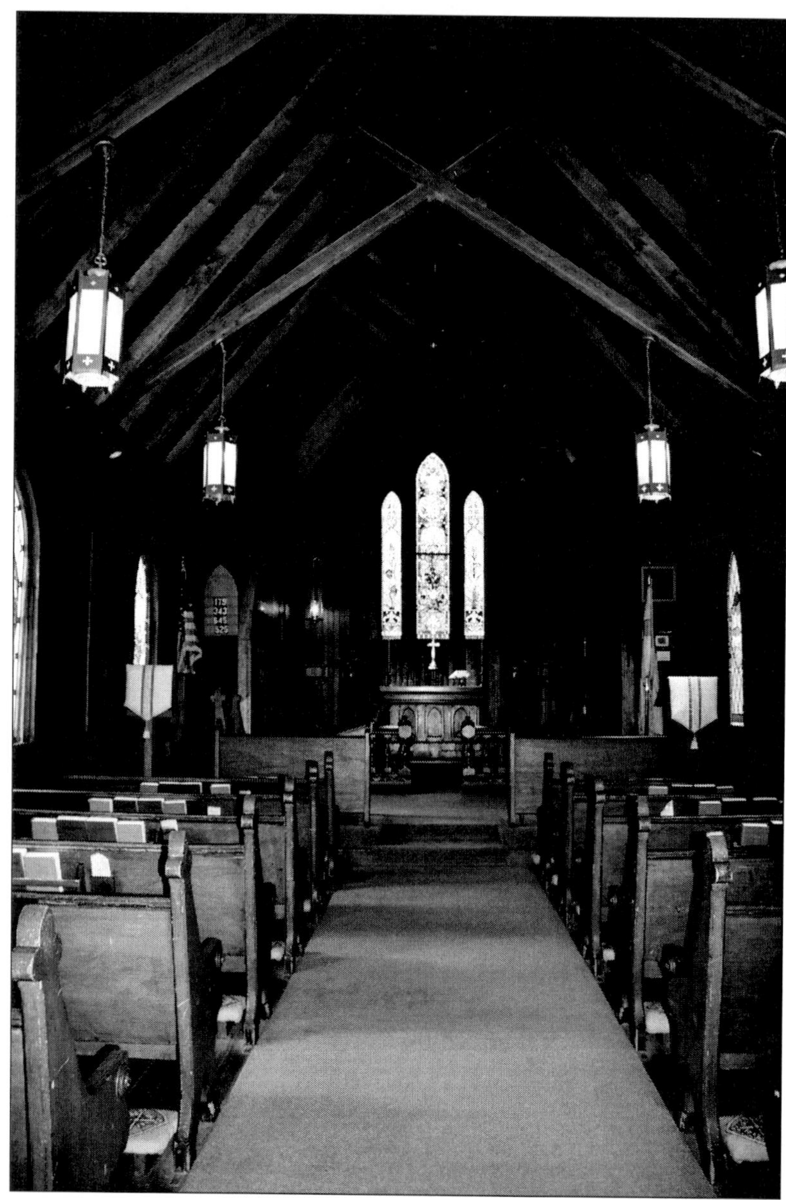

Photo: Dix Bruce

Also by Dix Bruce

Mandolin Picking Tunes-Early Music Gems, book/online audio – 34 wonderful songs from the 1200s to the 1600s, arranged for intermediate and advanced mandolinists. (Mel Bay)

Wedding Music for Mandolin, book/online audio – includes 23 of the most popular and best-loved wedding hits for intermediate and advanced mandolinists. (Mel Bay)

Mandolin Licks-ercises, (video and streaming) licks, tunes, and exercises for beginning and intermediate players.

The Parking Lot Picker's Songbooks – six separate books/online audio for mandolin, guitar, banjo, fiddle, resonator guitar, and bass. (Mel Bay)

Parking Lot Picker's Play-Along: Mandolin, book/online audio – 15 all-time great bluegrass, old time, and gospel hits recorded in play-along style. (Mel Bay)

Bluegrass Breaks: Mandolin, book/online audio – For beginning and intermediate mandolinists, this book contains a collection of various mandolin solos in a range of styles and levels of difficulty. (Mel Bay)

Gypsy Swing & Hot Club Rhythm Complete for Mandolin, 110-page book/online audio. Learn swing/jazz chords, rhythm, melodies, practice playing rhythm and leads with a real Hot Club-style band! (Musix)

Gypsy Swing & Hot Club Rhythm Complete for Guitar, 110-page book/online audio. Learn swing/jazz chords, rhythm, melodies, practice playing rhythm and leads with a real Hot Club-style band! (Musix)

All-Time Favorite Parking Lot Picker's Mandolin Solos, book/online audio. (Mel Bay)

All-Time Favorite Parking Lot Picker's Guitar Solos, book/online audio. (Mel Bay)

Christmas Favorites for Solo Guitar (30 Best Loved Traditional Songs for Bluegrass Guitar), book/online audio. (Mel Bay)

You Can Teach Yourself Mandolin, book/online audio and video. (Mel Bay)

Favorite Mandolin Picking Tunes, book/online audio. (Mel Bay)

Mandolin Uff Da! Let's Dance: Scandavian Fiddle Tunes & House Party Music, book/online audio. (Mel Bay)

Dix Bruce's Swing & Jazz Mandolin DVD: Chords, Rhythm, and Songs. DVD that teaches everything you need to know to get up and swinging on the mandolin! (Musix)

Getting Into Bluegrass Mandolin, book/online audio. (Mel Bay)

First Lessons®: Mandolin, book/online audio and video. (Mel Bay)

Other Mel Bay Mandolin Solo Collections